Children
and
Science

Children
and
Science

The Process of
Teaching and Learning

David P. Butts
The University of Georgia
Gene E. Hall
The University of Texas at Austin

PRENTICE-HALL, INC., Englewood Cliffs, N. J.

Library of Congress Cataloging in Publication Data

BUTTS, DAVID P.
   Children and Science.

   Includes bibliographical references.
   1. Science—Study and teaching (Elementary)
I. Hall, Gene E., 1941–   joint author.
II. Title.
LB1585.B818   372.3′5′044   74-8548
ISBN 0-13-132258-3
ISBN 0-13-132241-9 (pbk.)

© 1975 by Prentice-Hall, Inc.
Englewood Cliffs, New Jersey

Printed in the United States of America

10 9 8 7 6 5 4 3 2 1

PRENTICE-HALL INTERNATIONAL, INC., *London*
PRENTICE-HALL OF AUSTRALIA, PTY. LTD., *Sydney*
PRENTICE-HALL OF CANADA, LTD., *Toronto*
PRENTICE-HALL OF INDIA PRIVATE LIMITED, *New Delhi*
PRENTICE-HALL OF JAPAN, INC., *Tokyo*

Contents

Preface

This book is written for the teacher who is concerned about making science come alive—both for himself and for his students. For the teacher who perceives science as a huge altar of facts before which the priestly teacher bows while the observing students watch, this book will be of very limited value. For the teacher who perceives science as both what we know *and* how we find out, this book will be of practical use.

A multitude of science curricula are available from which a teacher can select experiences that fit both his own and his students' interests. Choices must be made, but based on what criteria? The chapters of this book have been designed to introduce a set of intellectual skills that have been found to be important in doing science as well as in contributing to mentally active life. With the exception of the first and last chapters, each chapter introduces the user to

1. an opportunity to learn about a specific skill by doing a series of activities using readily available household items.
2. a description of the skill, including quotations from various of the recently developed science curricula as indication of how they view the particular skill.
3. a selected sample lesson from several of the recently developed science curricula in order to provide the user with the opportunity to study several suggested ways for teaching the same skill.

A note of caution is needed, however. The ideas in each chapter require translation by a *thinking* teacher into *living* reality for his students. These ideas are presented as "first words" not "last words," as springboards and not coffin lids.

ACKNOWLEDGMENTS

We do wish to acknowledge the assistance and encouragement of more than 12,000 teachers who have helped suggest both ideas for classroom learning experiences and the generalized approach for planning instruction described in this book. We also wish to acknowledge the assistance of the students of the Mathematics–Science Teacher Education Program who have provided extensive feedback on the ideas of the book. These undergraduates were participants in the intensive Personalized Teacher Education Program which is jointly sponsored by The Research and Development Center for Teacher Education, The Science Education Center, and The Department of Curriculum and Instruction at The University of Texas at Austin.

We also wish to thank those who so faithfully assisted in the preparation of this manuscript: Barbara Boehme, Barbara Larson, Sue Tarlton, and Ida Fisher.

DAVID P. BUTTS

GENE E. HALL

*Children
and
Science*

1. Science Is...

This chapter is meant to perform a dual task: first, to give you a general picture of present and past science and science teaching, and second, to enable you to identify and name the resources found elsewhere in the book.

Science Is . . .

What do you have in mind when thinking of science? (Do not read any further until you have taken a minute to think about this question.) Consider the question and write down the answer for yourself.

When you think about science, many images and ideas may flash through your mind. Some people think of facts, atoms, and of memorizing the names of various plants, whereas others think of test tubes, and still others of space, planets, or nature. Some may picture a particular scientist or a stereotype image of a scientist: a frizzy- haired little old man in the white lab coat, surrounded by test tubes, beakers, and retorts, who is pouring a bubbling liquid from one test tube into another.

Science Is What Scientists Do

Just as the man with the bubbling liquid is a common image of a scientist, so the memorizing of all sorts of facts, names (probably in Latin), and formulas is an image of science. Most people have had science courses in high school or college and the above-mentioned impressions must be a reflection of those courses. Perhaps your experience was similar; at times you may have wondered how so many people could be so excited about and so thoroughly involved in anything as dull as science. Fortunately this impression of science and scientist is not all that there is to science. For that matter, it is not the most important aspect of science. Science does not consist just of a body of knowledge—the various facts and figures that you have memorized; it also is people actively using their minds to study as yet unexplained phenomena. A large part of science consists of the systematic investigation and study of the nature of the universe. The body of knowledge grows each time an investigation yields new information. Science is using what we *know* as a springboard to understanding what we do *not* know. Skills in using or processing information to augment the conclusions of the past (the body of knowledge) also belong to the field of science.

In order to investigate a phenomenon, a scientist needs scientific information pertaining to it. To solve the problem, the scientist has to use his mind. Knowledge by itself is of no value; it requires mind for the solution of problems. The intellectual activity of the scientist has been the missing link from most people's experiences with science. In many science classes the emphasis is on studying known facts rather than on learning how to use one's mind to investigate a phenomenon while processing existing knowledge, thereby creating new knowledge.

Science Teaching Is What You Do

By your having purchased this book, you are acknowledging the possibility that you may be teaching science. In order to represent science honestly, your teaching must convey to your students that science is not just the memorization of a body of knowledge, not just bubbling liquids in glass, but that it also includes the excitement of using one's mind in conjunction with the body of knowledge of science to solve a problem for which you are the first to have an answer.

Science Teaching Yesterday

As a perspective before progressing to the teaching of science in the 1970s, a few brief historical notes are in order. Science was first taught as an organized part of the elementary school curriculum in the mid-nineteenth century. At that time, most elementary school students were preparing for universities and future political and professional roles. Therefore, science teaching stressed the development of readiness for the university training to follow. It was called Object Study. The lessons consisted of the teacher identifying various objects from his environment, having the children observe them in as much detail as possible, and then making long lists of characteristics and properties of the objects. These lists could then be memorized and stored within each child's mind. There was little or no attempt to do anything with this information once it was stored, since it was generally felt that children's minds were not intellectually developed enough to process it.

As the nineteenth century came to a close, the science-curriculum materials for the elementary school were available in a textbook format. Earlier the science curriculum had been limited to the knowledge and ability of the teacher.

In the early 1900s the science curriculum shifted from Object Study to Nature Study. One of the main reasons for the popularity of Nature Study was the desire to encourage young adults to stay in the rural communities rather than migrate to the cities. Liberty Hyde Bailey is the principal person remembered for developing Nature Study materials. The major change from Object Study seems to have been the shift from studying objects to studying nature. Children were still not asked to go much beyond observing and memorizing the characteristics of objects of nature.

In the 1920s Dewey suggested that the method that the scientist employed was at least as important for children to learn as was the body of knowledge of science. In the late 1920s Gerald Craig proposed that the function of science in the elementary school was to be a part of the general education. Craig suggested that the laws, generalizations, and principles of science were relevant to all individuals, as they interacted with their enviroment. He suggested that such areas as health, safety, and economics were directly related to science and its interaction with the increasing technology of the times. Craig also thought that the affective part of science should be taught. He proposed that appreciations, interests, and attitudes were important aspects of science that should be included in the curriculum. The influence of Craig and Dewey on the materials for teaching science was quite profound and long-lasting.

By the mid-1950s science instruction was based on textbooks. In many ways these textbooks were not much different from those written in the 1930s. The pictures may have shown more contemporary scenes; however, the information to a great extent was not updated. There was still heavy emphasis on the body of knowledge of science and it was deemed important that children should read about science. The scientific method as proposed by Dewey was there; the main content emphasis was generally on practical technological applications of science. With the launching of Sputnik in 1957, a concern over the quality and quantity of science teaching in our schools was voiced by many people. Soon after, more funds were made available by the federal government and other funding agencies for the development of new science curriculum materials. By the early 1960s many millions of dollars were spent for this purpose.

Science Teaching Today

The big push for the development of new science curriculum materials began in the secondary schools with the development of such curriculum materials as Physical Science Study Committee (PSSC) for physics, the Biological Science Curriculum Study (BSCS) for biology, and CHEM. Study and the Chemical Bond Approach (CBA) materials for chemistry. As the 1960s continued, some efforts were made to develop curriculum materials at the junior high school level and attempts were started for the development of contemporary curriculum materials for elementary school science teaching. These new materials differ from those used in the past. Some of the characteristics are: few materials for the children to read, emphasis on activities and manipulating materials by children, direct input into the development of the curriculum materials provided by learning theorists, and more guidance and encouragement for science teachers.

One of the interesting features of the recently developed science curriculum for the elementary school consists of the varied approaches and emphases given to the teaching of science. Some of the curriculum developers have provided a great deal of structure and guidance for the teacher. Some have included a statement of objectives—descriptions of specific things children should be able to do by the end of the lessons; learning hierarchies (scope-sequence charts showing how the learning activities for children are related); and assessment items (ways to test children to see if they have been successful in achieving the objectives). Other curriculum projects have given the teachers very little structured guidance, no objectives, and have just outlined and described their philosophy for the teaching of science. Their reasoning was that the teacher could do a better job if left with less structure. Since there are commonalities and differences covering a wide range of areas in the presently available curriculum materials, you will find in this book sample exercises from several of the recently developed science curricula so that you may get an idea of the varied approaches which have been taken to the development of similar skills in children.

Science Teaching and the Organization of This Book

In this book you will find one way to categorize the tasks of a scientist:

He must have a notion of what science means to him.

He uses his senses.

He communicates what he knows to other people.

He compares his findings using measurement.

He describes his findings indicating change.

He explains or interprets his work.

He organizes and systematically investigates the part of the environment that is relevant to him.

He searches for causes and then effects.

He is concerned about precision and operational use of terminology.

He searches for regularities in nature.

He establishes with a base of evidence generalizations about the environment.

In short, he is at work using what he knows as a springboard to a better understanding of the world around him.

Each chapter is an invitation for you to experience one of these skills as well as to relate your experience to the ways others have suggested involving children. In each chapter you will find a set of similar resources.

Pretest. This is an opportunity for you to demonstrate to yourself whether or not you can do the science skill that is the main topic of the chapter. Before you teach an idea to children, you need to be able to do it yourself. As a homespun philosopher once said: "It is pretty difficult to come back from where you haven't been." Do the pretest yourself, and then check your answers with the "acceptable responses." If you did well on the pretest, you may want to omit the activities suggested for learning the science skill related to the chapter topic.

Introduction to the Topic. This provides you with a picture of the goal of the chapter. Included are both a description of what you should be able to do and the reason for the behavior being important to science and science teaching.

Your Skill with the Topic. This is a set of learning activities designed to help you. It is not a reading assignment. You will need to use objects and people for the tasks. Most of the objects will be on a desk or in a kitchen. As you do the activity, you will be asked to record your results. You will find brief discussions of what others have also found when they have done similar activities. "Your skill with the topic" is meant for you personally to become involved in learning important science skills.

Curriculum Developers' View of the Topic. It may not always be clear to you how the skill you have been learning is related to teaching children. Today we are fortunate to have the benefits of a number of science curricula developed by responsible groups of scientists, classroom teachers, and learning psychologists. As a part of their work, they have

had to ponder the questions, "What is science?"—and "How is it best related to children?".
In their writings, many excellent definitions are found of aspects of science and applications
of these definitions to teaching children. In this section, you will find ideas from these new
science curriculum groups.

1. *Science—A Process Approach,* a curriculum sequence for grades K-6, developed by the American Association for the Advancement of Science. John Mayor,
Director.

2. *Science Curriculum Improvement Study,* a curriculum sequence for grades 1-6,
developed at the University of California at Berkeley. Robert Karplus, Director.

3. *Elementary Science Study,* a series of nongraded science units developed at the
Educational Development Center. Joe Griffith, Director.

4. *Minnesota Mathematics and Science Teaching Project,* a curriculum sequence
for grades K-3, developed at the University of Minnesota. James H. Werntz, Director.

5. *Illinois Astronomy Project,* a series of units for grades 4–6, developed at the
University of Illinois. Michael Atkins, Director.

Involvement Experiences for Children Related to Topic. Being able to do a skill
yourself is essential. Knowing how it is related to an overall picture of science is important,
but still lacking is the specific way the topic is made part of the classroom experience of
children. In this section of the topic, you will find selections taken from the new curriculum
that illustrate how different people have translated the same topic into children's learning
experience. A common thread in these units is the direct involvement of children in active
learning to use the information of their experience. The manner in which they become involved is rather varied. An important clue to effective science teaching is found here. Many
different contexts can be used to help a child acquire the same skill. *You* and your students
will enjoy science if you select those contexts that appeal to both of you.

Before you leave the topic, you should have some feedback on how well you are
doing. For this reason, a *posttest* is the last section of each topic. Do it! Then feel the warm
satisfaction in your success as you check your answers with the "acceptable responses."

Science Teaching—And Your Part

At this point it is time to start the first topic and to check yourself as to whether you
can or cannot do the listed skill. In doing the various activities listed for developing the skill
take time to *think* about what this activity has to do with science as you perceive it; and most
importantly, think about how you would approach the teaching of this particular skill to
children. At the completion of the last chapter you should be able to identify, name, and
demonstrate twelve of the intellectual skills thought to be important in science, whether
you are a scientist or not.

When you have finished the book, it is hoped that—in addition to the fact that you
have developed skill in some of the intellectual processes of science—you will have had
an opportunity to reflect about which of the approaches suggested by the various curriculum
projects fits your style of teaching; and moreover, that you will have found in the approaches
new ideas to make your teaching more dynamic, varied, fulfilling, and even more efficient.
We hope that you will find the following pages worthwhile and fun and that you will have
difficulty in finding things to memorize. In turn, may your students find *your* science classes
worthwhile and fun, and may they have difficulty in finding things to memorize!

2. Using
Your Senses

By the end of this chapter, you should be able to describe the characteristics of an object or an event using more than three of your senses as sources of information.

Check yourself now. If you can successfully perform these tasks, omit this part of the chapter and go to page 11.

For this assignment, you will need a package of chewing gum.

Remove a piece of gum from the package. List seven characteristics of the gum that you can observe using your senses only.

1. _____
2. _____
3. _____
4. _____
5. _____
6. _____
7. _____

Now go to page 7 for discussion for acceptable responses on this pretest. *If* you were successful with the pretest, go on to the next part of the chapter, page 11. If you were *not* successful, the activities suggested on page are a way to help you develop skills in observing characteristics of objects or events.

6

Acceptable Responses for Pretest

In your list of the seven observable characteristics of the piece of gum, you should have included only those characteristics of the gum that were observable and not inferences as to how the gum was made or what will happen when you throw it away. You should also have used at least three senses. Some possible responses are:

1. It smells like spearmint.

2. It is brown.

3. It is rectangular in shape.

4. It bends easily.

5. It tears or breaks into smaller pieces when stretched.

6. It makes no sound.

7. It feels smoother than sandpaper.

Your senses are important sources of information about the world around you. In science, the information that you obtain through your senses is usually called observation. It is the basic stuff on which scientific thought is ultimately based. Observation using the five senses is basic to science because it is the first way of gathering information. It is basic to communication, prediction, measurement, classification, and other fundamental skills subsumed by science.

Often we use tools such as a magnifying lens or a ruler to amplify or to quantify the information gained through our sensory capacities and thus make our observations more precise.

In an attempt to explain a set of observations, we construct an inference. The inference is tested by making another set of observations. The attempt at explaining how observations fit together has characterized the history of scientific thought from the ancient view of the heavens to today's genetic research.

Just as observation is basic to the work of the scientist, so it is also essential to the work of the classroom teacher because it is important in the intellectual development of elementary school children.

To begin with, you will need two glasses of water, an Alka-Seltzer tablet, and a Polident tablet.

Place the two tablets about an arm's length away from you and list four characteristics of the tablets that you can observe by only looking at them.

Alka-Seltzer	*Polident*
1. _____	1. _____
2. _____	2. _____
3. _____	3. _____
4. _____	4. _____

You may now examine the two tablets in any way you wish. The water might also be helpful. Record six more characteristics of the two tablets.

Alka-Seltzer	*Polident*
1. _____	1. _____
2. _____	2. _____
3. _____	3. _____
4. _____	4. _____
5. _____	5. _____
6. _____	6. _____

Look back at your list of ten statements about each tablet. What was the source of information for each statement? _____

More than one source? To keep track of each source, code the statements as:

a.   Characteristics observed by sight.

b.   Characteristics observed by smell.

c.   Characteristics observed by touch.

d.   Characteristics observed by listening.

e.   Characteristics observed by taste (Note: It is extremely dangerous to taste unknown substances and very unusual to find taste employed as source of information in scientific investigation).

f.   Change in the tablets.

g.   Measurements of the tablets or of their change.

h.   Inference or explanation about the tablets or change that occurred.

In these experiences, codes a, b, c, d, and e are illustrations of observations of characteristics of the tablets. Codes f, g, and h are situations in which you have gone beyond observable characteristics to information you would only secure when you use more than your five senses.

You will find it useful to do these tasks. Write two more statements about the tablets to fit each of the codes.

Code A: 1. _____
          2. _____

Code B: 1. _____
          2. _____

Code C: 1. _____
          2. _____

Code D: 1. _____
          2. _____

Code E: 1. _____
          2. _____

Code F: 1. _____
          2. _____

Code G: 1. _____
          2. _____

Code H: 1.   _____

2.   _____

How would you define using your senses for scientific observation?   _____

Your definition probably included the idea that you should use at least four of the five senses in observing properties of objects. How is this related to teaching science to children?   _____

If you wish to reflect more on this subject, you will find it useful to read how skills in using the senses are discussed by curriculum developers. There are several current programs that have been developed by cooperating teams of scientists, learning psychologists, and classroom teachers. In most of these programs, using the senses is emphasized for a variety of reasons.

For example, in the Science Curriculum Improvement Study, *SCIS*, Hurd and Gallagher (1968) state some of the limitations of using one's senses:

The designers of *SCIS* are not suggesting that pupils learn only what they observe for themselves; in our complex world much learning must be based upon observations reported by others. To be able to utilize the experiences of others, "an individual must have a conceptual framework and a means of communication that enable him to interpret information as though he had obtained it himself." This understanding of science concepts is called scientific literacy and is identified as the principal objective of SCIS. It is through concrete experience that elementary school pupils acquire the concepts and communication skills essential to the development of scientific literacy.

Although the primary emphasis of SCIS is on concepts, attention is given to the development of attitudes, abilities, and skills including habits of careful observation, methods of recording observations and experiences, discrimination of fine differences and recognition of broad similarities, and the procurement of quantitative data along with the appropriate vocabulary to assist in the development of meaningful concepts. Children are encouraged to discuss their observations with others in the class and to use evidence to settle controversies that arise. Interest and involvement of children in the lessons is a major concern.[1]

In his description of initial skills needed by children, Gagné (1967) defines using your senses as *observing*. In *Science—A Process Approach*, he describes observing as:

Beginning with identifying objects and object-properties, this sequence proceeds to the identification of changes in various physical systems, the making of controlled observations, and the ordering of a series of observations.[2]

In a more detailed description the developers of the Minnesota Mathematics and Science Teaching Project (1967) MINNEMAST wrote:

---

[1] R. Karplus, "The Science Curriculum Improvement Study," *Journal of Research in Science Teaching*, 2 (1964), 296.

[2] Commission on Science Education, American Association for the Advancement of Science, *Science—A Process Approach* (New York: Xerox Corporation) Publication 67–12 (September 1967).

A child discovers the external world through the use of his basic senses of sight, smell, hearing, touch, and taste. He also reacts to the world in terms of his past experiences.

In the first . . . unit, . . . the child is encouraged to become a careful observer. His observations are based on a mixture of his sense impressions of the many objects surrounding him. (Then) . . . he goes on to discover the part each of his senses plays in making these observations.

The observer is not entirely outside and apart from what he is observing. We need to be aware of the limitations of sense data by taking into account the circumstances which affect perception. If, for example, an observer explores an ice cube by touching it, he is acting on it (melting it) at the same time that he registers the fact that it feels cold. Similarly, while he can see an object only by the light reflected from it, he is also to a degree reflecting light back to the object. For example, if a girl wearing a red dress holds a piece of white paper in her hand, it might look pink to her, while another child in different clothing might see it as pale yellow or pale green. Considerations of this type may of course be beyond the child's comprehension. But he can at least begin to be conscious of his role as observer. He can begin to learn the value of checking his sense impressions against those of others.

An important feature of (instruction) on the senses is the attempt to develop precision and objectivity in the child's observations and descriptions. At first these will be vague. With . . . guidance, he will begin to learn to distinguish between a statement that tells how he feels about an object and one that actually describes the object in ways that can be checked by other observers. For example, he might say about a rabbit, "It's nice." This kind of statement doesn't give any information about the rabbit. If he says instead, "When I touch it, it feels warm and soft; when I look at it I see it is white and has pink eyes," he is giving a description of characteristics of the rabbit as relayed by each of two senses.

. . . (The aim is not) . . . to discourage any offering of the child, the best way to lead him to an objective statement is to have him identify the sense impressions on which his comments are based. For example, if a child says, "I like that flower," ask him, "What do you like about it? The smell? The color?" . . . have the children consider what it is about a particular food that makes it pleasant to one child and unpleasant to another. Is it color, shape, texture, taste, or smell?

The five senses that the child is called upon to use in these lessons are sight, hearing, touch, taste, and smell. Each relates to an organ equipped with specialized nerve endings which receive appropriate stimuli. For example, the eyes receive stimuli from light sources and taste buds receive chemical stimuli.[3]

The Elementary Science Study (ESS) emphasizes the importance of the child's experience:

The originators of the Elementary Science Study (ESS) view the grade school years as a period of exploration, a time for children to examine relation-

---

[3] Minnesota Mathematics and Science Teaching Project, *Using Our Senses,* Unit 4 (Minneapolis, Minn., 1969), pp. 1–2.

ships between man and the physical and biological environments. Explorations are best done when teaching units are designed and tested with children to assure a good chance of providing experiences that are both interesting and enriching. This requires an abundance and a variation of activities within each unit to allow for differences among children in ability, interest, and background. It is also important that children have the freedom to work on their own. This means that much of the class time is spent in unguided activities when children have the opportunity, as Hawkins aptly put it, to "mess about in science."

The authors of ESS feel that the most fruitful way to help children develop useful concepts of science as well as cognitive skills is through free experiences with highly motivating materials. Moreover, they feel that science concepts and cognitive skills should be developed concurrently.

An essential part of the ESS program is that children need to use the instructional materials as they were intended: to raise all kinds of questions about them and to try ways of working that have not been preplanned by the teacher. It is expected that situations will be created in which children talk about their work with not only the teacher but also other children to compare observations and explain what they seem to mean.

The interaction of pupils and instructional materials may be illustrated by the unit entitled *The Behavior of Mealworms.* Each pupil is provided with a few live mealworms and given the opportunity to watch them. After a period of observation, pupils typically begin asking such questions as these: How do mealworms find food? Can they see? Can they feel heat? Can they move backwards? What would make them move backwards? These questions become the basis for experiments.[4]

Allowing the world around the child to have meaning through his experience is important in teaching him to use his senses. The following are illustrations of activities in which children are provided with opportunities to use their senses in a variety of ways. They were taken from different programs.

1. MINNEMAST LESSON: THE FIVE SENSES

PURPOSE

To enable the child to differentiate the kinds of information provided by each of his five senses.

To introduce to the child the idea that he often makes value judgments about sense impressions, and that these may legitimately differ from the value judgments of others.

---

[4] P. Hurd and J. Gallagher, *New Directions on Elementary Science Teaching* (California: Wadsworth Publishing, 1968), pp. 76–77.
From MINNEMAST, *Using Our Senses,* Unit 4 (1969), pp. 7–9. Copyright 1969 by the Regents of the University of Minnesota.

COMMENTARY

What kind of formal introduction to the senses does a five-year-old need? He has used his senses since he was born, but usually not with any special awareness. In order to increase his powers of observation, it will be helpful if he can become aware of what sort of information he can gather through each of his senses. When he isolates the contributions of each sense, he also will become aware of the limitations of a single sense. He should then realize that the information conveyed by several senses will be more complete than the information he can get by using one sense alone. For example, the many properties of an apple are revealed only when sight, smell, touch, taste, and hearing are all in operation.

A child will often describe an object by the way he feels about it. Each of us makes value judgments, and we do not always agree with each other. In this section, the children should begin to learn that it is easier to find agreement when they describe things objectively.

Lesson 1 : Exploring Sense Impressions

Select two or three of the fruits and flowers from the materials list. (The coconut is especially useful because of its unusual shape, texture, and the sounds it produces when shaken or tapped.) Have the children seated so that objects can be passed easily from one to the next. Pass an object. When it has gone around, ask a child:

> Tell me something about this. If the answer is general (for example, "It's a flower"), ask to be told something more. If a specific property is mentioned (for example, "It's red"), ask:
>
> How do you know?
>
> What part of your body were you using when you noticed the color? (eyes)
>
> We call this using the sense of sight.

Continue this discussion naming each sense and linking each with the appropriate sense organ.

Since the children are unlikely to use the sense of hearing, tap the objects and ask if they now can tell anything additional about them. The sense of taste can be introduced last by giving each child a sample of fruit to taste.

Lesson 2 : Do We All Agree?

Using materials from Lesson 1, ask a child to select the fruit or flower he likes best. Have him give a reason for his choice. Ask another child for his favorite item and the reason for *his* choice. Continue this procedure as long as the interest lasts. These will be value judgments. Try to elicit opposing ones. This activity should call attention to the fact that individuals differ in their reactions to the same sense impressions.

> Are there some things you might agree on in describing this object? What are they? (Color, shape, and so on)

2. ELEMENTARY SCIENCE STUDY LESSON: EGGS AND TADPOLES

A. Introducing the Eggs

If you have never handled frogs or tadpoles before, you may want to follow the plan suggested below for the first time, to help you start the children in their study. It includes notes of situations that have arisen in trial classes.

See that each child has ten to twenty frog eggs—if possible, newly laid—and a clear container in which to observe them.

Let them play with their eggs and equipment for some time. Naturally, the health of an egg or tadpole is not improved by a child's handling it and shaking it, sucking it up into an eyedropper, or poking it with his fingers—but the child's knowledge of the tadpole is increased. Some children may have to handle these gift eggs in order to feel that the eggs belong to them. In any case, the eggs and young tadpoles can stand a good deal of handling.

During the first week, the children should be encouraged to spend time with their frog egg containers whenever they can. If a child has finished his spelling lesson while the rest of the class is still working on it, let him bring his frog eggs to his seat and look at them. Older children may use available microscopes to examine the eggs quite closely.

To begin with, you may choose not to tell the children that they have frog eggs. Instead, you may want to ask them to guess what these things are and then verify their guesses by watching to see what happens. This approach can be quite successful, and you should not refer them to printed information. Let the children find out as much as they can about the living material in front of them. This means seeing what is happening, agreeing upon a description, and then trying to predict what will happen next.

It is important for you to give each guess your attention and not consider any answer silly. At first glance, after all, the eggs could be any one of a great many things.

Here are some examples of younger children's guesses about what the eggs are. "They look like fish eggs." "They're polliwogs—we got some last summer." "They're little beans." Rather than choose among the answers, your job at this stage is to lead the other children to be critical. By asking, "What makes you think so?" and, "How do you know?" and, "What can we do to find out if Raymond is right?", you can help them realize that the answering is really up to them.

Of course if the children can watch a female frog laying the eggs, they will be pretty sure of what the clumps contain.

In any case, the eggs will change hourly—sometimes subtly, sometimes dramatically. Within a week, they will hatch out to swimming tadpoles. Most children will know what the eggs are before that time.

In many trial classes the children have been firmly convinced from the start that they are dealing with some kind of eggs, and their discussions have included comparisons with what they know about chicken eggs. In general, such comparisons are very useful, because they lead to predictions about what will happen to their eggs. In one class, several children thought that the jelly around a frog egg is like the white in a chicken egg—a suggestive idea. One child thought that the jelly would turn into some specific part of the animal—probably, he guessed, the frog's white throat. This idea happened to be wrong, but it was useful because it directed his attention to watching for the jelly to take its place on the growing animal. With this theory in mind, he was able to observe the eggs in a specific way, and the observation helped him learn how to find the truth. The children were more uncertain about the relationship of the chicken egg yolk to what they were watching.

The teacher asked if eggs needed shells. One girl decided that her eggs didn't need shells because the eggs were for very small animals. It is hard to see how she reasoned, but she may have had the intuitive notion that the bigger something is, the more support it requires, and thus, a big chicken egg needs a shell to hold it together until it becomes a chicken.

Another child thought that "the eggshell keeps the chicken from drying up before it is grown." During the ensuing discussion, one boy decided to leave his frog eggs out of water to see what happened. The next day the results of his experiment were spectacular: the eggs had dried like paint on the paper towel. Many of the children became convinced that these shell-less eggs needed to stay in water to keep their wetness. This sort of discussion, resulting in a real test of some theory, is very satisfying to the children.

B. Discussions

On the second day of the study, the children will probably look at their eggs as soon as they come into class. Let them look and talk and compare observations and eggs for a while.

Ask them what they see when they look at the things in their containers. They should become critical of one another's statements and try to verify their own statements by looking at their eggs again. If some of them want to take an egg apart to see what is inside, they should be encouraged to try this. They should listen to one another and talk to one another rather than to you. If there are disagreements, it is sometimes better to leave them unresolved than to resolve them yourself, but do encourage discussion.

Whenever you discuss the eggs, the children should have their containers in front of them. You may find that many of them are looking at the eggs instead of listening to the discussion. This may be a sign that they need to spend more time just observing the eggs. Encourage them to talk about the changes that they see in words that come most naturally to them. There are many technical terms for the different parts of the growing animal and for the different stages in its development, but these would only cause confusion if they were to be introduced at this time.

Many of the children's descriptions may sound fantastic at first. For instance, one second grader said that the animal inside the jelly was "squeezing out like paint." The teacher had to use her imagination to realize that his comparison was actually very real for him. He had seen the spherical black thing elongate into a tubular form and was comparing it to some oil paint he had watched as it was squeezed from its tube. As you listen to your children's descriptions and find that most of the students are unable to explain exactly how they arrived at their comparisons, it is important that you refrain from implying to the children that they are not making any sense to you. They may, after all, be making sense to their classmates.

By the third day of the study, many of the children in the first and second grade trial classes noticed that the eggs had changed, and they asked many questions about what had happened. Some they could answer from their own observations, such as, "Did the egg start out black or white?" Some were more difficult: "Do they eat the jelly?" Most of the questions were impossible to answer: "How did the black thing get that way?" The children ask such questions because they have never had the opportunity to learn how to find out things for themselves directly from the material. The best way to handle this kind of question is to ask the questioner if he can figure out a way to find the answer.

C. Descriptions

Children can sharpen their observations by making drawings of what they are trying to describe. Give a big piece of paper to each child who wants to draw, and encourage him to fill it with a large drawing. Have the children compare their drawings, and let each child make new drawings as he learns more about this animals. If you can get the students to understand that the drawings are for them to use among themselves when they discuss the eggs and are not to be "graded," the discussions will probably progress better. If a child criticizes another's drawing, ask him how he would change it to make it look more real.

In several first grade classes, the children were enthusiastic about drawing pictures of eggs and tadpoles on the chalkboard. The teachers found it best to have each draw his pictures on large paper first so that he would not be influenced by the others. Crayon drawings are best in the lower grades, because the children do not feel that they have to be so accurate, and the resulting pictures are satisfyingly colorful.

During the study of the first set of eggs, you will probably find that the children cannot remember by the fourth day exactly what has happened. If they have made several drawings, you might begin a discussion by asking them to arrange other children's drawings in the order in which the changes depicted occurred. This may help them to become more critical of their own observations, and it will usually encourage them to keep more accurate records. For instance, children have asked whether the eggs started out all black or all white, and if there was white, what happened to make it look all black. Such discussions should eventually lead the children to the realization that they could answer many of these questions if they could observe a new set of eggs.

Remember, however, that drawing pictures and keeping records are not essential. A child will want to keep records when he feels a need for them. This often comes too late, but it is far better for a child to wish he had kept records and plan to do so next time, than for him to keep them because you tell him to if he is not convinced of the necessity. Do not urge record keeping, then, but hold it in mind as something to talk about when the need for a second batch of eggs is being discussed.

You may be surprised how few children can describe the overall appearance of the eggs. Do not worry about this. Looking at something new is one of the things they are learning how to do. Post a few of the children's drawings and leave them up. Agreement is not immediately necessary, and self-correction is the most helpful kind. Just encourage the children to listen to one another, to consider one another's statements, to be critical, and to verify ideas by looking themselves. Ideally, the children will become aware enough of their own ability to make accurate observation to trust themselves to make valid statements about things they see.

In one class, for example, discussion centered around the color of the jelly. The children began by calling it white, but the teacher asked them what things in the room the jelly most closely resembled. The children thought that the jelly was like the face of the clock, the window, and their egg containers, but not like the white chalk or paper. The teacher wisely let them draw their own conclusions.

Let new ideas come up naturally. When the notion of looking at the eggs through the bottom of the container occurs to someone it will sweep through the class like a new fad. It is better if this comes from the class than from you even if it takes a few days. You will probably not even need to mention the magnifying glasses. If they are available, someone will be sure to think of using a glass to look at the eggs and then the others will want to try this too.

D.   Questions

During the first few days after the children receive the frog eggs, many things will be happening. The questions that arise are much more important to remember than any individual observation. A class should come through the first week or two with many unanswered questions—how their eggs looked yesterday and the day before, how they looked at the very first, what they looked like as they changed, how the changes took place. You can encourage a critical and questioning atmosphere from the very beginning, so that by the second week, when you make the film loops available to the class, the children will be eager to use them to help answer questions that have been raised and are not resolved.

Using the second batch of eggs is even better than showing the film loops, but both probably should be used for comparison. You can introduce the idea of a second set when you feel that the children have questions which they can no longer answer because the first eggs have developed too far. The second batch offers a way of answering these questions. A good time to introduce it is at the beginning of the third week of the study. The first time the children observe their eggs, they have little idea of what to expect, perhaps little idea even of how to look. The second time they approach the eggs with specific questions in mind. Throughout the unit, each child will be concerned with his own particular questions, so what each learns will be different from what his neighbor learns. This is good, because the children are observing their animals not because they have been told to do so or because the rest of the class is doing so, but in order to get answers to their own individual questions. Their learning will relate to them specifically.

3. SCIENCE—A PROCESS APPROACH LESSON: OBSERVING USING SEVERAL OF THE SENSES

Using the delight of the smells and sounds of popcorn the main context for this unit is an opportunity for children to experience and then share. Within this context the objectives are for children to learn to:

1. Identify objects, or changes in objects, by using several of the senses.

2. State which sense or senses he used to make his observations, by saying, for example, "I smelled it," "I saw it," and so on.

Beginning with the unusual event of popcorn popping—out of sight and not expected —the springboard activity leads children and teacher to telling what they know and observe and what they think might have happened. Here the teacher can skillfully guide children in identifying both what they think happened and its supporting evidence—gained from each sense: (1) *heard* it popping; (2) *smelled* it popping; (3) *feel* it now; and with butter, enjoy its *taste*.

Children can then explore the problem of popped corn—a great new way to describe things by comparison. They will have much fun talking about other things that get larger— bread dough, cookies, and, in the last activity, an entire can of whipped cream or shaving cream, sprayed on a large sheet of paper.

4. SCIENCE CURRICULUM IMPROVEMENT STUDY LESSON: AIR AND WATER

While investigating some of the properties of air samples, students again observe and recognize that an air sample may be considered an object.

Children observe that air occupies space, takes the shape of the container enclosing it, and is compressible. They also observe that air must leave a space before water can fill that space. . . .

Introduction

Hold up a plastic bag, and ask the children to describe this object. After some properties have been mentioned, give each child a plastic bag. Tell him to put one or more objects inside but not to use objects from his desk. Some children will put hands or fingers into the bags, and others will probably trap

From *Science, A Process Approach* (1967), Part B. Exercise N, p. 1. Reprinted by permission of the American Association for the Advancement of Science, Washington, D.C.

From *Science Curriculum Improvement Study* (Chicago: Rand McNally and Co., 1970), pp. 74–75.

air inside. Accept these decisions, and encourage pupils to describe the properties of the objects they have selected. Check to see if they are able (especially in the case of air) to think of the object or objects as being distinct from the bags.

Putting Air in the Bags

Trap some air in your plastic bag, and ask the children to do the same; then discuss the properties of the enclosed air. You or the children should mention that the air (1) is colorless ("see-through color," according to one first grader); (2) can be squeezed; and (3) takes the shape of the bag. The properties of a bag filled with air should then be contrasted to the properties of another bag filled with solid objects. Either fill one demonstration bag with some solid objects or, if you feel the group is having trouble, give each child a few solid objects so that he can directly experience the difference.

Using the Syringes

Give each child a syringe. Encourage the children to explore possible uses of the syringes. After a few minutes the children may discover that the syringes can be used to trap and move samples of air. When the free activity has been completed, demonstrate the following two situations; then let the children explore each one.

After pulling the syringe plunger to the end of the barrel, place your finger tightly over the nozzle and try to push the plunger in. This demonstration should help to emphasize that there is a sample of air in the syringe and that, until you remove your finger from the nozzle and let the air out, it is very difficult to push the plunger in.

After pushing the plunger all the way in, put your finger on the nozzle and try to pull the plunger out. This is hard to do, because the pressure of the air outside the plunger tends to push it back. This is a very complicated idea for first graders, but the important point is that they experience the difficulty of pulling the plunger out.

Connecting Two Syringes with Plastic Tubing

Invite a child to assist you in demonstrating the following three problems to the class. Then let the children work in pairs and try each problem themselves; allow enough time so that all can experiment with the syringes. Discuss each problem before demonstrating the next one.

Close two syringes and connect them to the tubing. The problem is to pull one of the plungers out without disconnecting the tubing. Discuss the difficulty encountered. (Do not worry if only a few children have an adequate explanation; the main purpose of this investigation is to enable the children to experience the problem.)

Push the plungers halfway in, and connect the syringes to the tubing. The problem is to push one of the plungers in without pushing the other plunger out.

Push the plungers halfway in, and connect the syringes to the tubing. The problem is to predict what will happen when one plunger is pushed all the way in or pulled all the way out. In your discussions, help the children understand that the movement of the second plunger is related to the movement of air in both syringes and the tubing.

Experimenting with Air and Water

Gather the children in the class demonstration area during the next session. Show them the setup of the syringe, vial, and one-holed rubber stopper. Tell the children that the problem is to fill the vial with water. Now pour some water into the syringe. When it does not run into the vial, let the children discuss the problem. Accept and try out their suggestions for solving it; if they do not guess the solution, tell them that you must let the air out of the vial before the water can flow in. Repeat the demonstration a few times, still using a syringe and vial, but this time employing a two-holed rubber stopper. By putting your finger over the second hole, you can demonstrate its importance. The flow of water into the vial will stop when you prevent air from leaving through the second hole.

When the vial with the two-holed stopper is full of water, present the problem of emptying the vial first with, and then without, your finger over the hole in the stopper. You must take your finger off the hole in order to let air out when filling the vial or to let air in when you pour the water out.

Using a Syringe to Fill a Vial with Water

A vial in a dish of water poses a more difficult problem. Fill the dish with water before laying the vial in. Then show the children a syringe with tubing attached, and ask them how one could use this to fill the vial with water. Try all their suggestions, or let the children carry them out to decide if the methods are successful. Your pupils' suggestions will help you evaluate their understanding of the properties of air.

The most effective way to fill the vial with water is to remove the air with a syringe. Push the plunger all the way in, place the tube in the vial, and then pull the plunger all the way out. Remove the tubing from the vial, push the plunger back in, and repeat the process until the vial is filled with water. Once the vial is filled, similarly present and carry out the problem of emptying it.

On another day, set out the dishes, syringes, tubing, vials, and water to encourage interested children to independently review the problems or invent new ones.

Using the Student Manual

...The children are asked to indicate how moving the plunger would affect the size of the balloon attacked to the end of the syringe.... Have they understood the changing distribution of air in the syringe and balloon when they moved the plunger?...you can set up this experiment as an interesting optional activity. All you need is a small one-hole stopper (No. 00) and a balloon for each syringe. The children can then experiment with the many possibilities provided by this apparatus.

Coconuts, flowers, frog eggs, popcorn, magnets, and bags of air. These sound like an improbable collection. They have one common thread—they are useful experiences by which children can be guided to use their senses more effectively.

Using one's senses to observe the world around him is an important part of many science curricula. Is it equally important to each of the lessons included here? _____

In what ways do they emphasize children's using their senses? _____

_____

_____

_____

By now you should have developed sufficient skill in using your senses. Check yourself before you go on.

Posttest

To take this test, you will need a teaspoon from the kitchen. List seven characteristics of that spoon, using only your senses.

1. _____
2. _____
3. _____
4. _____
5. _____
6. _____
7. _____

Following, you will find acceptable answers. If you are having difficulty, you may wish to discuss this with your instructor.

Acceptable Responses for Posttest

Your answers should be such that you could code them by a, b, c, d, or e. Some answers might be:

1. Bowl of spoon is shaped like an ellipsoid (Code A)

2. It sounds like metal (Code D)

3. It feels cool to the touch (Code C)

4. It has no odor (Code B)

5. It is gray or silver in color (Code A)

6. It has a handle that is longer than the bowl (Code A)

7. The handle is shaped like a rectangle (Code A)

---

3. Telling
Another Person

By the end of this chapter, you should be able to:

1. Distinguish an object or event from similar ones in a set by identifying its unique observable characteristics.

2. Identify and name two-dimensional and three-dimensional shapes as part of objects in the environment.

3. Construct a classification of a collection of objects using observable properties of the objects.

4. Construct a graph when given the manipulated and responding variable data.

Check yourself now. If you can successfully do these tasks, omit this part of the chapter and go on to page 34.

For this assignment, you will need a collection of kitchen silverware.

First, name the two-dimensional shapes that you can see in a fork and a spoon.

	Fork		*Spoon*
1.	_____	1.	_____
2.	_____	2.	_____
3.	_____	3.	_____

Second, make two groups of all the silverware you have in your collection. What is the name of the first group? _____

_____

What is the name of the second group? _____

_____

If there is more than one object in your first group, divide that group into two smaller groups. What are the names for the new groups? _____

_____

Third, make a graph of your collection.

Check the following discussion for acceptable responses on this pretest. If you were successful with the pretest, go on to the next part of the chapter, page 34. If you were *not* successful, carry out the activities suggested on page 23 as a way to help you develop skills in telling another person about your experience.

Acceptable Responses for Pretest

Suppose in your collection you have a dinner fork, a table knife, a teaspoon, a tablespoon, and a paring knife. The two-dimensional shapes in the dinner fork would be rectangular handle, triangular point on the four prongs, square or rectangle in the large, flat part of the fork. The spoon would have a rectangular handle, an ellipse in the bowl of the spoon, and so on.

With the items listed you could have several groups, such as:

Sharp cutting edge	*No sharp cutting edge*
paring knife	fork
table knife	teaspoon
	tablespoon

or

Holds liquid	*Does not hold liquid*
teaspoon	fork
tablespoon	knife
	paring knife

The first group could be reorganized as: used for peeling vegetables—not used for peeling vegetables; or: holds less than two teaspoons—holds more than two teaspoons.

Your graph must have the left side and the base line labeled. For example, the title could be "Collection of Kitchen Silverware." On the side put "Number of Objects," and across the bottom put "Type of Objects" : one fork, two knives, and two spoons.

"Collection of Kitchen Silverware"

Type of Objects

Telling another person about what you have observed requires you to organize your thoughts and find ways to communicate them to the other person. Verbal communication demands that you be precise in your descriptions, whereas visual communications, or graphs, make it necessary for you to carefully select and order your thoughts. This is another way of saying that you must classify your information.

You will need a friend or at least someone who will listen to you and a collection of things from your desk drawer, such as paper clips, pencil, rubber band, and ruler.

Look at the furniture in your room. Make a list of each piece of furniture that has a gizmo on the the end of it.

1. _____

2. _____

3. _____

4. _____

Have your friend check your list. Did you agree? Do you know what a gizmo is?

Now look around the room and identify each piece of furniture that has cylinder-shaped legs.

103783

1. _____
2. _____
3. _____
4. _____

Have your friend check your list now. Did you agree ? What was the difference between the gizmo task and the cylinder task ? _____

_____

You may have noted that in the gizmo task there was no clear definition in your mind and in the mind of your friend of what it was you were talking about, whereas in the cylinder task both of you had a workable idea of what a cylinder was.

Look again at the furniture in the room. Name three things that have a shape like

a. a circle

1. _____
2. _____
3. _____

b. a square

1. _____
2. _____
3. _____

c. a rectangle

1. _____
2. _____
3. _____

d. an ellipse

1. _____
2. _____
3. _____

e. a triangle

1. _____
2. _____
3. _____

f. a cube

1. _____
2. _____
3. _____

g.   a cone

   1.   _____

   2.   _____

   3.   _____

h.   a pyramid

   1.   _____

   2.   _____

   3.   _____

i.   a cylinder

   1.   _____

   2.   _____

   3.   _____

j.   a rectangular parallel pipehead or rectangular prism

   1.   _____

   2.   _____

   3.   _____

You may find it useful to look back at those three-dimensional shapes (the cube, cone, pyramid, cylinder, and rectangular parallel pipehead), and identify the two-dimensional shapes (circle, square, rectangle, ellipse, and triangle) that are part of them.

Select a book in the room and hold it up to the light so that you can observe its shadow.

What is the shape of the shadow of the book? _____

What is the shape of the shadow of a ball? _____

What is the shape of the shadow of a tin can? _____

What is the shape of the shadow of a pencil? _____

Can you get more than one shadow from any of these objects? _____

You may have noted that the shape of the shadow of the book was like a rectangle, whereas the shape of the shadow of a ball was like a circle. The shape of the shadow of a tin can, however, could be both a circle and a rectangle, as the shape of the shadow of a pencil could have a triangle in the point, and a longer narrow rectangle with also the shadow of a circle. In the case of the tin can and the pencil, more than one shape of the shadow was possible.

What shadows do you get from an object that is shaped like a cube? _____

_____ Like a cone? _____

_____ Like a cylinder? _____

Shapes are useful, too, in telling another person what you have seen or experienced. There are other times that you will want to describe more than a single thing. You will need to describe a series of things. For example, think about what you must do to open a bottle of Coke. Write out the directions for your friend so that he will know what to do.

Did your directions include where to find the Coke bottle and the opener? How to open the bottle? Which end of the opener to use? How to push or pull on the bottle with one hand and what to do with the other hand?

Would you like a very nice one? Write out a description to tell your friend how to unlock the front door or how to phone your nearest neighbor.

Check your description by having your friend do *only* what you have included in your written description.

One way in which you can improve your description is to group objects and then to use the idea that the group has in common. For example, use an unopen drawer or a closet (or a refrigerator if you have one available). As both you and your partner watch, open the door for fifteen seconds only. Then close the door. Now both of you make a list of what you saw.

Compare the two lists.

1.   How many objects did you list? _____
2.   How many objects did your partner list? _____
3.   How many objects were on both of your lists? _____
4.   How many objects were on only one of your lists? _____

Open the drawer again and check your lists. What items do you now need to add?

On a sheet of paper, make a list of your objects according to this scheme:

All objects	
Listed on both lists	Not listed on both lists
Listed on one list	Not listed

From your desk drawer, take out a collection of miscellaneous objects such as rubber band, pencil, pen, paper clip, and so on. Place these in a large circle on a sheet of paper. Name the circle so that it will include all the objects.

Now group the objects into two groups and name the characteristic that is common to each group on the chart. Continue this subgrouping until you have each object in a separate circle

In your chart, identify where these objects would not fit into your scheme.

1.   A pencil.
2.   A chalkboard eraser.
3.   A dime.

4. A thumbtack.

Some useful keys for classifying information are: first, each time you regroup, select a characteristic shared by about half of a total group of objects. Second, make sure that your groups are mutually exclusive. That is, that an object will always belong in one or the other groups, such as "blue" and "not blue" rather than "blue" and "red." In the first case, anything will belong in one of those two groups, but if you had "red" and "blue," where would you put a yellow object?

Let's sweeten up this subject now. Make a list of seven kinds of candy that you have eaten.

1. _____
2. _____
3. _____
4. _____
5. _____
6. _____
7. _____

List the smallest number of characteristics needed to distinguish each kind of candy from the others.

1. _____
2. _____
3. _____
4. _____
5. _____
6. _____
7. _____

Construct a classification key for the entire set of candy. And then show on your chart what you would do to add a carrot and a Milky Way candy bar to the group.

Let's go back to that group of miscellaneous objects that you took out of your desk drawer. Suppose that you have at least six objects in the group. How many of them have a shape

    a. like circle? _____
    b. like a triangle? _____
    c. like a square? _____
    d. like an ellipse? _____
    e. like a rectangle? _____

Imagine that you were trying to tell somebody the results who could not read or hear words. In what way might a graph help? _____

_____

What information or story should a graph include? _____

_____

A graph is a useful picture of information, an economical way of showing the results of your experience. The information or story included in the graph should be contained in the labeling of both axes as to what is being encountered or grouped; the title would show a reason for the graph being made.

Using either a sheet of graph paper or of plain paper on which you can draw lines, what will you use as the label for the horizontal axis, that is, the base line? _____

_____ The choice is arbitrary, but it is customary to use that set of categories that *you* selected for the base line and the set of categories that you counted or measured for the vertical axis. After you have labeled your two axes, did you wonder whether you labeled the lines or the spaces? Custom says to label lines only. Now complete your graph. What title did you give your graph, that is, of the relationship of what ideas is the graph a picture?

To get some more information, write down the names of:

1. Your governor. _____

2. One U.S. senator from your state. _____

3. The mayor of your town. _____

4. The secretary of defense. _____

5. The chief justice of the Supreme Court. _____

6. The mayor of New York City. _____

In one group, the results were as follows: Out of twenty-six individuals, twenty-four named the governor, twenty-five named the senator, twenty-six named the mayor, eleven named the secretary of defense, four named the chief justice, eighteen named the mayor of New York. Add your own results to these data and construct a new graph on this information of important people today.

In Table 1, you will find a set of data showing the results of student achievement scores in spelling between the first test and the last test of a new approach to spelling. Construct the graph that will best communicate the effectiveness of this approach.

TABLE 1. Spelling Achievement of Miss Ima Genius's Class.

Child	January	March
Bill	89	91
Marie	61	82
Janet	86	93
Don	40	81
Marilyn	50	84
Ken	72	88

Figures 1 and 2 are graphs of this information. Did your graph look like either one? As you think back about the graphs that you have just constructed:

1. What kinds of categories do you place on the base line?

   _____

2. What kinds of categories do you place on the vertical axis?

   _____

3. Why are categories placed on line and not on the space?

   _____

In answer to the questions, you may recall that on the base line, or horizontal axis of the graph, you place those categories that you selected, whereas on the vertical axis you place those categories that you measure or count. Categories are placed on the line and not on the spaces in order to be consistent with the line representing the completion of an interval rather than the space that is in between intervals.

When you think about telling another person in science, how would you define the skill of telling another person? _____

_____

Your definition should indicate that telling someone about your experience requires *a.* that you have had an experience, and *b.* that you are able to organize the information of your experience. This organization may include distinguishing similarities and differences in parts of the experience and grouping the different aspects of the experience (*classifying*). As an additional tool, unambiguous communication is aided by use of shapes in describing objects and by use of graphs to picture relationships.

How is the skill of telling another person related to teaching science?

If you wish to read more on this subject, you will find it useful to read how the use of verbal and written communication skills has been emphasized by curriculum developers in such current programs as *Science Curriculum Improvement Study, Science—A Process Approach, Minnemast Elementary Science Study*, etc.

Communicating is a process not only of science but of all human endeavors. Clear, precise, unambiguous communication is desirable in any activity, and is fundamental to all scientific work. Scientists communicate with oral and written words, diagrams, maps, graphs, mathematical equations, and various kinds of visual demonstrations.

In *Science—A Process Approach* the Communicating process begins with oral communication. The children practice describing objects so that they can be identified by other children. Most children find this fun and enjoy doing it. Next the children learn to describe objects whose properties are changing. For example, they describe butter melting or water evaporating. This is more difficult, both for children and adults, than describing objects that do not change. But it is an important skill and should be practiced whenever an opportunity occurs.

Later in the Communicating process, the children use diagrams to communicate change. . . . maps, diagrams, and graphs are also used for communication. Since graphs are used so frequently in scientific communication, the children are given frequent opportunities to construct and interpret graphs of data they collect in their investigations.[1]

In the Science-Curriculum Improvement Study, skills in telling another person clearly emphasize the need for a frame of reference—or a common language:

The principal new idea introduced in *Position and Motion* is that of a reference frame, a systematic selection of reference objects and directions. The use of a reference frame makes possible the complete and accurate description of relative positions. For example, when you say "Boulder is 27 miles northwest of Denver," you use Denver and the set of compass directions as a reference frame. In connection with this new idea, the unit introduces techniques for measuring, comparing, and recording distances and directions.

REFERENCE FRAMES

The Relativity Concepts

The relativity concepts are explained in the *Relativity* teacher's guide, which is included in the equipment kit for this unit. It is pointed out there that the position and motion of an object can be perceived and described only with reference to other objects. When you say, "The paper fell on the floor beside the desk," the desk serves as a reference object in your description of the position of the paper. When a passenger says, "The clouds are drifting past the airplane," the airplane is his reference object for the motion of the clouds. An observer on the ground, however, will say the airplane is flying through the clouds, thereby using the clouds as reference objects for the motion of the airplane.

Starting Point and Directions

Actually, the description of the position of the paper relative to the desk was incomplete, because the desk has two "sides" (right and left) and the paper could have been on either one. A single reference object usually is not adequate and must be supplemented with other reference objects ("The paper is on the side of the desk nearer the door") or with directions ("The paper is on the left side of the desk"). You can make a complete description of the position of an object when you use a starting point and a set of directions extending from the starting point. In the statement "Bermuda is about 800 miles southeast of New York City," the city is the starting point, and a compass provides a set of directions. A starting point and a set of directions form a *reference frame*.

Examples of Reference Frames

The description of the location of Bermuda illustrates a reference frame consisting of a starting point and compass directions. Any reference object or landmark can be used as starting point in such a reference frame. For practical reasons, however, the starting point must be easily recognizable by any potential user. Landmarks are especially suitable (Empire State Building in New York,

---

[1] *Science—A Process Approach, Commentary For Teachers* (1970), pp. 97–98.

the Capitol or the Washington Monument in the District of Columbia, and so on). Furthermore, the directions should be clearly identified; thus, compass directions, as shown on the face of a compass, are frequently used.

The artificial observer Mr. O, introduced in the *Relativity* unit, is another reference frame. The figure of Mr. O (more exactly, the point where his arms cross his body) is the starting point, while "right, left, above," and so on form the set of directions. Even though the phrase "reference frame" was not used in the *Relativity* unit, the children in fact learned to treat Mr. O as a reference frame.

A person's body can also be used as a reference frame. When you give the instructions, "Look fifty feet ahead" or, "Take three steps to your left," you are using the listener's body as your reference frame. This reference frame is very similar to Mr. O, and each can be called a *personal reference frame*. Note that personal reference frames may be positioned arbitrarily. A landmark and the set of compass directions, however, is an *earth-based reference frame;* such a reference frame is fixed on earth and cannot be repositioned arbitrarily.

Two important directions which are part of an earth-based reference frame are "up" and "down." Man's erect posture, the direction of tree growth, falling objects, and buildings all help to define "up" and "down." Our intuitive notion of these earth-based directions is so strong that they are usually included along with the personal directions right, left, front, and back in our everyday use of reference frames.

The reference frames we have described make different use of reference objects than most people do in everyday life. When many reference objects are present, and this is usually true, you can describe the position of almost anything with the help of some nearby reference objects. For instance, you could say, "The clock is near the left side of the door." You probably would not say "The clock is five feet west of the door." The first kind of description is more convenient for anyone who is in the classroom and is looking for the clock. For someone who is *not* actually in the classroom and has never been there, the second kind of description is more informative.

Coordinate Frames

The clock example shows how a description which is adequate for casual use can be improved for a person who is not present or where accuracy is important. This unit introduces children to two different artificial reference frames which require minimal use of reference objects in the immediate environment and which permit the complete and accurate numerical description of relative positions. These reference frames are called *coordinate frames*.

Probably the most familiar coordinate frame is the one in which every point on earth is given a latitude (degrees north or south of the equator) and a longitude (degrees east or west of Greenwich, England). The two reference objects used to orient this frame relative to earth are the observatory in Greenwich and the geographic North Pole.[2]

---

[2] "Position and Motion" (preliminary edition), *Science Curriculum Improvement Study* (University of California, 1969), pp. 5–8.

In the MINNEMAST materials, definition of characteristics and their comparison is the key factor for verbal communication skills.

In the first two MINNEMAST units, the children have been encouraged to observe events and objects in their environment. The activities in this unit focus on more specific observations and descriptions. The children now use their observations as a starting point for further activities; e.g., not only do they observe and describe an object as green, but they also sort objects into sets, classified as green, and not green, or green, blue, and so on. Characteristics or qualities of objects such as color, hardness, or shape are called properties; the children observe objects, describe their properties, and sort them according to properties.

Classifying, or sorting, is a means whereby we can cope with large assemblages of objects, grouping them until we can see some simplifying relations in the complex situation. Sorting requires attention to properties of objects. Children, as well as adults, tend to emphasize name and function. When looking at an object, we tend to answer the question "What do you see?" by stating the name or the kind of object (it is a pen, a book), or by stating its use or function (it is to write with, to read). The activities in this unit concentrate on many properties of objects more basic than name and function.

Focusing on properties allows for more flexible or creative problem solving. If an object is unfamiliar, description by name or function becomes difficult or impossible. In such situations, it is still possible to describe the object in terms of its properties. Or if we need an object that is not available, a description of its properties could suggest another available object with similar properties that satisfy the original requirements.

Description by properties is also stressed because later units involve studies of changes that occur in properties. This requires careful description of objects at various times (and the recording of such data) so that any changes in properties can be noted.

Sorting or classifying objects according to their properties involves separating them into collections that are known as sets. Set concepts are important in the operations of mathematics and science and are basic to studies of logic and probability, yet they are simple enough to be easily grasped by a child. Thus, this unit begins the treatment of material that will form the foundation for much further study in later units.

This unit has two major emphases:

1. *Defining a set.* The children learn, after observing, describing, and sorting many objects, that they can define a set by one or more properties or characteristics common to all members of the set. A defining property gives us a way to tell which objects are and which objects are not members of our defined set. Every object that has the property is a member and every object that does not have the property is not a member of the set. Every object that has red coloring is a member of the set of red objects and only red objects are members. The property of redness is the defining characteristic of the set.

A set can also be defined by listing or tabulating all of its members. This is usually done when the set has relatively few members and when there is no obvious common property that identifies the set. When a set has been defined by listing all its members, whether or not an object is a member of the set can be determined by consulting the list. If it is on the list, it is a member; if it is not on the list, it is not a member. For example, if the set is composed of an apple, Mary, a car, and a pencil, Mary is a member of the set, whereas a dog is not a member.

Two other ideas that are part of set theory are subset and the empty set. A subset of a set is any selection of the members of that set including all or none of the members. For example, the set B is a subset of set A *if and only if* every member of set B is also a member of set A. For example, if all the blue books in the classroom are represented by B, all the blue books are a subset of the set of all books in the room, or B is a subset of A. In addition to subset B, the list of subsets of set A includes the subset of red books, of picture books, and so on, as well as the entire set A and the empty set—which has no members.

It is important that the children acquire an early understanding of the concept of the empty set primarily because of its significant application in ...developing the concept of the number zero. The idea of the empty set also will be used in other units.

It is appropriate and interesting to introduce the empty set by examples such as "the set of children with green hair," "the set of all elephants in this classroom," and "the set of books with no pages." Teachers report that children are ingenious and original in thinking up their own descriptions of the empty set.

It may seem strange to say that "the set of children with green hair" is the same as "the set of all elephants in this classroom." But these sets are equal, since neither contains a member that is not in the other. In fact, neither contains a member! Although there are many descriptions of the empty set, there is only one empty set.

2. *Comparing sets.* After being led to discover that a set is the same set if its members are simply rearranged without removing or adding members, the children learn to compare the numbers of members in two sets without counting them. They make the comparison by pairing one member from the first set with one from the second, continuing until each member of one set has been used in a pair. If there are no leftovers, the sets have the same number of members. If there are leftovers, the set that contains the leftovers has more members and the other set has fewer members.

Conservation of the number property of a set—the idea that the number of members in a set does not change when the members are rearranged—is emphasized. If one set has more, fewer, or the same number of members as another set, this relation is not changed by moving members of either set around. Nor is the number property changed when another object is substituted for a member of a set, regardless of how large or small the substituted object may be. For example, the number of a set of 4 mice is the same as that of 3 mice and an elephant. The set is changed, the number of members is not.

Experience indicates that, although many children can recite the number words by rote, they make mistakes in counting because they do not properly pair the words from the number set with members of the object set and do not understand such concepts as "one to one pairing," "same set under rearrangement," and "conservation of the number property of a set under rearrangements," or "substitution." This unit stresses set comparison and conservation as background for counting activities. . . [4]

Communication or telling someone else what we have experienced is a significant task. Helping children communicate unambiguously is an equally challenging task.

Taken from different curriculum materials, the following are illustrations of activities in which children are provided with opportunities to tell another person a variety of experiences.

1. MINNEMAST LESSON: USING BUTTONS

SORTING

In this lesson the children should have the opportunity to discover for themselves that a set of objects can be divided into subsets according to properties. The specific subsets they make are not so important as the process of separating a set into two subsets. The idea suggested to the children is that the objects within each subset go together because of some common property. . . .

PROCEDURE

A. Give each child a paper or plastic bag. Have him collect a few objects. How and when the collection is made depends upon the circumstances. You may want it done at home, at the school playground, on a walk, or in the schoolroom, and so on. Have each child take out his set of objects and separate them into two subsets, each with objects that he thinks go together. As this is done, have some children individually try to explain their sortings to you. Have them push the objects together and sort them into two different subsets. Continue with other children, asking for their explanations. There are no right or wrong answers here. The emphasis is on sorting and then describing why the objects in a subset go together. The objects that go together do so because they have some property in common, whereas the other objects that do not have that property do not go in the subset. Keep in mind that it is possible that the child may be responding to some similarities that he cannot verbalize. You or other children might try to "guess" the properties that might connect the objects.

A clear, verbal description from the child is not necessary, however, as any combination of objects is a set.

B. Have varied colored pieces of construction paper cut into odd shapes. Make these available for sorting during free-time activity.

---

[4] MINNEMAST, *Describing and Classifying,* Unit 3 (1967), pp. 1–4.
From MINNEMAST, *Describing and Classifying,* Unit 3 (1967), p. 9–10. Copyright 1967 by the Regents of the University of Minnesota.

2. *MINNEMAST LESSON: USING SHAPES*

Before class begins, draw a 2-branch concept tree on a large sheet of newsprint (or make it with a rope on the floor). The children may want to examine it before the activity begins. Ask them what the tree could be used for. Remind them of the classifying activities...and lead them to suggest using the tree for classifying and sorting objects....

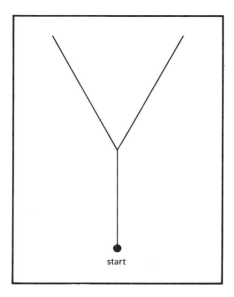

start

Activity A

1. Have the children sort themselves by sex, using the tree. The boys should walk up the tree to the top of one branch and the girls to the other. For more practice, have the children sort themselves by hair color. The children with blond hair go up one branch and those with not-blond hair up the other.

2. Now have the children label the branches with the names of two colors, say red and yellow. Suggest that the children put a red dot on one label and a yellow dot on the other. Then let them sort the property blocks, carrying all the red ones up one branch and yellow ones up the other.

3. With pieces of yarn, extend the tree to include branches for the properties circle and square on each original branch. Help the children sort the blocks according to two properties....

From MINNEMAST, *Curves and Shapes,* Unit 2 (1967), p. 47. Copyright 1967 by the Regents of the University of Minnesota.

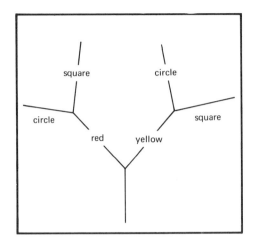

4. Let the children sort many objects until they understand how to use the concept tree. When they are ready, review the concept of open and closed curves. Then distribute the curve cards (or let the children make new curves of their own) and have them sort open and closed curves with the tree. Remove the yarn pieces and label the branches "open" and "closed." Put an example of the correct curve on each branch label to guide the children in their sorting. (Save the tree for Activity B.)

Activity B

From construction paper, cut a leaf for each child. Have each child draw a curve on his leaf. Some should draw open curves and others should draw closed ones. Hang the concept tree used in Activity A on the bulletin board and let the children tape their leaves to the correct branches. You or the children may wish to paint or color the tree to make it look more realistic.

3. SCIENCE—A PROCESS APPROACH: VARIATION IN OBJECTS OF THE SAME KIND

Pets, peanuts and pansies offer ways to keep children observing similarities and differences in their environment. In this unit which emphasizes classification skills, children use such different objects as dogs, cats, peanuts, balls,

From *Science—A Process Approach* (1967), Part B, Exercise E, p. 1. Reprinted by permission of the American Association for the Advancement of Science, Washington, D.C.

flowers, tree leaves, insects, frogs, paper and potatoes to help them learn to:

1. Identify and name variations among objects or organisms which have many features in common.

2. Describe features which are common for each member of a group.

From an initial task—in what way dogs are the same—children then proceed to describe how they are *not* the same and how they can be grouped.

With peanuts, the ways in which they are not the same are called variations. The variations are their basis for grouping. Volume comparison here is possible and should be encouraged.

Other collections of objects are then used to keep children focused on how the objects are *alike* and *not alike*.

4. SCIENCE CURRICULUM IMPROVEMENT STUDY LESSON: RECTANGULAR COORDINATES

A DAY IN TOWN

J. P. leaned against the pickup truck and looked across the wheat fields. He took a deep breath of the warm clean air and smiled. It had been fun to explore Yellowstone National Park with Uncle Jim. Now J. P. was happy to be back at Aunt Hildegarde's farm. He and Homer were waiting to go to town with her today.

Aunt Hildegarde came out of the house and got into the truck. J. P. and Homer climbed in beside her, and J. P. quickly fastened his seat belt. As they rode, J. P. looked at the compass he had bought in Yellowstone. He found that they were riding westward.

Aunt Hildegarde planned to do some shopping. She was going to let J. P. and Homer explore the town by themselves. She would meet them later at the candy store. She parked the truck and gave J. P. instructions for finding the candy store. J. P. and Homer started in the direction Aunt Hildegarde had shown them.

J. P. liked the stores in the town. Each store sold something different. J. P. looked into the store windows, and Homer tagged along behind him.

J. P. and Homer stopped in front of a barber shop and looked at the old-fashioned striped pole. It reminded J. P. of a peppermint stick, and he suddenly remembered the candy store. But when he looked around, he couldn't

From Science Curriculum Improvement Study, *Relative Position and Motion,* Teacher's Guide (Chicago: Rand McNally & Company, 1972), pp. 20–23.

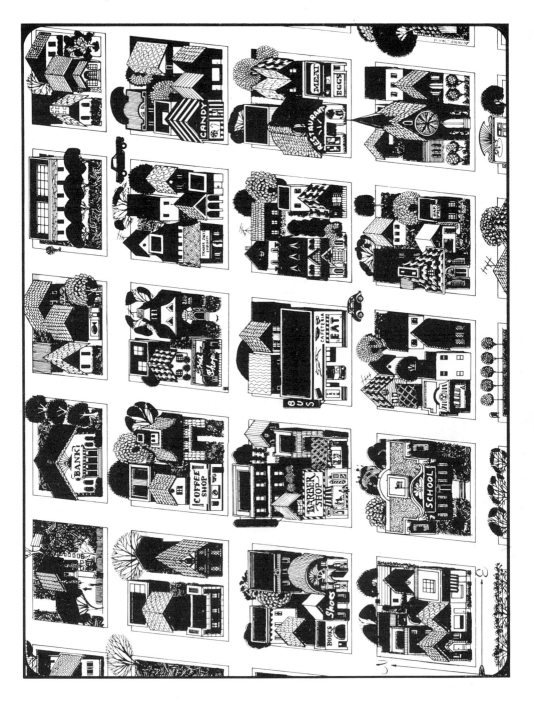

see the store. He didn't even know where to look for the candy store. He had forgotten Aunt Hildegarde's instructions.

Write instructions to guide J. P. and Homer to the candy store. On the opposite page, a picture of the town shows the positions of the barber shop and the candy store.

SQUANGLE

Choose a partner and challenge another team to play Squangle. Make the other team lose pegs by calling the rectangular coordinates of a hole where they have placed a peg.

Rules:

1. Hide your pegboard behind a book or another object.
2. Place four blue pegs in holes to form a square.
3. Place three orange pegs in holes to form a triangle.
4. Place two green pegs in holes to form a line.
5. Take turns calling rectangular coordinates of holes.
6. If the other team calls coordinates of a hole where you have a peg, you must take out that peg.
7. Let everyone see the pegs you take out. Those are "lost."
8. The team which loses the fewest pegs is the winning team.

Look at this pegboard. Which pegs are not correctly identified?

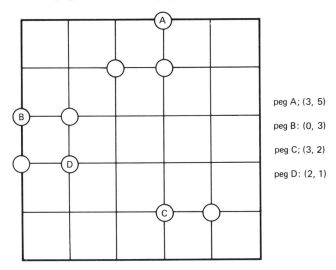

peg A; (3, 5)

peg B: (0, 3)

peg C; (3, 2)

peg D: (2, 1)

5. ELEMENTARY SCIENCE STUDY LESSON:
LIGHT AND SHADOWS

In exploring *Light and Shadows,* try to respect the individual paces children set for themselves and the depth to which each is willing to work. Some children, for example, will readily accept your suggestion to chalk along the shadow cast by the corner of the building at different times of day; others may prefer to mark some other fixed object; a few may reject the idea entirely. Some children may figure out that changes in a shadow's position—morning, midday, and afternoon—provide a kind of clock; others may set themselves the task of finding out why there is no shadow at all at a particular time of day, or why the shadow is directly in front of the building one time, skewed off in another direction later; some may barely see the relation between the position of the shadow and the position of the sun. Try to content yourself with the inevitable: a crumb satisfies some children; others seek the full fare.

Nor is it always easy to tell what any one child has absorbed. Some will attempt to analyze; others may have notions they are far from ready to talk about. A scientist engaged in research often feels this way, too. If he is unwilling to nail his words down hard and fast while his knowledge is still intuitive, may not children also have that privilege?

When children are exploring shadows they are experimenting with spatial relationships in simple but truly scientific ways.

Shadows

What kind of shadows do various objects make?

Lacy things...things with holes...square things...round things

What is the biggest...roundest...smallest...flattest...umbrella shadow?

6. ELEMENTARY SCIENCE STUDY LESSON: SELECTED ACTIVITIES FOR ATTRIBUTE GAMES AND PROBLEMS

Commentary 3

This [section] introduces the students to two activities that recur throughout the problem sequence: classifying by attributes and identifying a piece added to or removed from the subset (group). Students form subsets and play take-away games to become familiar with the attributes, *color, shape,* and *size,* as well as with different ways of classifying the pieces in the set. Those working directly from the [section] should work with a partner, alternating turns in the take-away games and making up variations of the suggested activities.

Younger children can be introduced to the attributes *shape* and *color* and to orderly arrangements quite naturally in a free-play situation. After two or four children have been building freely with a set of *A Blocks* for a while, ask them to share the pieces equally. If their method of dividing the set is random at first, see if you can get them to think of more systematic ways of sharing the pieces. Four children may do this by color, each child taking all the pieces of one color, or by shape. Two children sharing a set can each take two colors, or two shapes, or one child can take the large pieces and the other the small ones.

There are several ways of introducing the take-away game. For example, ask one child to close his eyes or to turn around while you, or another child, remove or add a piece. Another way is to slide a piece of cardboard between the child and the array of blocks in front of him and then remove or add a piece. Initially you may want to take turns playing with the children; afterwards, they can play this game (or any other they think of) with a partner.

Take-away games may be difficult at first for some children. Perhaps the easiest way to introduce them is to encourage a child who has all the pieces of one color to place each small piece on top of the corresponding large piece. When a single piece is removed from such an array, it is quite easy to identify what is missing. Two pieces at a time may then be removed. Finally the eight pieces can be scrambled and a piece removed.

Commentary 4

Size is an attribute many students find troublesome in working with *A Blocks;* color and shape distinctions are clear and absolute, but size comparisons are relative. There is, in fact, a great deal of variation between pieces within the two size groups. Older (or more analytic) students may point out, for example, that two small triangles are the same size as one small diamond and, similarly, that two large triangles will just cover one large diamond.

Students may be encouraged to check the relative weights of the blocks, as we did. (In weighing one set, we found the small diamond slightly heavier than the small circle, but the large circle was heavier than the large diamond.)

With accurate measurements, your students' may be able to find eight different values for the attribute *weight;* two or four are more likely. Investigations of this sort can be very useful, especially in helping older students understand that classification by three attributes represents an arbitrary decision to pay attention to certain features and not to others.

Commentary 5

To communicate clearly, it is necessary for us to make the distinction between *attribute* and *value.* One way of looking at the distinction between the terms is to think of them as representing different levels of abstraction. The word "color" is more abstract than the word "blue" because "color" refers to all possible colors, while "blue" refers to a limited portion of the spectrum; so in this case "color" is the attribute and "blue" is one of the values. The relationship between attribute and value is, however, strictly relative. For example, suppose one were dealing with a large group of objects of different shades of blue, but all of them blue. One might then refer to blue as an attribute of the particular group, and terms such as "sky blue," "light blue," and "navy blue" would be values. Few students will be familiar with this distinction, but those at the junior high school level may be able to grasp the implications of their experience with these materials and to extend the idea of attributes and values to other situations. By the time your students are working with *Creature Cards,* they will be inventing attributes and values for their own "creatures."

Especially with the younger children you should look for chances to use the value and attribute names informally, playing games and talking with the children: Which color would you like? Choose a shape...do you want the circles or the diamonds? Which size would you prefer, large or small? Your consistent use of the terms will help the children learn them naturally. Although they may start using these names quite rapidly, it would still be a good idea to check them occasionally and to help those who do not seem to understand.

Here are three blocks.

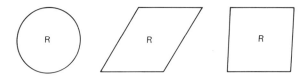

How are they alike? How are they different from these?

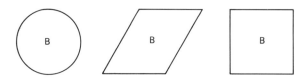

Can you think of one word that will describe this difference? The child who is still in doubt should be shown some pairs that differ in only one attribute:

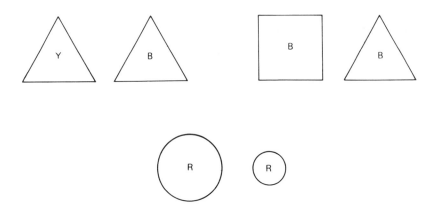

If the child is encouraged to find one word for each of these differences, he will soon become quite familiar with the attributes we are using.

Our title, *Attribute Games and Problems,* may prove helpful in familiarizing children with the word, whether or not they fully understand its meaning. There is no need for children to memorize or repeat any of the words used in these activities: what is important is that they feel at ease with the ideas the words imply.

7. ELEMENTARY SCIENCE STUDY LESSON: MAPPING

Locating a Landmark

The children go outdoors in pairs and find a simple feature somewhere near the school, such as a hill, a stream, a valley, a field, or a small cliff. If the school is in the city, they can use nearby buildings or features of the schoolyard, such as a basketball court, an enclosed or steep area, a tree, or a fence. When they return, they try to describe the feature on an index card without naming it. They may use pictures, words, or both to help another team recognize and find their feature.

It may be necessary for you to locate ten or so appropriate landmarks in the vicinity beforehand to suggest to particular teams.

The activity could be organized in terms of a treasure hunt or as a part of a project, such as planning for a fair in the schoolyard.

The children swap cards and try to locate each other's features. Many problems will come up:

It took too long.

We made a drawing, but it looks awful.

We tried to give directions, but we didn't know which was north or south.

The children will be quick to identify problems they had with other people's directions:

I couldn't tell which way to look at.

Her picture doesn't look much like a church.

I couldn't tell which side of the fence they meant.

They said, "It's 50 feet away from the tree toward the brick wall of the new building." Boy that was confusing! What part of the wall?

After the children have looked at several people's pictures, they can discuss some general problems. It may be helpful to put some of the drawings and directions on transparencies for use on an overhead projector.

Reprinted from *Mapping,* pp. 23–25, by the Elementary Science Study. Copyright 1971 by Education Development Center, Inc., 55 Chapel Street, Newton, Massachusetts 02160.

What were some ideas that might have helped other people know what you meant?

Directions for north and south.

Write the names of things on the paper.

Neat drawings.

Where were you standing when you drew your land features?

We walked all around it.

You need some other landmarks near it to tell you which hill it is.

You can't draw everything; you need symbols.

Practically every problem dealt with in this unit will come up in some form right away. Some children will indicate that they have extreme difficulty in recognizing or constructing configurations when they cannot reconstruct them in a familiar context.

How can I tell what something looks like if I can't see all of it?

I just didn't know how to do it.

Many of the problems that the children raise have to do with distortion and changing points of view. They have difficulty drawing three-dimensional figures, and easily confuse side views with overhead views and combine the two.

Other problems involve describing the location of something by its orientation and its position in relation to other things. One thing is certain: most of the students will not solve these problems right away. As the unit progresses, they will have chances to confront the same questions again and again.

8. ILLINOIS ASTRONOMY PROJECT LESSON:
THE SHAPE OF THE EARTH

The Shape of the Earth

How big is the earth? What is its shape? You may know the answers to these questions already, but probably you do not know *how* the answers were obtained. Scientists are as much concerned with how we get answers as with the answers we get.

On land, the earth's surface appears to be flat—except for such objects as mountains, hills, and valleys. But on the ocean you may discover that the surface of the earth is really curved.

Watch a ship disappearing in the distance—preferably one with tall masts.

From *Charting the Universe*, Elementary School Science Project, University of Illinois (New York: Harper & Row, 1966), pp. 4–7.

Through binoculars you can see that the ship does not simply get smaller and smaller until it is too small to see. The ship would disappear this way only if the earth were flat. Instead, the ship sinks out of sight. The hull disappears first and the top of the masts last.

First, sight along a table top at a tiny paperclip boat. Move the boat farther and farther away. Then sight the boat as a friend moves it away from you over a curved piece of cardboard or over a globe.

Even if you haven't been able to see the curvature of the earth, you may have seen photographs which show this effect. Some of the pictures taken by astronauts show the curvature clearly.

We know, then, that the earth's surface is curved. But several shapes have curved surfaces. An ant can travel around a telephone pole, a beach ball, or a hot dog. Which of these shapes is most like the earth?

Try holding objects of various shapes in the beam of a strong light and notice the shadows they cast on a wall or screen. Turn each object in various ways and see whether the shapes change.

Sometimes the shadow of the earth falls on the moon. Then we can observe that the edge of its shadow is always circular, no matter how the earth is turned. The only object which *always* has a circular shadow is a sphere. About 2,000 years before Columbus, ancient Greek thinkers concluded from their observations that the earth must be a sphere.

Even when you take long trips you aren't really aware that you are traveling *around* the earth. Why? The reason it doesn't look round is that you don't see enough of it at one time. A small part of the surface of a very large sphere looks flat.

To demonstrate this idea, get some balls of various sizes—a beach ball and a ping-pong ball, for example. Cut out small paper squares. Press a square firmly against each ball. Notice how much flatter a square appears on the largest ball.

You can determine the *shape* of your island by looking from a high hill. But to find its *size*, you need to measure it. The earth appears to be a sphere. But to find its size, you need to make some measurements. A yardstick might solve your problem on the island. But you can't very easily stretch a tape measure across the oceans to find the size of the earth. You'll have to learn how to measure the earth indirectly—without walking around it.

Blocks, dishes, crayons, colors, shapes, peanuts, dogs and cats, flowers, leaves, rubber bands, sandpaper, coordinates, light and shadows, maps and the shape of the earth—these represent a wide variety of experiences. They also illustrate the general need and opportunity for communicating. Telling another person is an important dimension of each of the preceding lessons.

In what ways did the lessons emphasize children's communication skills?

By now you should have developed sufficient skill in telling another person. Check yourself before you go on.

Posttest

To take this test, you will need a collection of at least five keys.

1. Name the two-dimensional shapes you can see in one key:

    1. _____
    2. _____
    3. _____
    4. _____

2. Make two groups of the keys in your collection. What is the name of the first group? _____ What is the name of

    the second group? _____

    If more keys than one are in your first group, divide it into two smaller groups. What are the names for the new groups? _____

3. Make a graph of your collection of keys.

Following, you will find acceptable answers. If you are having difficulty, you may wish to discuss this with your instructor.

Acceptable Answers for Posttest

1. Your answer will depend on your keys, of course. They probably had a circular hole, maybe an ellipse for the top part, a rectangular-shaped narrow part with triangular points.
2. One possibility is square-shaped heads—heads that are not square-shaped. Building keys—not building keys.
3. Your graph should have a title, for example, "Collection of Keys." Verticle axis would be number of keys and horizontal axis category of keys.

4. Finding How Much More

At the end of this chapter, you should be able to: (1) Compare objects based on characteristics that they have in common; (2) Describe the objects to another person using arbitrary or standard units of measure. (3) Estimate measurable dimensions.

For the pretest, you will need three rubber bands of different sizes.

1. Name three measurements you could make with the rubber bands.

   a. _____

   b. _____

   c. _____

2. Using one rubber band as the measuring unit, describe the other two rubber bands.

   a. _____

   b. _____

3. Estimate the length of the rubber bands using centimeters.

   a. _____

   b. _____

   c. _____

Acceptable responses to the pretest follow. If you did satisfactorily, go now to page 57. If not, you will want to carry out the activities on page 48.

Acceptable Responses for Pretest

1. Measurements you could make include the:
   unstretched length of the rubber bands;
   stretched length of the rubber bands;
   width of the rubber bands;
   diameter of the area enclosed by the rubber bands;

area enclosed by the rubber bands;
stretchability of the rubber bands.

2.   Selecting one of the rubber bands as unit of measurement, you should describe how much larger or smaller the other two are. For example, band A is between one and two times as long as band B and band C is slightly longer than band B.

3.   To check your estimates, you should use a metric ruler; in the previous illustration, for example, band A was 9, band B was 6, and band C was 7 centimeters long.

How comfortable are you with the metric system? If you need more help, the activities that follow will provide you with an opportunity to practice.

In perceiving objects or events, it soon becomes desirable—because of sheer quantity, indeed essential—to contrast or compare the observations in order to consider similarities or differences. Intuitively, these comparisons are made in terms of specific properties of the object or event, which seem to be held in common contrast. To compare a glass of iced tea with a cup of hot tea, comparisons could be made of color (brown,) phase of matter (liquid), or amount (volume). Usually, however, when the two substances are compared, temperature will probably be the property selected.

To describe a contrast, observations of specific properties are essential. To refine observations, it is necessary to say *more* than the hot tea is warmer than the other; or equally accurate, the iced tea is cooler than the hot tea. In either case, it is relevant to know that neither substance is hot or cold; that is, one substance is compared with the other and it is hotter or colder based on this comparison. When compared with dry ice, the iced tea would, of course, be warmer. Establishing a frame of reference for the comparison (that is identifying with *what* the object or event is being compared) is one way in which observations are extended.

Even though a frame of comparison has been established, in order to extend the observations of the two tea substances the five senses are inadequate to distinguish the temperature differences. Now it is essential to have a means by which smaller differences can be detected and these differences contrasted. Throughout the history of science, creative men have constructed instruments to aid the five senses in comparing. These instruments are now highly refined and serve as very useful means to aid in extending the five senses.

However, instruments as a means for securing comparative data present a concern—communication. Although scaling the comparison is an arbitrary choice, communicating the scale to another individual is necessary, for the scale and divisions to be meaningful. Thus, the fascinating history of linear scales, temperature scales, etc. has developed. Once a common scale has been made, the task of communicating with others is a simpler one. . . .

Extending observations through comparisons, or contrast, or against scales that have common acceptance (standards), describes the task of measuring.

Inherent in this task is the decision as to what type of comparison to make and what instrument to use.[1]

To do this activity, you will need a toothpick, a pencil, a paper clip, and a felt pen.

Arrange the four objects in front of you. Write down eight items to describe the objects.

1. _____
2. _____
3. _____
4. _____
5. _____
6. _____
7. _____
8. _____

Look back at your list. Was any of the eight items useful in comparing a characteristic such as length or mass?

List now four comparisons or measurements that you could make with the objects.

1. _____
2. _____
3. _____
4. _____

Your list may have included length, width, volume, mass, or weight.

Think back to the length of the objects. Arrange them from longest to shortest. Which object did you start with? What was your reason? (Usually you start with either the longest or the shortest and make your arrangement accordingly.)

Using the pencil as your unit of measurement, complete these statements:

1. The paper clip is _____ as long as the pencil.
2. The toothpick is _____ as long as the pencil.
3. The felt pen is _____ as long as the pencil.

Now use the paper clip as your unit of measurement and complete these statements:

1. The pencil is _____ paper clips long.
2. The felt pen is _____ paper clips long.
3. The toothpick is _____ paper clips long.

What is the difference in using the pencil or paper clip as your unit?

You may have had results like these:

_____

[1] MINNEMAST, *Introducing Measurement,* Unit 5 (1967).

The paper clip is 1/5 as long as the pencil.
The toothpick is 1/3 as long as the pencil.
The felt pen is 4/5 as long as the pencil.

and:

The pencil is five paper clips long.
The felt pen is four paper clips long.
The toothpick is two paper clips long.

You probably found that it was easiest and most accurate to measure using the smallest object as your unit. In fact, your measurements will always be much more accurate if your unit is smaller than the object being measured.

For the next activity, you will need any three containers, for example, a coffee cup, a drinking glass, and an empty Coke bottle.

Which of the three containers will hold the most liquid? _____

_____

Which will hold the least liquid? _____ Arrange the three containers from the one that will hold the most to the one that will hold the least liquid.

Now, describe a way that you could use to find *how much more* liquid your largest container holds than the next largest size.

One way to do this is to fill the smaller container and then pour it into the larger one. Continue to do this until you have filled the larger one and then describe the larger one in terms of how many of the smaller ones it can hold.

If you were now asked to describe the volume of each of the three containers using one of them as a unit of measure, which would you use? _____

_____ Why? _____

_____

You should use the smaller unit and then describe the others using it as your unit of comparison. Thus the Coke bottle is $2\frac{1}{4}$ times as large as the cup and the glass is $1\frac{1}{4}$ times as large as the cup.

For the next activity, you will need three strips of cardboard.

Strip A should be 1 meter long.
Strip B should be 10 centimeters long.
Strip C should be 1 centimeter long.

Using strip A, how may strips long is the table? _____

_____ The door height? _____ The table height? ____

_____

Were your measurements exactly as long as two, three, or four strips? _____

If not, for example, was the table more than one strip but less than two? _____
By custom, we round off to the number of strip lengths that is closest to the actual length of an object.

How many *A* strips wide is your desk? _____

The page in this book? _____

When you measured the paper, you found that it was between zero and one strips long but closer to zero, so that when you rounded off you had to describe the paper as about zero strips wide.

Try measuring the page of the book with your *B* strip.

How many *B* strips long is it? _____

How many *B* strips wide is it? _____

How many *B* strips long is your pencil? _____

How many *B* strips wide is your pencil? _____

What happenes when you round off here? _____

How many *C* strips wide is your pencil? _____

Arrange the *A*, *B*, and *C* strips in front of you.

How many *C* strips long is the *B* strip? _____

How many *B* strips long is the *A* strip? _____

How many *C* strips long is the *A* strip? _____

By now you have undoubtedly seen that the *B* strip is equal to 10 *C* strips, and that the *A* strip has the same length as 10 *B* strips or 100 *C* strips.

The *A* strip is a meter.

The *B* strip is a decimeter.

The *C* strip is a centimeter.

To carry out the next activity, you will need a metric ruler.

Take out a sheet of paper from your notebook. Make these estimates.

1. The paper is _____ centimeters wide.

2. The paper is _____ centimeters long.

3. The lines are _____ centimeters apart.

Now check your estimates with a metric ruler. Which was the closest? Try it again with the size of the book, the length of your pencil, the width of your hand, and your height.

Estimated length of book _____ centimeters

Measured length of book _____ centimeters

Estimated length of pencil _____ centimeters

Measured length of pencil _____ centimeters

Estimated width of hand _____ centimeters

Measured width of hand _____ centimeters

Estimated height _____ centimeters

Measured height _____ centimeters

You are probably finding that your estimates are much more accurate for smaller objects.

Make these estimates of your shoe length:

My shoe is about _____ centimeters long.
My shoe is about _____ decimeters long.
My shoe is about _____ meters long.

If you found that your shoe was 30 centimeters long, it was also 3 decimeters or .3 of a meter long.

30. centimeters
= 3. decimeters
= .3 meters.

The simplicity of the metric system is elegant indeed.

If you wish to know more about the topic of measuring and how it fits into the teaching of science, you will find the following comments useful.

Relating the adult world of measuring to the child's views is emphasized in these comments by the writers of the Elementary Science Study Materials.

Long

Tall

Big

Small

Young children use these terms every day in conversation and play.

I'm going to make a *long* garage for my trucks.

I can build a tower *taller* than myself.

Davis is *small,* so he'll play my little brother.

Children make comparisons and note similarities and differences long before they are ready to consider such questions as How long...? How tall...? How much bigger...? How much smaller...?

Like everyone else, children use size words to describe things as they perceive them. A child, even more than an adult, sees the size of one thing in relation to the size of something else. What he classifies as "big" in one instance, he may call "small" in another. A piece of cake served to him is "tiny" when all the other pieces are larger. It is "huge" when all the other pieces are smaller.

That a child uses size words does not, however, mean that he understands what size is. For an adult, an object has an exact, consistent, measurable size. For a young child, the size of objects really is changeable. His notion of the size of something depends on how it looks to him at that moment. Even looking at it from a different angle may make it "be" more or less. Water poured from a drinking glass into a tall, thin tube may immediately become "more water," since the level of the liquid is higher in the tube than it was in the glass. A row of blocks flat on the floor may look shorter than the same row standing up as a tower. A ball of clay may lose or gain weight when it is broken into little pieces.

Likewise, a child uses number words in a descriptive, rather than a precise, way. When he sees a full box of dominoes, he may say that there are "a hundred," when actually there are many less. What he means is: There are a lot. Numbers used to describe quantity have little or no value to a child at this stage in his development. He may count out ten dominoes in a pile and say that there are ten, but when the same dominoes are spread out, he may think that there are more because they appear to take up more space.

Similarly, the standard units of measurement used by adults make little sense to most children. What is an inch, a quart, a pound, if the quantity of size changes as the substance changes position or shape? What do the numbers attached to inches, quarts, and pounds really stand for? How does 5 feet differ from 5 inches when both are 5?

By matching and comparing, thinking about his results, and generalizing from any experiences, a young child gradually comes to accept the idea that number, length and quantity stay the same even when the appearance of objects changes. He finally realizes that ten dominoes are ten no matter how he places them, and that a piece of string stays the same length whether he arranges it in a circle or in a straight line. He knows for sure that one cup of water remains one cup, regardless of the shape of its container. As he arranges and rearranges his dominoes and pours liquids from one container to another in different situations, he develops his ability to pay attention to several kinds of measurement at once—height and width, number and spatial arrangement.

The same experiences which enable a child to accept the fact that quantity is constant are necessary prerequisites of his grasp of the "how" and "why" of measuring. He begins by expressing the size of another, goes on to establish standard units of his own, and gradually learns to handle conventional measuring tools with understanding. Conventional measuring devices lose much of their mystery if a child uses them alongside other tools of his own invention. Lacking this sequence of experiences, children frequently assume that conventional units of measurement are somehow essential to measurement. For some children, it seems as if length exists only when they have inches with which to measure it or that an object too large for the available scales will weigh "nothing."

Perhaps the most urgent message in this Guide is that measuring should not—"really cannot"—be "taught," either through problems in arithmetic or through a series of planned lessons. Learning to measure is a gradual process. Until a child has had a chance to establish in concrete, comparative terms what a foot and a yard are, "3 feet plus 2 feet" is meaningless to him.

People measure to obtain information for some purpose or to satisfy curiosity. They seldom measure simply for the sake of measuring. Measuring in the classroom will be most effective and interesting if it grows out of situations in which children are actively involved. Sewing, cooking, carpentry, and caring for animals are examples of activities that capture children's interest and provide opportunities for measuring. To make use of these opportunities, children need encouragement to pursue questions that interest them, access to a variety of measuring tools, and the freedom and time to use the tools as they see fit.[2]

---

[2] Elementary Science Study, *Match and Measure* (1969), pp. 1–2.

Continuing to help children acquire the skill of measuring, the writers of MIN-NEMAST suggest:

Children have had experience with describing and classifying objects by their properties. The next step is to have them measure some of the properties of objects. Often a meaningful description of an object can be given only after some of its properties have been measured.

A measurement is generally thought of as an association of a number with some property of an object, but measurement also includes a simple comparison of the properties of objects in terms such as "greater than," "less than," or "appears to be the same as.". . . Actually, comparison is the basis of all measurement. In all probability, early man made very gross comparisons of the sizes of animals, lengths of time durations, and so on. It was later, after the idea of number was developed, that measurements were made more precise by comparing with reference units and by counting such units. . . .

A comparison can be made between two—and only two—objects at a time. In other words, no matter how many objects are to be arranged in order, the procedure must be to break down the operation into numerous comparisons of two objects at a time. This comparing of objects in pairs is called *binary comparison*. Measurement is essentially a series of binary comparisons. For example, in measuring lengths, we either compare the objects with each other or compare the object we want to measure with a reference object such as a ruler. In measuring time durations, we may be comparing two events themselves or comparing an event with a reference event such as the movement of the hands on a clock. Whenever two objects are brought together for comparison, the measurement is called *direct*. If a reference object is used to compare objects that cannot conveniently be brought together, the measurement is *indirect*.

A series of binary comparisons will enable the child to order or rank objects and events according to certain properties. The properties investigated in this unit are length, area, and volume for objects, and time duration for events. *Length* is considered as a measure of a line segment, area the measure of a region on a surface, *volume* the measure of the space occupied by (or within) an object, and *duration* the measure of the time an event lasts. We will also investigate the time order relation between events, which is similar to the space order relation between objects. . . .

The results of comparing length, area, or volume are found to be *invariant* under many conditions. Invariance implies that the result of the comparison remains the same regardless of where, when, or how the comparison is repeated. There is absolutely no way of knowing whether the length of an object has changed when the object is observed in a different location or at a different time. One can only measure the object by a binary comparison with the same reference object at both locations or times. If, by comparison, an object has greater length than the reference object at one location and time, and this same relationship exists at another location or time, the comparison can be called invariant.

An underlying principle that is emphasized. . .is that of *transitivity*. Transitivity is illustrated in the following example. If the area of object A is greater than the area of object B, and the area of object B is greater than the area of object C, we can predict, by transitivity, that the area of A is greater than the area of C. This principle, which permits us to predict a comparison on the basis of two other comparisons, applies to length, volume and time duration comparisons, as well as to time ordering.

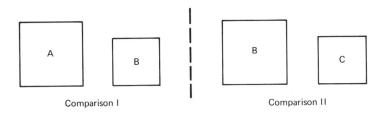

Comparison I   Comparison II

In the activities dealing with time duration, some very simple *before and after* concepts of time ordering will be introduced. In this case, as probably in many others, the ideas will not be completely new to the children. The intent is to clarify their thinking and broaden their experiences.[3]

MINNEMAST writers also suggest that measurement is one of the important operations of science.

It usually includes the process of assigning numbers to various properties of objects or events, so that we can indirectly compare those properties by comparing the numbers without bringing the objects together for direct comparison. To compare the property of length, we might ask, "Which is longer— the teacher's desk or the principal's?" We need not bring the desks together, nor rely on our memories of how they look. Instead, we can ask, "Which desk has had the greater number of units assigned to its length by a measuring process?"

Obviously the measurements must be made in the same way if we are to be able to make comparisons. We must use the same standard units. The number thirty-nine is greater than the number four, but thirty-nine inches are not greater than four feet. And we should not compare the length of the teacher's desk with the width of the principal's if we want to know which desk is longer.

We can assign numbers to any kind of property or event that we can describe precisely, provided we can specify a measuring process—a way of making the assignment. We can even measure properties of "things" that are not objects, for example, time duration.

There is a basic kind of measurement in which we compare properties of two objects directly, repeating such comparisons until we have ordered or ranked the objects from least to greatest in magnitude.

---

[3] MINNEMAST, *Introducing Measurement*, Unit 5 (1967), pp. 1–2.

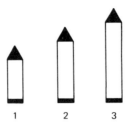

No numbers need be involved in this; our ordering just ranks them, according, say, to length. Such a ranking has many of the properties of numerical ordering. It is transitive: if object 2 is longer than object 1, and object 3 is longer than 2, then object 3 is longer than 1. We need not compare objects 3 and 1 directly.

If we order the numerical measurements of objects 1, 2 and 3, we shall find the same relationships. If the number assigned to object 2 is greater than the number assigned to object 1, and the number assigned to object 3 is greater than that assigned to object 2, then the number assigned to object 3 is greater than that assigned to object 1.

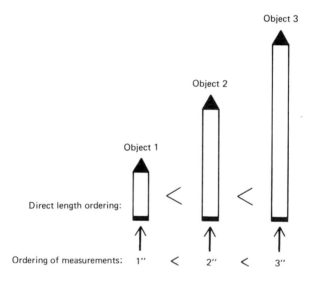

Without using numbers assigned by measurement, the children have done a good deal of work comparing and ordering objects according to the magnitude or size of some common property.... It is important, for making comparisons and for communicating with others, to have standard units of measurement that are as nearly alike as possible and that everyone uses. The standard unit chosen is arbitrary. To demonstrate this, paper clips and handspans are used at first. But the initial determination of the magnitude of the familiar inch, centimeter, foot, etc. was equally arbitrary.

The main considerations in choosing measurement units are convenience in use and in communication. When the length of a king's arm was chosen as a measuring unit, it would have been impossible for the king to be present whenever it was desirable to compare the length of some object with the length of his arm. Therefore replicas of that length unit were made and the unit became the basis for what we now call a "yard." While a handspan is convenient for approximations, people's hands differ in size and handspan length changes as the owner of the hand grows. It even changes from time to time, according to how one spreads his fingers. Handspans are not accurate, even if we do not care much about communicating our measurements. Measurements reported in paper-clip lengths may be convenient, but they will provide accurate comparisons only for those who use paper clips of just the same size. Thus people have agreed on certain arbitrary units, such as inches, centimeters, ounces, grams, seconds, and so forth. The process of measuring has been standardized, so that measurements made by everyone will be communicable and comparable.

The importance of using a standard unit (such as the inch or centimeter) which has been commonly agreed upon is so obvious that we tend to assume that this approach is known and understood even by young children. It is true that at an early age children may accept and use the common measuring standards or scales of their culture, but a child may understand neither the arbitrariness of the choice nor the principle of defining a common standard. That is why children begin their measurements, in these lessons, by using paper-clip chains to measure length, corks to measure volume, and pendulums to measure time durations. Then, in later activities, they use common standard units such as inches, centimeters, quarts, seconds, etc.[4]

We can agree that measurement is relevant and even essential to science. A more important question is, "How does one teach a child measurement skills?"

The following units illustrate how this question has been approached by the various curriculum developers.

1. ELEMENTARY SCIENCE STUDY LESSON: MEASURING LENGTH

Growing Plants

Children who have planted seeds and are watching them grow may be interested in measuring their plants as they develop.

How tall is your plant today?

Do you think it will be the same height tomorrow?

What about three days from now?

---

4 MINNEMAST, *Measurement with Reference Units,* Unit 12 (1967), pp. 1–4. Reprinted from *Match and Measure,* pp. 14–17, by the Elementary Science Study. Copyright 1971 by Education Development Center, Inc., 55 Chapel Street, Newton, Massachusetts 02160.

Can you keep a record and find out? Some children have done this with strips of paper and made a graph.

Does corn grow faster than peas?

Is the tallest plant bigger all over?

Some children have kept track of a plant's growth by cutting strips of paper to match the plant's height each day. Placed alongside one another these strips make a visual record.

Shadow Play

Shadows are intriguing. They can shrink; they can grow; they can disappear altogether. After playing such games as tag and follow-the-leader with shadows, children may become interested in looking more closely at their own shadows and at shadows of things around them.

How can you tell whether your shadow is as big as you are?

Can you make your shadow grow bigger?...smaller? Can you make it disappear?...

Compare your sun shadow with yourself in the morning and again in the afternoon. Did anything happen to the shadow?

Try doing the same thing with something that won't be moved—in the room or outside of the building.

Some children thought of lying down on their shadows. No matter how they tried, this never seemed to work.

Keeping Animals

Animals in the classroom present possibilities for children to explore many kinds of measurement.

A group of youngsters had just about given up trying to measure their class guinea pig. A ruler was useless—the pig wiggled too much.

Aware of the children's frustration, the teacher made an effort to help them without telling them what to do; she simply stood near the group with a piece of string in her hand. It wasn't long before one child hit upon the idea of using the string to measure the guinea pig from nose to tail. After taking this measurement, someone asked for more string to find out how big the guinea pig was around the tummy. To everyone's amusement, the two measurements were nearly the same.

Children in a second grade were very impressed with the way a tiny gerbil could dig in the dirt. Taking careful measurements, they found that he was able to send the dirt flying behind him a distance greater than his own length (including tail) and that the mound of dirt he piled up was much taller than he was. The children speculated about whether they could accomplish such a feat themselves.

Choosing a suitable cage for an animal may raise questions.

Is there room enough for the hamster to stand up?...lie down?...stretch out? ...run around?...hide in a corner?

Measuring the "Impossible"

After children have had some experience measuring ordinary things, they may look for something really difficult and challenging to tackle. Two boys in a third grade wondered if they could measure the distance from their classroom window to the ground. They decided to try using ticker tape.

The next question was about the classroom itself. How far was it from the ceiling to the floor? Reaching the ceiling posed a problem at first, but they soon solved it by attaching tape to a long pole and standing on a table. When the tape was stretched out on the floor, the children were surprised to see that it reached almost all the way across the classroom.

How would the first tape compare with the second one? As they unwound the tapes side by side, it became obvious that the distance from window to ground was much greater than the distance from ceiling to floor.

The teacher then asked the children if they could use the two measurements to figure out how many classrooms would fit between their window and the ground.

Some children guessed that three rooms would fit; others said four. A classmate interrupted the discussion with, "That's silly. You know Miss Smith's room is under us and Mr. Robbons' is in the basement. There are only two rooms. Mr. Robbins' room is partly underground. But we measured from the windowsill in our room, so that makes it right."

2. MINNEMAST LESSON: LENGTH

Lesson 1: Introducing Length

In this lesson the children will begin to consider the length of the greatest obvious dimension of an object. They will compare objects two at a time and tell which has the greater or lesser length. In some of the situations they will not be able to see a difference—the objects will appear to be the same length.

The children will use *Minnebars* in this lesson for the first time. They should be allowed to play with these during their free time before and after the unit activities....

PROCEDURE

A. Place two strips of the same length on the flannel board so that the ends are on different levels.

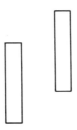

Which is longer?

Which is shorter?

How can you be sure?

How can we find out which has greater length?

Have a volunteer show a method of comparing.

The children should realize that to show that the objects apparently have the same length, both pairs of ends must line up with nothing left over.

B. Divide the class into groups of four. Give each group eight of the strips of paper described in the material list. Ask each child to pick out two of the strips from his group's set and to describe and compare his two strips.

Which of your strips is longer? Hold it up.

Find a way to show which of your strips is longer.

Now have everyone in each group put his first pair of strips back in the group's pile and choose two different ones.

Which of your new strips is longer? Hold it up.

Can someone show us one way of telling which of his strips is longer?

Have several children show their methods of comparison. Try to have all the following methods shown. Method 3 is not a decisive test.

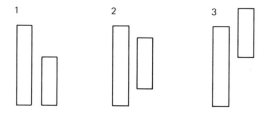

C. Ask the children to find two objects in the room that appear to have different lengths. Have them tell which is the longer and test their decision by making the comparison.

D. Give one set of Minnebars to each pair of children. One child should choose two Minnebars and ask the other child which bar has the greater length. They should take turns telling and check by actually making the comparison.

E. *Game: Giant or Dwarf.* Have many strips of heavy paper of different lengths prepared. Minnebars might also be used here. Select two children to demonstrate the game. Give each child six strips (or Minnebars) of different lengths and ask that he keep them out of his partner's sight. At a signal, each child secretly chooses one of his strips. The partners then compare the two strips they have chosen. The child with the longer strip wins both strips and places them in a separate pile. If the strips are of similar lengths, each keeps his own strip. The game continues through six matchings. The child with the most strips at the end is the winner. After the demonstration, the entire class should have opportunities to play in groups of two. For variation, the winner could be the one with fewer strips.

Lesson 2: Using Reference Objects in Comparing Lengths

In this lesson, the children will compare one object with other objects, and become more familiar with describing an object in comparative terms. They will see, for instance, that a pencil has greater length than a crayon but less length than a yardstick. Emphasize such comparative descriptions in all measurement discussions throughout this unit and the rest of the year. Also use comparison terms for properties other than length:

Is this block harder than this ball of cotton?

Is this sheet of green paper darker than that one?

Now the children should begin to see that all comparisons are relative—the results depend on the objects compared. . . .

PROCEDURE

A. Place the set of objects where all the children can see them. Hold up one object (for example, a pencil).

Find an object which is longer than the pencil.

Find an object which is shorter than the pencil.

Show me how you test which is longer.

(When they see the comparative aspect, ask similar questions without holding up the object.)

Find an object which is shorter than the book.

Who can find an object which has greater length than the crayon but less length than the straw?

B. *Game: Grab-Bag Matching.* This is played by two children. Give each pair an opaque bag of assorted Minnebars. Without looking in the bag, each child draws one bar to serve as his reference object. The child with the longer reference object collects bars that are longer than his reference object and the other child collects those shorter than his reference bar.

The child with the longer reference bar begins the play by drawing another bar from the bag and comparing it with his reference. If it is longer than the reference he keeps it. If it is the same length or shorter than the reference, he puts it aside (not back in the bag). The other child then makes his draw and retains the bar only if it is shorter than his reference. Each takes his turn until all the bars are drawn. The child having the greater number of bars is the winner.

As children play the game, some will come to realize that selecting the reference and other bars by touch gives an advantage.

3. ELEMENTARY SCIENCE STUDY LESSON: MEASURING AREA

Measuring Area

PAPER AND CLOTH

Doll corner and playhouse activities and simple building at the work bench abound in opportunities for children to deal with two-dimensional measurement. Odds and ends of yard goods and cast-off materials provide them with opportunities to cover surfaces of different sizes and shapes—to make tablecloths for the playhouse table, a cover for the doll's bed, costumes for dressing up. Even wrapping a present for mother calls for matching the gift to the right amount of paper.

Patternmaking—for puppets, doll's dresses, costumes for dress-up, and the like—takes children a step further and challenges them to experiment with different ways and means of measuring surface area. Newspaper or large rolls of wrapping paper should be on hand for these purposes.

A class of first graders undertook to make paper patterns of themselves. The children stretched out full length on large sheets of wrapping paper. The patterns were cut out and matched against their models.

After painting in faces and clothing on their patterns, the children decided to arrange them by height.

It's taller because it's on tiptoe.

Now we're both on flat feet.

It wasn't always easy to tell who should follow whom. Often live models had to be checked against each other.

Finally, the paper figures—"flat feet" and all—were lined up along the school hallway. The lineup soon started some youngsters guessing about how

Reprinted from *Match and Measure,* pp. 30–32, by the Elementary Science Study. Copyright 1971 by Education Development Center, Inc., 55 Chapel Street, Newton, Massachusetts 02160.

many "paper children" it would take to reach the ceiling. One child said, seven; another, nine.

The teacher good-naturedly accepted the rather hazardous job of stacking the patterns feet on head up the wall.

Everyone was surprised when it took only three children to reach the ceiling.

In their early efforts at making clothes, children rarely think of allowing for seams or the thickness of the body. Rather than warn them of this, it is better to let them find out about it for themselves. After they have experienced the frustration of turning out costumes that don't fit, they will try other techniques for making patterns, such as wrapping paper around themselves or the models they are working with. Arranging a pattern on a piece of cloth is not easy. With practice, children develop an eye for conserving space and getting the most out of a piece of material.

4. SCIENCE—A PROCESS APPROACH LESSON: ORDERING PLANE FIGURES BY AREA

Footprints of various animals make for an interesting and involving introduction to measuring area. The exercise begins with a discussion of what kinds of animal tracks the children have seen. The discussion then focuses on the size of the footprints. The objectives are for the children to learn to:

1. Order groups of plane (two dimensional) figures of various shapes of sizes from smallest to largest on a basis of area. They will do this by visual comparison, by superimposing one upon the other, and by comparison with some selected unit.

2. Stay and demonstrate the area of plane figures in terms of some selected unit, for example, "This large square has an area as great as nine of these small squares."

The children are given paper handouts which have animal footprints on them. The children cut out the footprints and then compare the sizes of the various footprints using one footprint as the unit of measure.

Next the children are given colored paper triangles and asked to compare the area of these. Generalizing from what they have learned so far, the children proceed to measure the surface area of various structures within the classroom such as a wall, a window, a door and perhaps various surface areas outside of the classroom.

From *Science—A Process Approach* (1967), Part B, Exercise U, p. 1. Reprinted by permission of the American Association for the Advancement of Science, Washington, D.C.

5. MINNEMAST LESSON: VOLUME UNIT

Lesson 14:   Using a Standard Volume Unit

This lesson extends the children's experience with quantification by having them measure the capacity of containers.

The children are guided to use an arbitrary standard (a cork) as a unit of volume measurement. They then use the standard corks to compare the capacity of a fruit-juice can with that of a Jell-O box. The results are recorded in the form of histograms. . . . These histograms show that—even with standard units—we may get variation in the results of measuring a quantity. This point is not emphasized, however. The histogram is constructed by placing an O or X in the column corresponding to the number of corks a child reports he used to fill his container. In this case, the columns of tallies are placed *over* the numerals, rather than between them, since they represent actual counts of corks. The recording should be done as a class activity, each child placing a mark in the appropriate place on the histogram. Note that the histogram should have a zero point on the scale, even though only a portion of the chart is used. . . . Pegboards and golf tees may be used for the histogram. If these are used, the numerals should be placed *under* the columns of holes. Histogram and worksheets should be saved for use in the next lesson.

The lesson cannot be conducted until the children each have a juice can [6 fl. oz.] and Jell-O box [3 oz. size]. . .so they should be requested to bring these in advance.

The procedure of this lesson is continuous; it is not divided into separate activities. The suggested questions are structured to give children an understanding of capacity, direct comparison, and indirect comparison. . . .

Hold up the soup can and the cheese container.

> Which of these would hold more ice cream? Is the capacity of the can greater than, less than, or about the same as the capacity of the cheese container?
>
> How could we compare the capacities—how much they will hold?

Some children may be confident they can tell which container has the greater volume simply by looking at them side by side.

> How can we be sure?
>
> Can we decide by fitting one container inside the other? By a direct comparison?
>
> Is there some other way of comparing what they will hold? By an indirect comparison?

If some child suggests that you fill the containers with ice cream to make the comparison, explain that it would be a good way but, unfortunately you haven't any ice cream.

> Could we use this sand? How?

From MINNEMAST, *Measurement with Reference Units,* Unit 12 (1967), pp. 131–36. Copyright 1967 by the Regents of the University of Minnesota.

Let children demonstrate to the class that the comparison can be made by filling one container (level with the top) with the sand and then pouring the sand into the other.

Show the class a frozen-juice can and a Jell-O box.

Which would hold more ice cream, this can or this box?

How can we compare them to find out? (We could fill one of them with sand and then pour the sand into the other.)

To bring up the idea of an indirect comparison of volume, use an imaginary situation like this:

I know a girl named Jeannette who is a first grader in Canada. She likes ice cream, too. Her ice cream comes in a box. If we compared our box and can, do you think it would help us decide how much Jeannette's container would hold? (No)

Why wouldn't it? (Because we don't have one of Jeannette's ice cream boxes here. We don't know what kind of boxes they are.)

In the discussion, lead the children to recall that numbers helped when we compared lengths and areas.

What could we use to fill our containers and then count?

Would the sand be good to use? Would the grains of sand be good units of volume? Why not?

The children probably will see rather quickly that it would be impractical to try to count the grains of sand.

What might we use as units of volume?

Suggestions to use peanuts in the shell, cranberries, or popcorn would be good. Elicit from the children that these objects could be used to fill the containers and the number in each container could be counted and compared with a similar count which Jeannette could make.

I don't know whether Jeannette could get the things you suggested, but I know that she has a lot of corks like these. How could we use them for a comparison?

Guide the discussion toward the following activity: Divide the class into pairs and see that each pair has a juice can, a Jell-O box and about sixty corks (12-oz. container full). Have the children estimate which container will hold more corks and record their guess on the top of Worksheet 18. Then have them fill one container with corks and pour the corks into the other container, recording their results by filling in line 2 of the worksheet. Next ask them to determine—by actual trial—the number which each will hold. Point out that by "full" we will agree to mean level with the top, not heaped up. After they have made the trials and recorded the results, they are to complete the sentence at the bottom of the sheet, by putting the proper symbol (, , or =) in the blank.

Worksheet

Name_____

WHICH CONTAINER HOLDS MORE CORKS?

1. I <u>think</u> that the _____ will hold more
   corks than the _____.

2. By pouring, I <u>found</u> that the _____
   holds more corks than the _____

3. The box holds _____corks.

Jell-O

box

4. The can holds _____corks.

Juice

can

5. Volume of box _____Volume of can.

To develop the idea that there is variation in such measurements and to further illustrate the use of a histogram, have the class record their results on two histograms—on pegboards...and on charts.... Make the charts on large sheets of paper.... Each pair should record its data by having a child put an O or X in the appropriate column. Emphasize that there is no single "correct" result, only a "most likely" result. Give these reasons to help the children accept different results: the top of the container is not well defined; corks are packed in different ways; or corks and container vary slightly. Have each child repeat his measurements; this should bring out the variation in packing....

This is a copy of the chart which Jeannette's classmates made for their boxes. What does it tell us?

The children should see that the histograms indicate that Jeannette's class had boxes which would hold more ice cream than the Jell-O boxes but less than the juice cans.

If each child recorded a box on the chart, how many children are in Jeannette's class?

Note: Save the juice cans and Jell-O boxes for the next lesson.

6. ELEMENTARY SCIENCE STUDY: BALANCING

Distinguishing mass and weight and their measurement is a part of measuring. In this unit, from Elementary Science Study *Balancing,* children begin an intuitive feel for this task.

Each child, to start, should have a balance stand, a pegboard beam, and a supply of small washers and paper clips for himself.

For the first few lessons, teachers have found it best to give the children free rein with all the balancing equipment, allowing them to explore the materials for themselves and devise their own experiments. . . .

Teachers are often upset at the fact that the children don't start with simple problems. Rather, their earliest work would often require the most complex analysis if the children were really to understand it. Don't worry. After a few sessions, they usually go back to more basic problems; yet many children do come back to these hard questions later on, when they have the understanding necessary to attack them.

As you look around the room, you may find children involved in problems such as the following:

Symmetrical arrangements—hanging a single washer on one side and then a single washer on the other side in the corresponding place; continuing to add washers in pairs, one on each side. The board might end up looking something like this.

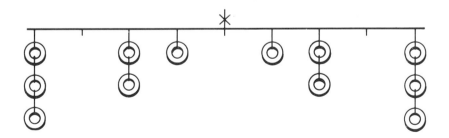

This sort of arrangement can be turned around into a problem: Can you add washers to this board to make one side the mirror-image of the other? Don't move the washers already there.

Reprinted from *Balancing,* pp. 11–15, by the Elementary Science Study. Copyright 1966 by Education Development Center, Inc., 55 Chapel Street, Newton, Massachusetts 02160.

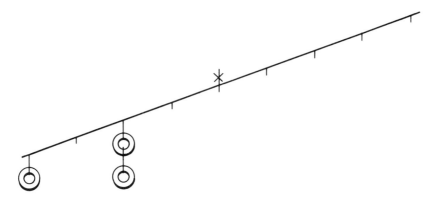

How about this arrangement?

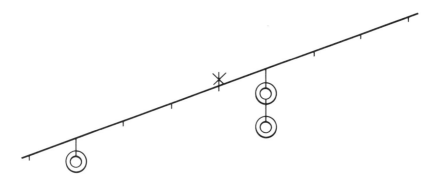

MOVING AWAY FROM SYMMETRICAL ARRANGEMENTS TO OTHER
WAYS OF BALANCING THE BOARD

Problem:

Can you make the board balance by adding two washers on the same paper clip?

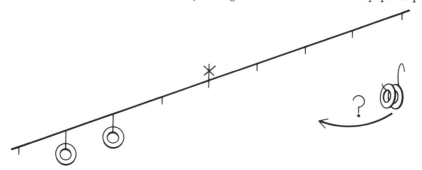

This perhaps leads on to *balancing one washer with two....*

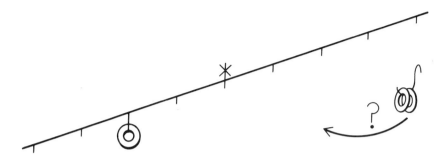

Many children balance washers with long *chains of paper clips.*

Problem:

Will a chain of six washers balance six washers hung on one paper clip? (What about the extra paper clips?)

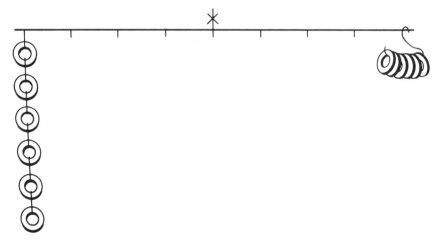

Problem:

Will a washer hung at the bottom of a paper-clip chain have the same effect as one hung at the top?

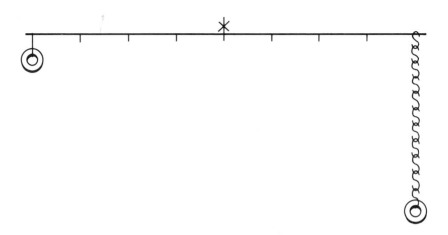

Problem:

Where can you put six washers on one paper clip to balance a chain of six washers hung as shown below?

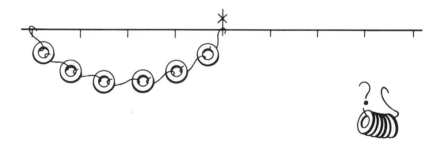

BALANCING THE BOARD WHEN THE NAIL IS OFF-CENTER

A few washers cut out on the long side, an intriguing situation.

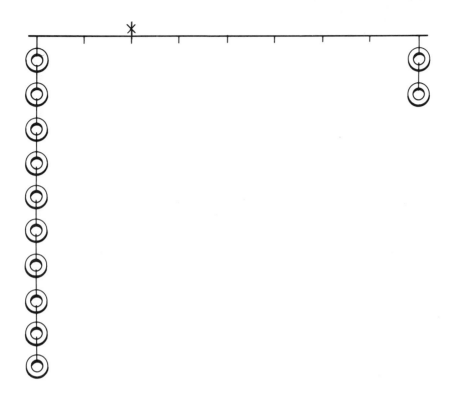

Problem:

If the board is supported near one end, how many washers will be needed to make it level?

USING THE BOARD TO WEIGH THE WASHERS

One girl did this: Using the pegboard as an equal-arm balance, she hung a single washer on a paper clip from the end hole on one side and kept adding paper clips to the end hole on the other side until the board was balanced. It took 33 paper clips. She announced that the washer weighed the same as 32 paper clips.

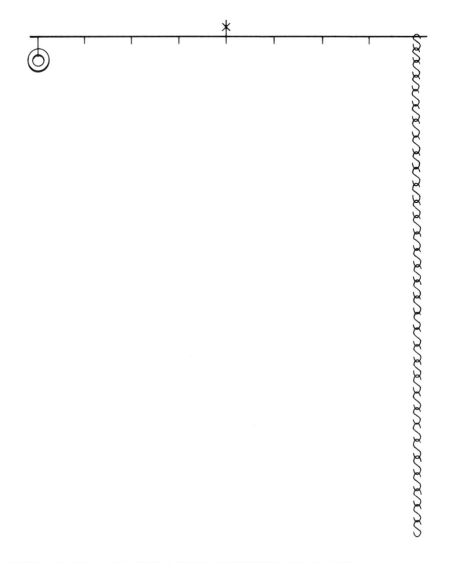

WHEN CAN THE BOARD "FEEL" SMALL DIFFERENCES IN WEIGHT?

One student announced at the end of the first class that when there were no washers on the board, one paper clip made it tilt a lot; after he had hung many washers on it, one paper clip didn't have any effect. He found this out in the course of balancing the board by itself while he was trying out the equipment for the first time. Children often want to investigate this sort of thing more carefully later on.

Problem:

What's the lightest thing you can weigh with the board?

Problem:

What difference does it make when you put the nail in the middle-row center hole instead of the top-row center hole?

7. SCIENCE—A PROCESS APPROACH: MAKING COMPARISONS USING A BALANCE

Children compare the weights of common objects from around the classroom in this exercise. Many of the objects have nearly the same weight which necessitates the use of the equal arm-balance.

The objectives are for the children to learn to:

1. Order objects the weights of which differ appreciably, by lifting them and by comparing them on an equal-arm balance.

2. State that one object is heavier than another because the earth-pull on that object is greater than it is on the other.

3. Demonstrate how to compare small objects by counting the number of arbitrary units, such as paper clips, pins, or tacks, needed to balance the objects on an equal-arm balance.

4. State the results of their measurements, as in the following example: "The object weighs the same as six paper clips," or "The object weighs more than ten paper clips, but less than eleven paper clips."

In the introduction, children find need for a more sensitive means for comparing weights than their lifting objects with their hands. The class is then divided into groups with each group having an equal arm-balance.

The groups of children do several tasks such as ordering a set of objects from lightest to heaviest and finding out how many paper clips it takes to balance each of the objects.

The balances are kept available to the class between science lessons so that during free time the children may work with them.

From *Science—A Process Approach* (1967), Part B, Exercise N, p. 1. Reprinted by permission of the American Association for the Advancement of Science, Washington, D.C.

8. SCIENCE—A PROCESS APPROACH: MEASURING FORCES WITH SPRINGS

In the introduction, children are asked to examine a spring and to think about what they can do with it. They are asked to observe what happens when they pull on the spring and to suggest possible uses of the spring. Next the teacher shows the children two cylinders which are alike in size but different in weight. The problem is posed of figuring out if there is a way to use the springs to tell something about the cylinders.

The objectives are for the children to learn to:

1. State that if an object does not move, the forces acting upon it must be in balance.

2. State that attaching a weight to a spring increases the force pulling on the spring so that it stretches.

3. Demonstrate with a spring whether two objects have the same or different weights.

As the exercise continues, the class is divided into groups of four or five children with each group having two cylinders of unequal weight and an equal arm-balance. The groups are asked to determine which cylinder weighs more and how they might determine the difference. The children are asked to think about how they might be able to use springs in comparing the earth pull of two different cylinders.

Next, one child is asked to stand in the front of the classroom and hold a ball in his hand while the remainder of the children analyze the forces acting on the ball. In the end they decide that the earth pulls down on the ball and the hand pushes up on the ball, and that these forces are in opposite directions. A force diagram is drawn on the board and there is a short discussion based upon the question: "Why doesn't the ball move?"

A wooden box is then given to one child to hold. Through discussion, the forces acting on the box are analyzed. Then by using a spring, the amount of force necessary to lift the box and to pull the box sideways under various conditions is observed.

The class is then divided into groups with each group having a spring. The groups are to determine how far an object will stretch the spring. This amount of stretch is then compared with the number of some other uniform objects, such as washers or paper clips that are needed to stretch the spring the same amount.

String, rubber bands, ticker tape, paper, cloth, pieces of wood, animal footprints, Jell-O boxes, balls, balances, cylinders, and washers are all useful sources of experience for children in developing the skill of measuring or the ability to find out how much more.

To take the posttest, you will need a straight pin, a thumbtack, and a staple.

1. Name three measurements you can make of the collection of objects.

From *Science—A Process Approach* (1967), Part C, Exercise F, p. 1. Reprinted by permission of the American Association for the Advancement of Science, Washington, D.C.

a. _____

b. _____

c. _____

2. Use the staple as your unit to measure the length of the thumbtack and the straight pin.

a. _____

b. _____

3. Estimate the length of the three objects using centimeters.

a. _____

b. _____

c. _____

Acceptable responses to the posttest follow. If you did satisfactorily, you are ready for the next chapter. If *not*, you should talk with your instructor.

Acceptable Responses for the Posttest

1. Measurements you could make include
    Length.
    Width.
    Mass.
    Weight.
    Diameter of stem or head.

2. Your answer should include how many times the straight pin was longer than the staple; the same for the thumbtack.

3. Check your estimates with a metric ruler. If you are within two centimeters you are doing quite well!

5. Communicating Change

At the end of this chapter, you should be able to: (1) describe objects' locations using a two-coordinate system; (2) construct vector diagrams to describe change; (3) describe change based on the rate of change that is measurable; (4) describe change in terms of the net change or resultants.

To do the pretest, you will need only the following grid.

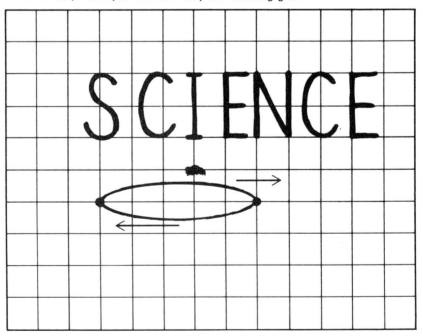

1. Without showing another person this grid, write out the directions he would need to know to locate the letter *I* in *Science*.

2. Two small bugs were having a race on the letter *I*. The results of this race were not completely clear as they tried to tell a third bug. Both bugs started in the middle of the letter *I*; the brown bug went one block north and the green bug went one-half block south. Both raced for the same time. Draw arrows that they could use to communicate their *displacement:*

velocity:

3. On the next day, the two bugs raced over the same course. The brown bug went from the middle to the north end of the *I* in two minutes. The green bug went from the middle to the point halfway between the middle and the south end of the *I* in one minute. Draw arrows that they could use to communicate their
displacement:

velocity:

4. To show her superiority, Marie has been demonstrating her jogging ability to Bill. She has been using a moving-belt machine that moves west from the starting switch at a rate of three meters per minute.

   a.   What is Marie's velocity relative to Bill if she jogs west at one meter per minute north? (It is assumed that Bill is not moving.)

   Show how you could find out using arrows.

   b.   What is Marie's velocity relative to Bill if she jogs east at three meters per minute?

Show how you could find out using arrows.

c.   What is Marie's velocity relative to Bill if she jogs east at two meters per minute?

Show how you could find out using arrows.

5.   In which of the above situations is rate of change involved?

How do you decide what the rate of change is, that is, what is the rule for computing a rate of change?

Acceptable responses for the pretest follow. If you did satisfactorily on the pretest, you will want to omit the activities and go to page 92 for more suggestions on how to use these ideas with children. If you did *not* do satisfactorily, you will want to carry out the activities beginning on page 80.

Acceptable Responses for Pretest

1.   To perform this first task, you must first establish a frame of reference between you and the other person. The best way to do this is to number or name the lines along the base line of the grid and along the vertical axis, such as:

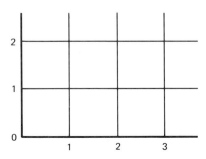

Using this system, the *I* can be described as a straight line from (7, 6) to (7, 8).

2.   The displacement of the bugs would be the same as one block on the grid for the brown bug and one-half block on the grid for the green bug. Displacement arrows would show not only the distance but the direction, like this:

Velocity arrows will show both speed and direction. Since the brown bug in the same time went two times as far as the green bug, the arrows would be:

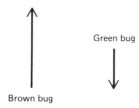

3.   We now have a change in the race. Both bugs went the same distance and direction away from the starting point, so the displacement arrows would be the same as in number 2.

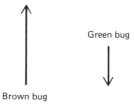

However, the *time* it took them to do this was different. The brown bug took two minutes to go one block on the grid, whereas the green bug took one minute to go one-half block on the grid. Their speed was the same, so their velocity arrows would be:

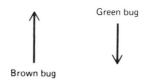

4. a.   Since the belt is moving west at three meters per minute, Marie would be moving relative to Bill at four meters per minute.

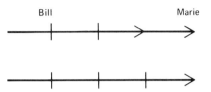

b.   In this situation, Marie would appear to be standing still.

c.   Now Marie will appear to be running backwards to Bill.

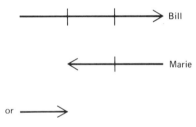

5.   Since nothing in task 1 was moving, no rate of change was involved. In tasks 2 and 3 the bugs were moving, and the rate of change involved their speed.

In task 4 Marie was moving, and her speed was the point of attention.

The rule for computing a rate of change is the amount of change divided by the time needed for that change.

The task of scientists is to describe the behavior of the physical world. Similarly, the young child, experiencing science activities in the classroom, inquires into the why and how of physical phenomena and communicates his knowledge to others.

Consider this description of a recent phenomenon. In their craft, three passengers shot off into orbit. Escaping the earth's gravitational pull, the three directed their vessel toward its target. Utilizing extraordinary speed, the craft reached its destination in several days and after nearly an additional day it raced back home. A successful mission!

Consider this description of the same extraterrestrial journey. At 7 : 51 A.M. of December 21, 1968, from Pad 39A at Cape Kennedy, Florida, three astronauts were launched into earth orbit. Accelerating to a speed of 24,200 miles per hour, they left the earth's gravity and sped on a curved path toward the moon. At a point of displacement 234,100 miles from earth, their craft slowed its speed to 3,625 miles per hour to orbit in a nearly perfect seventy-mile-high circle around the moon, just sixty-nine hours away from liftoff. After ten orbits, they accelerated to 5,980 miles per hour and were propelled out of lunar orbit, returning to earth. Entering the earth's atmosphere, their velocity mounted to 24,765 miles per hour toward the earth. The return trip of $57\frac{1}{2}$ hours ended in the Pacific Ocean only 7,000 yards from the waiting rescue ship *Yorktown*.

Which description communicates more specifically what happened? Might this depend on *what* is being communicated to *whom?* A word of caution then : the purpose of the communication and the audience to whom it is addressed will determine how specific to be.

Basic to communicating these happenings is a description of the physical environment, the location in space and in time. The child learns to describe relative location of objects in his environment. The keyword is *relative*. The need for a frame of reference is essential. One reference frame which children can use for describing location is a coordinate system.

When objects are in motion and the location or position changes, description of location becomes increasingly complex. Motion is characterized by speed and velocity; hence, time is now considered. Speed is the rate of change of position; it is a statement of the division of distance per time intervals. Speed is describable in terms of simple magnitude, as is volume, energy, mass, and time. These are scalar quantities and their magnitudes are indicated by a real number, such as 50 miles per hour, 20 cubic centimeters, 15 seconds.

Velocity, however, communicates *more* than simple magnitude. It indicates direction. When the child wishes to communicate the direction of change of position in addition to the rate of change, he is describing the velocity and a more sophisticated "describer" is required—a vector quantity. The term vector is used as the name for a quantity that has direction as well as magnitude. Vector quantities are used to describe velocity, as well as force and displacement. The term *arrow* has been used in this module to refer to the diagram of a vector quantity. If preferred, the term *vector* may be utilized.

All events are not characterized by motion and speed. The rate of change of other properties is encountered in every child's experience. Though most are familiar with height, weight, mass, length, volume, or area as properties that change, few are able to describe or apply a rule to determine the rate of change of these properties.

But words may not be adequate to express to us what is meant by communicating change.

In this activity, you will need a friend and possibly a telephone !

A splendid challenge is to play tick-tack-toe on the phone. Your friend will know how to arrange his grid as :

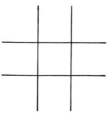

In this telephone version, however, have him connect the outside lines of the box, such as:

One rule for telephone tick-tack-toe is that all *X*'s and the *O*'s must be hung on the intersection of lines and not in spaces. Are you ready?

You place the first *X* on your grid and then tell your friend where to put his. What will you say? _____

_____

Suppose you put your *X* in this position:

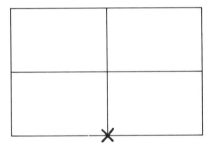

How would you describe that to him?

You may have observed that thus far the simplicity of the system has not caused much of a problem for you can say, "the middle of the bottom line," and it is quite clearly the exact location of your *X*. Try the game again, using only names for the locations of *X* and *O* based on this grid.

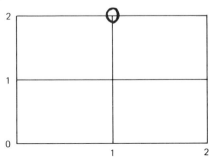

Note that it is a mere convention that you start with the horizontal name first and then add the vertical part of that name. So the *X* position name would be (0, 1). What would the *O* position name be? _____ [Did you go over 1 and up 2 (1, 2) ?]

In this grid, name the position of the winner's choices. _____

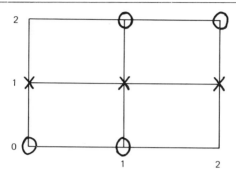

Since you don't know what was the order of the winner's choices, it does not make any difference as to how you listed them. The choices were (0, 1), (1, 1), and (2, 1).

In any two coordinates like this grid, there are two axes. One of these is usually called the *X axis* or the *across axis*. The second is the *Y axis* or the *vertical axis*. When describing the position on such a grid, it is conventional to name the *X* axis first and then the *Y* axis. (Note: In the alphabet, *X* comes before *Y* !)

For the next activity, you will need a sheet of graph paper and four paper clips.

Grids are useful devices for describing location, such as on maps. They can also be used to describe change in locations. Name the lines on the graph paper grid. Now place the four paper clips in each of the positions as indicated.

Clip #1   (0, 2).
Clip #2   (3, 6).
Clip #3   (6, 6).
Clip #4   (7, 1).

Did you have any difficulty recalling that the first number referred to "going over" and the second number referred to "going up" ?

Do what this statement says to Clip #1.

(0, 2) ⟶ (7, 4).

You probably noted that the arrow in that statement is used to indicate *moving* the clip.

Complete these moves:

Clip #2   (3, 6) ⟶ (4, 0).
Clip #3   (6, 6) ⟶ (5, 0).
Clip #4   (7, 1) ⟶ (5, 5).

In these statements, what does the head of the arrow indicate? _____
_____ What does the line of the
arrow indicate? _____ What

do the numbered pairs indicate? _____

_____

As you think back to this situation, the arrow head tells you the direction of the move. The line or the stem of the arrow has no special purpose other than to indicate path, whereas the number pairs name the starting and ending positions.

On your graph paper grid, draw arrows that will picture this event. A ladybug began its trip at (6,3) and walked to (2, 3). Then it went on to (2, 5) and over to (6, 6).

Mark these positions on your grid. From the marked positions, can you tell where it started and how it traveled? _____

Use arrows now to complete the picture so that another person could tell both where the bug started and the sequence of its trip.

What was the total distance traveled by the bug? _____

_____ How far is it from where it started? _____

You may have noted that you described distances in both of these questions. However, in the first answer you described the total distance moved, whereas in the second answer you were describing total distance *away from starting point*. The distance of an object away from its starting point is called *displacement*.

To apply this idea, place a paper clip at (1, 4). Now move it to (4, 1) and then to (7, 4). Use arrows to show

1. The total distance moved.
2. The displacement.

In this situation, when you used the arrow to indicate displacement,

1. What did the head of the arrow indicate? _____
2. What did the line of the arrow indicate? _____

For arrows indicating displacement, the head always points out the direction of the displacement, and the length of the line indicates how far or how much displacement.

Arrows are useful tools for communicating changes other than displacement. Move two paper clips from position (0, 1) to (0, 11). Draw displacement arrows. Now repeat this move, only make Clip #1 go twice as fast as Clip #2.

What would the displacement arrows look like for both of the clips? Suppose you wanted to draw arrows indicating speed, which pair would fit?

Set A   Clip #1 $\longrightarrow$
         Clip #2 $\longrightarrow$

Set B   Clip #1 $\longrightarrow$
         Clip #2 $\rightarrow$

Set C   Clip #1 $\rightarrow$
         Clip #2 $\longrightarrow$

If you selected Set B, you are correct. You may have noted that in both *displacement* and *velocity* arrows, the head of the arrow indicates the *direction* of the change. The length of the arrow indicates *how much change* (if a displacement arrow, how far from the beginning point, or if a velocity arrow, how much speed).

You will find the next activity an interesting application. To carry it out, you will need two pieces of foil.

After making sure that the pieces of foil are about the same size, wad one into a small ball. Hold both pieces at eye level and drop them at the same time. Here are three sets of arrows. Which set of arrows describes the displacement of the event? _____ _____ Which set describes the velocity of the foil? _____

Set A   Set B   Set C

Since the displacement, that is, the total distance away from the starting point, is the same for both pieces of foil, and since the direction of the displacement is the same for both pieces of foil, Set A is the best description of the displacement. You probably did not measure the time, but observed that the wadded foil dropped much quicker than the sheet. Therefore, Set B would be the best indicator that the wadded foil had moved at a greater speed.

For the next activity, you will need a map of your city.

Find the location of your home on the map. Use the grids to name that position. Now find a school that is near your home. Name that position. Suppose you left home in the morning and went to school. Draw a displacement arrow for your trip. After school, suppose you returned home. Draw a displacement arrow for your day's trip or a combination of the two trips.

You may have noted that your displacement at the end of the day was 0; that is, when you added the two displacement arrows of equal length but which were in opposite directions, you got a *resultant* of zero displacement.

On your map, locate your favorite shopping center. Suppose that after going to school, you went on to that shopping center. Draw a displacement arrow for those two trips.

In this case, you should have drawn an arrow from your home to school, with the head indicating that the direction was *away* from home. Your second arrow would be drawn from school to the shopping center with the head indicating travel from the school. Your *resultant* displacement is found by drawing an arrow from your point of origin to the head of the last displacement arrow. In what direction will the head of the resultant displacement arrow point?

Resultant arrows are useful in communicating the total change both for displacement and for velocity. Just for fun, use your imagination in this situation. Suppose your ladybug is sitting on the top of your car. As you drive to school, suppose you are driving at a careful speed of 10 mph. Your ladybug is also walking from the back of the car toward the front at a speed of 1 mph. (Speedy bug, isn't she!)

Here is a set of arrows.

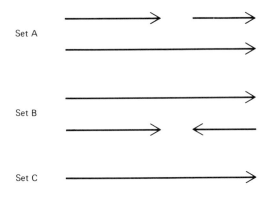

Which set of arrows would best describe the velocity of the bug? _____

Suppose the bug is tired and does not change its position on the car roof. Which set of arrows would describe its velocity then? _____

Suppose the ladybug decides to return from the front to the rear of the car roof. Which set of arrows would describe its velocity? _____

Which set of arrows best describes *your* velocity? _____

You probably selected Set A for the first situation, for the velocity of the car would be added to the velocity of the bug. In the second situation, Set C is best, for the bug's velocity is the same as that of the car. In situation three, Set B is appropriate, for the bug's total velocity is the resultant of subtracting its velocity from that of the car, if you are thinking relative to the map! In the last situation, your velocity relative to the car is zero, but relative to the road it is the same as that of the car.

Arrows are useful tools in communicating change, but they are not the only tools. In some situations, ratio of a numerical comparison is equally efficient.

For the next activity, you will need several cubes or teaspoonfuls of sugar, three glassfuls of water, a source of heat such as a kitchen stove or a hot plate, and a thermometer.

Begin by putting half a cup of water in each glass. The water in the first glass should be at room temperature, in the second glass heated for two minutes, and in the third glass at the boiling point. Put two cubes of sugar into each of the three glasses.

Make a list of the things that you think are important in order to communicate what happened.

1. _____
2. _____
3. _____
4. _____
5. _____
6. _____
7. _____

Did your list include comparing the appearance of the water before and after you put the sugar in? Did it include a measurement of the time it took for the sugar to disappear? Name the properties of the objects in this event that changed.

1. _____

2. _____

3. _____

4. _____

Did your list include the taste of the water and the phase or state of the sugar? Now to compute the rate of change for each glass, what information will you need?

1. _____

2. _____

In this case, the rate of change will be related to sugar dissolving. It will be the relationship between the temperature and the dissolving time. How do you decide on what the rate of change is?

Your answer probably included the idea of identifying the property that changes, the way of measuring it, and the length of time required for the change. Thus, speed is a rate of change, that is, 25 miles (linear distance is the property) per hour (the unit of time).

One dimension of communicating change is the frame of reference of the observer. The writers of the Science Curriculum Improvement Study describe this:

Relative Position

REFERENCE OBJECTS

For practical purposes reference objects must be easily located and identified. Otherwise they cannot be used as guides in finding the object whose position is being described. It would be hopeless, for example, to try to find the girl in the daisy field if her position were described by saying, "The girl is between two daisy blossoms." Specific reference objects such as the corners of the field, a rock, a tree, or perhaps a scarecrow are necessary.

The use of reference objects in everyday life is highly varied and adapted to many special circumstances that arise. A piece of furniture, a pointing finger, corners of a room, street intersections, a tall building, a railroad track, or the sun—these and many others are commonly used as reference objects.

J. P., his dog Homer, and his Aunt Hildegarde took a long walk on the farm.

Aunt Hildegarde: J. P., do you see the falcon sitting in that tree over there?

J. P.:   What falcon? In which tree? Where?

Aunt H.:   In that big, broken tree over there (pointing her finger).

J. P.:   Oh, that tree in front of us! I see it, but I don't see the falcon.

Aunt H.:   It's on the branch.

J. P.:   There are too many branches. I give up. Let's forget it.

Aunt H.: No, let's start over again. Do you see that broken branch about halfway up the trunk on the left side?

J. P.: Yes, I do.

Aunt H.: Fine. Now look at the second branch above it, on the same side of the tree. Now move to the left and you just have to see the falcon.

J. P.: Oh sure, but that's a hawk.

...What happened in this conversation? What finally allowed Aunt Hildegarde to communicate the location of the falcon without confusion, ambiguity, or absurdity? She established her first reference object by pointing to the proper tree. Then she selected a large, easily identifiable branch on that tree as a second reference object. J. P. could identify these two reference objects. Aunt Hildegarde also specified dirctions ("...above it...") and distances ("...the second branch..."), so that it was easy for J. P. to locate the falcon.

Note that the reference objects must be readily identifiable. Aunt Hildegarde's initial attempt to use the tree as a reference object failed because there were several trees. Her next attempt to identify the tree by pointing (her arm served as a reference object) succeeded, but the position of the falcon was still not specified accurately enough to enable J. P. to find it.

THE DESCRIPTION OF RELATIVE POSITION

It is very difficult to give instructions for locating an object to a person who is not familiar with a particular location. For example, suppose you are describing the placement of a book to a person who is not familiar with the room in which the book is kept. Since none of the objects in the room can be conveniently used as reference objects, it is most helpful to use the person's body. This can be done by telling the person to stand in the doorway to the room, to look for the bookcase on his left, and then to look on the middle of the second shelf of the bookcase. This example illustrates how we may use large objects in the environment (the room and its door) to locate smaller ones (ourselves), then still smaller ones (the bookcase, the book) in a narrowing-down process.

The problem of describing position is more difficult when you do not have any reference objects to use in a narrowing-down process. As an example, imagine yourself as a passenger on an ocean liner observing something in the ocean. Here, you have to start with the ship on which you find yourself and work outward. You may sight a flying fish "500 yards off the starboard bow" which means ahead and to the right of the ship. You could also say the fish is "500 yards northwest" if you and your listener knew the compass directions.

Travelers in a spaceship, sighting a meter, face a similar problem in trying to describe its position to their shipmates. For a spaceship traveler, there is no north and south, no up and down because the earth is far away. How can space travelers describe the position of an object outside their spaceship?

One method would be to label all the portholes with letters and report, "The meteor is in the direction of porthole F." A second method would be to use the pilot sitting at his controls as a reference object. Relative to him, a report could take the form, "The meteor is above me and to my right." A third method would be to select several particularly bright stars for use as reference objects.

MR. O

The lack of environmental reference objects on the ocean and in space creates a problem when we try to apply our usual procedures for describing position. Another problem arises because young children always view objects from their own point of view. The invention of Mr. O introduces an aid to help students overcome the limitations of conventional observations and their egocentric view of spatial relationships.

Mr. O is called an observer because he "reports" the position of any object we wish. In his reports Mr. O uses his own body as a reference object. The distance is measured from wherever he is—more precisely, from the point on his chest where his arms cross his body. He describes directions relative to the major directions established by his shape. His head and feet define up–down, his arms define right–left (his right arm is distinctively colored for easy identification), and his body defines front–back as though he were a person (buttons are indicated in front for easy identification).

Relative Motion

So far we have considered ways of describing the relative position of objects that are stationary. Now let us consider objects that change position. When an object such as a truck on a roadway changes position, you commonly say that it "moves," that it is "in motion." But what do you mean by "motion"? Since position can only be described relative to reference objects, it is plausible to expect that motion would also be described relative to reference objects. It is therefore more precise and helpful to use the phrase "relative motion."

EXAMPLES OF RELATIVE MOTION

Imagine that a truck on the roadway is being observed relative to two different reference objects. The first reference object is the roadway; the second reference object is a crate on the truck. To make the descriptions simpler and more concrete, we shall introduce two artificial observers, one associated with each reference object.

As the truck moves down the road, observer A on the roadway reports its position first to his left, then in front of him, then to his right. The position of the truck relative to observer A has changed. But observer B on the crate always reports the truck as being in the same position, with the platform under him and the driver's cab to his left. The position of the truck relative to observer B, therefore, has not changed from the beginning to the end of the experiment. Thus you find that you have two different reports, one from each observer. Relative to the roadway, the position of the truck has changed, but relative to the crate, the position of the truck has not changed. If we define relative motion as the change of position relative to reference objects, then the two observers disagree not only about the relative position of the truck at various times during the period of observation, but they also disagree about the truck's relative motion.

The discussion can be extended to the motion of other objects. For instance, does the earth move? This depends on the reference objects used to define the earth's position. Relative to an observer standing on the sun—something you have to imagine—the earth moves in its orbit and spins on its axis.

Consider some of the consequences of this concept of relative motion, consequences which may seem fascinating or merely strange, depending on how willing you are to break out of habitual modes of thinking. In order to describe the position and motion of objects in an experiment, it is important that you decide upon the reference objects. Already you have noted that observers may disagree about the relative motion of an object. You must also recognize that an artificial observer will always report an object to be stationary relative to himself as long as he is attached to that object. Such an observer's report about the rest of the world will seem unusual indeed if he is attached to a merry-go-round, a satellite in orbit, or a sewing machine needle.

SPEED OF RELATIVE MOTION

Another consequence of the relative motion concept is that two observers might disagree about the direction and the speed of a moving object which they both observe. Think about this example in which an object travels at different speeds relative to two observers.

The speed of a riverboat going upstream as reported by its passengers looking at the shoreline is a snaillike 1 mph, but the speed as reported by the captain is a respectable 10 mph. Who is right?

All navigation and propulsion of the riverboat take place relative to the water. The motion of a riverboat relative to the shore is different from its motion relative to the water unless the water is still. Since the water is flowing downstream at a speed of 9 mph (relative to the shore), and the riverboat is traveling upstream at a speed of 10 mph (relative to the water, as reported by the captain), the speed of the riverboat (relative to the shore as reported by the passengers) is 1 mph. Thus the contradictory reports of the two observers can be reconciled. The question "Who is right?" can only be answered, "Both are right."

The Relativity Concepts in Modern Science

The concepts of relativity of position and motion were seriously applied to the motion of the bodies in the solar system by Copernicus, Kepler, and Galileo. These scientists questioned the geocentric (earth-centered) frame of reference, in which the planet earth was absolutely stationary and celestial bodies were in motion. They found that a much simpler geometrical description of the motion of the sun and the planets was obtained when the sun was considered to be stationary and the earth to be in motion. Even though this revolutionary point of view shook social and religious institutions of the time, it came to be accepted because of the new insight and understanding of the solar system which it provided.

Now scientists believe that there is no absolute frame of reference which is "at rest," with everything else moving about it. Instead, they believe that an observer can, hypothetically at least, be associated with any object or system.

He may be associated with the sun, with the earth, with a moving automobile, with an arching football, or with an orbiting satellite. An observer on any one of these objects can describe the position and motion of other objects. The observer on the satellite may observe the earth and the moon, the observer on the football may observe the passer and the receiver, and so on. Several observers of the same phenomenon will, in general, give different descriptions of the motion of the same object.

Albert Einstein formulated a theory by which the observations of different observers can be related to one another, just as we related the reports of the observer in car A to the reports of the observer at the roadside. Light signals, as phenomena to be observed, played a special role in Einstein's studies because they were the most rapid means by which the observers could communicate with one another. Einstein concluded that no observer could report an object moving with a speed greater than the speed of light.

The Relativity Concepts and Children's Thinking

The young child's concept of space is egocentric. He relates the objects in his environment to himself rather than to one another. For this reason, his descriptions and drawings are not realistic. In one picture he may show objects seen in a side view, yet their relative placement may reflect an inaccurate top view. He does not make perspective drawings, even though most objects are usually seen from an angle, and exact side views are very rare in nature. He is unable to describe or recognize the view of a scene from an observation point other than the one he occupies at the moment. He may even combine observations that he has made over a period of time, so that he thinks objects (e.g. home and school) are spatially close to one another only because they are closely associated in his thoughts. The young child's egocentrism distorts his awareness of the spatial relations in his environment.

During their upper elementary school years, most children begin to overcome their egocentrism. The Relativity unit is introduced at this point to help them accomplish this change. The theme of the unit is that there are always several correct, though differing, spatial points of view. By comparing their observations with one another and with the reports they ascribe to Mr. O, children begin to consider other points of view and transfer their awareness away from themselves.[1]

Change implies that the observer has identified what is changing. The writers of the MINNEMAST program focus on this topic.

In this unit we want them to focus their attention on the way two changing properties in a system are related to each other. The children are guided to discover the relation between two changes by setting up a number of experiments. In an early experiment the children plant corn. They observe that there is a change in the height of their plants that is related to the change in the number of days since planting. Similarly, as they drop marbles into a container

---

[1] Science Curriculum Improvement Study, *Relativity* (Lexington, Massachusetts: D.C. Heath and Company, 1968), pp. 14–17.

of water, they see that with each change in the number of marbles, there is a change in the height of the water, and that there is a relation (or rule that operates) between the two changes.

Relations between changes like these are called functional relations. If measurements of the changes can be made, the relation can be vividly shown on a graph. Therefore the children are given experience with several different methods of graphing the changes. . . .

But even where measurement is difficult or impossible, the relation between changes can still be investigated by observation and/or experimentation. For example, the children do an experiment where they let one potato sprout in the light and another in the dark. It would not be difficult for them to measure and compare the longest sprout on each potato, but it would be impossible for them to measure precisely how much light (or heat) each potato received during the growing period. In such a case, the children can still observe the rule (the functional relation) that operated. They can make a fairly accurate statement saying that the potato that had less light had the longer sprout, or that there is a relation between darkness and the rate of growth.

The concept of functional relations is emphasized at this point in the curriculum because it is basic to man's attempt to understand the world around him. Ability to recognize and interpret the relation of one change to another and to express that relation in concise form is an important aspect of scientific and mathematical investigation. The limited understanding which the child acquires now will aid him in his attempts to explain his environment. His understanding will gradually be extended as his studies continue.[2]

The entire task of communicating change is important to the study of science, but the challenge of helping children communicate change even more so. In these units, the developers of various curriculum programs illustrate alternative ways to approach the topic of change and its communication.

1. MINNEMAST LESSON: CHANGE IN PLANTS

COMMENTARY

Plant growth and development is seen most dramatically in a germinating seed. The change from a small dry object to an elongated, rapidly-growing seedling with roots, stem, and leaves takes place within a few days. Each child should grow his own plant and observe it every day. He should be helped to see that while all its visible properties change, the plant is at all times the same living organism.

---

2 MINNEMAST, *Comparing Changes,* Unit 19 (1969), pp. 1–2.
From MINNEMAST, *Observing Properties,* Unit 8 (1969), pp. 111–15. Copyright 1969 by the Regents of the University of Minnesota.

The seeds...are easy to procure. They are relatively large and easy to handle, and they produce attractive young plants. Other seeds you or the children might like to try are grapefruit or flower seeds. Some teachers have used seeds from the Halloween pumpkin. Some parents may be able to supply seeds. You should plant a few extra seeds in case some of the children's do not grow. Commercial seed companies are your best source of flower seeds. Various kinds of beans and peas are packaged for groceries. These are inexpensive and can be used but you should try out a few first to make sure they are still viable. . . . If this lesson is begun on a Friday, results should be evident before the end of the next week. . . .

Give each child several different kinds of seeds, a section of kitchen paper toweling, and a small container. Tell the children they are going to plant these seeds in the containers, but first ask them to describe the properties of each kind of seed, including its shape, size, color, hardness, markings, or grooves. Label and save some seeds of each kind. These seeds should not be germinated, but should be saved for reference by the children.

Now show the children how to plant the seeds. Have them press each seed against the inside of the glass or jar with a wet wad of toweling in such a way that the seeds can be observed as they germinate. If a single piece of paper toweling does not keep the seeds against the glass, stuff another piece in the center of the jar. . . .

Tell the children that the paper toweling must be kept moist. They can do this by putting a little water in the bottom of the jar and then covering the jar with a small index card. (An alternative method is to fold the seeds inside moistened toweling and put this "package" in a plastic bag.) When the children have finished planting, have them mark or initial their containers. Put them in some convenient place in the classroom where the children can easily observe them. The seeds should germinate well at room temperature.

Remind the children to look at their plants every day and to record any changes with drawings or with marks that indicate measurements. They can keep these records on a folded sheet of newsprint or in a small notebook.

Ask questions that require the children to look closely:

What is happening to the outside of your seeds?

Is the outside wrinkled?

Is the outside split?

What is happening at the lower end of your seed? At the upper end? At the side?

I notice that we have planted our seeds in many different positions in our jars. Some seem to be turned one way, some another. Some seem to be placed sideways and some lengthways, while others are in a slanted position. Does this seem to change the way the roots come out?

Did any of your seeds send out roots from the top position? From the side? What direction did the roots take then? Did all the roots grow in the same direction? Which direction? (After a while, the roots all grew down.)

Watch to see how the stems grow. Did the stems all grow out from the top position? Which way did they grow? Did they all grow or turn in the same direction? (Yes, after a while all the stems turned toward the top of the container.)

Some children may be able to remove their own plants from the containers carefully enough to draw the changing outlines in their record books. Each day after recordings are made, you may wish to have the class discuss briefly the changing properties of their different plants. Have them make comparisons of each germinating seed with its appropriate reference seed.

When the seedlings are two to three inches long and when the leaves and roots are strong, the class should examine these structures with magnifying lenses. A discussion should follow, as children identify changed and unchanged properties of the plant. You might extend the discussion by asking:

Is the plant you are looking at today the same plant you looked at yesterday?

Was the plant you looked at two days ago the same plant you looked at three days ago? How do you know?

References to their seed notebooks should help the children recall that the same plant was a seed a week before. The class should recognize that although the plant looked different at different times, it was always the same plant—its biological identity was retained. If you use several kinds of seeds, the children can see that not only the original seeds but also the seedlings are different.

After the plants are a few inches high, you could terminate the observations, as plants will not continue to thrive in paper toweling. But the young plants could also be used for an interesting experiment and continued observations:

Do you think these plants will continue to grow well in this paper toweling? (Predictions.)

Would they grow better if we planted some of them in soil? How can we find out? (By leaving some in paper toweling and planting some in pots of soil.)

Have the children do this, if you wish, reminding them to water the plants and to make observations of them from time to time.

Read the story, "Surprise Packages," to the children and provide some morning-glory seeds and a narcissus bulb or two for them to plant and care for, as the children do in the story. Children will enjoy watching the growth of these interesting and beautiful plants.

2. MINNEMAST LESSON: CHANGE IN PEOPLE

Changing Properties of Humans

COMMENTARY

Here the children have opportunities to observe changing properties in themselves. In Activity A they describe themselves and make some predictions about possible changes in their appearance. In Activity B, using some of the items requested in the letter sent home at the start of Section 4, the children examine evidence of how they have changed and of how they will continue to change. In Activity C they use baby pictures to see some of the changes. Activity D, which concludes this unit, reviews some of the children's learnings in a story, "The Unidentified Object," which you read to them. . . .

Activity A

Let's pretend we are writing a letter to a Martian. We want him to come and visit us. If he came, how would he know people from houses or trees? How could we describe ourselves so that he could recognize us?

List the children's replies. Some suggestions might be that a person can run, has a head, clothing, etc. The descriptions of their hands, legs, feet, and so on, can be as detailed as you find appropriate. But specifically, children should recognize that humans have two legs and two feet, two arms and two hands, one head with a nose, mouth, two eyes, two ears, hair, and teeth. Put this list into the letter. At the close of the letter, invite the Martian to visit your class of children.

On the next day, read an imaginary reply from the Martian. Say that he would like to visit the class, but it will take him a year to arrive. The Martian wants to know if the children will still look the way they do now.

Will you children still look the same a year from now?

Review the list of human characteristics from the letter written to the Martian and ask the children to predict in what ways they may have changed. They will have changed in height, weight, size of feet, and number of teeth.

How do you know you will become taller?

Were you ever shorter than you are now?

Were your feet ever smaller than they are now?

How can you tell that your feet are not the same size they used to be?

Could we tell from outgrown clothing? From photographs? From family charts of your height and weight?

If you haven't already brought something you used to wear when you were a baby, try to bring one thing tomorrow. Then we will try to find out whether we have changed and which properties have changed.

Activity B—Clothing as Evidence of Growth and Change

Use the articles of clothing the children have brought to school. Mark them with their names or initials. Collect these items in a box. (Be sure to label all photographs and put them in an envelope in a safe place where the children will not see them until the next activity.)

One way to handle this activity is through dramatization. Ask for volunteers to play the parts of the parents. You will need to select the "children" from those who brought outgrown clothing. Tell the children to pretend that mother is unpacking their last year's clothes. "Mother" will ask the "children" to get the clothing from their box and try them on. "Children" can demonstrate how they have outgrown their old clothes. "Parents" can make appropriate comments, such as Father: "What, another pair of shoes! Why can't you wear these shoes?"

If someone has brought something too large, then "Mother" can say: "Let's see if this fits." "Mother" may then comment that the child will "grow into it" later. You will need to repeat this until all children who have brought articles and who want a turn have had it.

Activity C—Pictures as Evidence of Growth and Change

Make temporary mounts of the photographs on separate sheets of paper. Ask the class to identify the person in each picture. The owner must not tell. Compare a few photos with the children whose pictures they are.

How has he changed?

How has he not changed?

If the parents of your children cannot supply many photographs use pictures of kittens and cats, puppies and dogs, calves and cows, etc., or a series of pictures of famous personalities at different ages (presidents, actors, etc.) or bring some of your relatives or some of yourself. The children will find it almost impossible to believe that teacher was ever a baby!

3. SCIENCE CURRICULUM IMPROVEMENT STUDY LESSON: RELATIVE POSITION

ADVANCE PREPARATION

The words "position" and "motion" occur frequently in this unit. Plan to include a discussion of words ending in "-tion" in your language-arts program before you begin to teach *Relativity*. This preparation will help your students understand "position" and "motion" as they study this unit. Also please refer to the suggestions regarding word meanings which are included in the Optional Activities at the end of this chapter.

To prepare for "Which Object Am I Thinking of?" fold the six pieces of construction paper in half, and stand them in various places around the classroom.

LOCATION OF OBJECTS

Begin by asking the class where various objects are located in the classroom. Where's the door? Where is my desk? and Where are you? are examples of questions you may ask. The children will reply in a variety of ways; they may point toward the object (Over there), they may describe its position in relation to other objects (The door is opposite the windows), or they may describe its position relative to themselves (The desk is in front of me). The

---

From Science Curriculum Improvement Study, *Relativity*, Teacher's Guide (Chicago: Rand McNally & Company, 1968), pp. 28–31.

children's responses to further questions will indicate a preference for one or another of these approaches and will enable you to estimate their ability to answer accurately. The children's accuracy in describing directions (Right–left) and distances (The vase is two feet from the corner of the desk) is feedback to help you determine the appropriate time and pacing for you to introduce Mr. O. . . .

GAME: WHICH OBJECT AM I THINKING OF?

Select an object for the children to identify from your description of its position in the classroom. For example, you might say, "The object I am thinking of is behind me and to my right. It is between the door and the chalkboard. It is above the pencil sharpener." Give a fairly complete description before you let the children answer so as to discourage guessing on the basis of incomplete information. You might use an incomplete description that would fit several objects to illustrate the inadequacy of such a description. Follow this with a discussion of what is needed in order to be more precise. Let children take turns describing the position of an object for the rest of the class to identify.

Children will frequently give property clues (The object is red, or, The object is round) in addition to position clues (The object is near the windows, or, The object is in a corner of the room). When that happens, remind them that the rules of the game restrict the person giving the clues to tell only where the object is, not what its properties are. To illustrate, let one child select one of the pieces of construction paper, and describe its position so the others may try to identify it. Since the pieces are identical, property clues do not help to distinguish the pieces. The first time a paper is used, the identification will probably be quite easy because it can be accomplished by using a nearby major piece of furniture as reference object. To make the task more challenging group two or three of the papers, or possibly all six, close together on a window sill, desk, or table.

GAME: WHERE IS THE OBJECT?

In a slightly different game, one child acts as detective and leaves the room. In his absence the remainder of the class chooses an object somewhere in the room. When the detective returns to the room, he tries to identify the mystery object by asking about its position, using questions which can be answered with "yes" or "no" (Is the object near the front of the room? or, Is the object on the window sill?). For variety you may want to limit the number of questions that the detective may ask, or you might have a contest, keeping a tally of the number of questions needed to identify the object. The winner is the detective who asks the fewest questions.

In another version of the same game, have one child select the object to be identified, and have the other children ask him "yes-or-no" questions about its location. When only one person is being quizzed, it is helpful to ask questions such as, "Is the object behind you?" This type of question is not as helpful when a group is being questioned because different members of the group may have to give different answers.

In the previous games the children used themselves as well as prominent objects in the classroom to describe position. "Blindman Statue" is designed to give the children practice in describing the position of objects relative to their own bodies. While they can easily describe objects "in front" and "in back" of themselves, many children may have difficulty distinguishing right from left. Those children who have such difficulties will benefit from extra practice. . . .

For this game one child is the Blindman. While he stands blindfolded on a chair (pedestal) near the center of the room, the class secretly selects an object in the classroom. With the aid of instructions from the class, the Blindman is to try to point with an outstretched arm toward the selected object. He may not walk, but he may turn his body, and move his arm until the class succeeds in getting him to point toward the selected object. At this time the blindfold is taken off, and the Blindman may guess the identity of the object toward which he is pointing.

The children will discover that instructions making reference to objects in the classroom are of no help to the Blindman because he cannot see. The instructions that help the Blindman are those that make reference to the "statue" himself (front, back, right, left) and to the "statue's" sense of up and down.

Having the Blindman stand on a pedestal avoids the confusion of his pointing toward several objects that are in line with one another (this might happen if the child's arm is close to table level). The children who give instructions may stand behind the Blindman to observe his direction of pointing more clearly.

REFERENCE OBJECTS AND INVENTION OF RELATIVE POSITION

Play the game "Which object am I thinking of?" two or three times. Each time, as you describe the position of a mystery object, write on the chalkboard the names of the reference objects used in your description of its position. When the children are able to identify the object, write its name next to the names of the reference objects.

After you have several groups of names on the chalkboard, explain to the children that the objects you used to give clues are called *reference objects,* and write this phrase on the chalkboard near the names of the reference objects. Explain that clues describe the position of a mystery object relative to its reference objects. Write the phrase *relative position* on the chalkboard. (Note: Both the words "relative" and "position" have several meanings and may be misunderstood by some children. . . .)

Repeat one or two of the previous games, and call attention to the use of reference objects as the children describe or inquire about relative position. You might, for instance, write a list of five or six reference objects on the chalkboard, and require that all questions and answers make use of some of these reference objects but no other reference objects. The reference objects you choose may be your desk, the flag, the clock, the aquarium, or David's desk. In the game "Where is the object?" the questions would then take the form, Is the object near the flag? Is the object between David's desk and the aquarium? and so on. Restricting the number of reference objects makes the game much more difficult. In "Blindman Statue," of course, the statue himself is the only useful reference object because he cannot see any other objects.

4. *SCIENCE CURRICULUM IMPROVEMENT STUDY LESSON: USING MR. O*

FLASH CARDS

With a small group of children gathered around you, give each child a punch out sheet. Show the children how to prepare Mr. O and a small cardboard block from the punch out sheet. . . .

Explain that you will hold up flashcards with the words that Mr. O would use to report the position of the block. Each child is to arrange his Mr. O and his block so that Mr. O's report fits the report on the flash cards. Encourage the children to check on one another.

You might begin by holding flash cards for just one major direction and a distance (*in front of me* and *close*), and gradually work up to more complicated problems showing two or three major directions at once (*behind me, below me, to my left,* and *close*). If the children ask about the meanings of the terms for distance, let them choose the units they would like to use for measuring *close, far,* and so on. They may use the length of Mr. O as a unit of distance: *very close* might mean a distance less than one Mr. O length, *close* might mean a distance of one to two Mr. O lengths, and *far* might mean a distance greater than two Mr. O lengths. Or they may suggest using a hand width or something else for the unit of distance.

Variations of the problems can be created by imposing certain requirements. For example, you may require all the children to lay Mr. O flat on the table (buttons down or buttons up) and not to move him from that position. Only the cardboard block may be moved to fit the flash card report. For the flash card *in front of me,* the block will have to be held under the table if Mr. O faces down on the table. Since Mr. O reports the position of an object as though there were no visual obstacles, the fact that the table is between him and the block does not affect his report. This obstacle may cause some of the children to hesitate, however.

Another variation is to have each child place the block on the table, and manipulate only the Mr. O figure in order to fit the flash card reports. Still another is to have one child arrange the Mr. O figure and the block, and a second child to select from the set of flash cards those that correctly report the position of the block. The rest of the group may judge the accuracy of the report.

From Science Curriculum Improvement Study, *Relativity,* Teacher's Guide (Chicago: Rand McNally & Company, 1968), pp. 48–49.

5. SCIENCE—A PROCESS APPROACH: RELATIVE POSITION AND MOTION

As an introduction to the concept of relative position, several children from different parts of the classroom are asked to estimate the distance to an identified object such as the classroom door. Then the actual distances are measured. Through a class discussion and by having the children point to various objects the idea of each child being at different position relative to an object is introduced.

The objectives are for each child to:

1. Describe observed changes in the position of objects relative to his own position.

2. Describe observed changes in the position of objects relative to the position of another observer.

As a next step toward clarifying the concept of relative position, one child is placed in a wagon and pulled across the room by another child. The child in the moving wagon points at the class while the class is pointing at the wagon. They then describe and discuss the motions they have observed.

As generalizing experiences the teacher may read two stories to the class. One story is about a little girl lying on the bottom of a boat while the boat moves away from the dock. The second story is about the same little girl while she is riding on a train.

6. SCIENCE—A PROCESS APPROACH: ROTATIONS AND LINEAR SPEED

This exercise begins with a bicycle wheel and a round waste basket in front of the classroom. The children are asked to make an estimate of the distance around the wheel and the top of the waste basket. The name for the distance around, circumference, is then introduced. The class is then divided into groups with each group having one pair of power driven wheels from which the battery and motor have been removed. Each group also has one pair of tires and a data sheet which outlines a sequence of activities which the children are to undertake using the wheels.

The objectives are for the children to learn to:

1. Apply a rule for finding the distance a wheel rolls given the circumference of the wheel and the number of rotations it makes.

2. Apply a rule for finding the linear speed of a rolling wheel given its angular speed and its circumference or diameter.

From *Science—A Process Approach* (1967), Part D, Exercise U, p. 1. Reprinted by permission of the American Association for the Advancement of Science, Washington, D.C.

From *Science—A Process Approach* (1968), Part E, Exercise T, p. 1. Reprinted by permission of the American Association for the Advancement of Science, Washington D.C.

3. State and apply a rule relating the circumference and the diameter of a circle.

The children measure the circumference of the wheel and make predictions about how far the wheel will travel for different numbers of rotations. As the activities continue wheels of different diameters are used with the children making predictions and measurements based upon the diameter and circumference of the wheels as well as the linear speed of the wheel and the angular speed of the wheel.

The generalizing experiences include estimating distances traveled once the diameter of a bicycle wheel has been measured. More complex problems are suggested as optional tasks such as measuring the sprocket wheel and comparing its angular speed to that of the rear wheel.

7. SCIENCE CURRICULUM IMPROVEMENT STUDY LESSON: INVENTION OF THE REFERENCE FRAME CONCEPT

On a piece of chart paper, write "reference frame = starting point + set of directions" for use in this and later chapters. Post the chart paper.

For the compass activity, assemble the compass arm by placing the magnets in the grooves at the ends of the arm. To orient the two magnets properly, make sure that ends which attract one another point toward the center of the arm. Do not yet place the arm on the base. Plan to use a wooden table or, if you must use a steel table, make a pedestal of three books to raise the compass out of interaction range of the table.

TEACHING SUGGESTIONS

Introduction

Point out the chart you prepared. Explain to the children that they will work with several reference frames, and that each one consists of a reference object called the "starting point" and a set of directions aiming outward from the starting point. Perhaps one of the children will recall using such a reference frame in Yellowstone Park—Madison may have been his starting point and south the direction in which he headed for a trip. If no one remembers such an example, you might mention one.

Mr. O Reference Frame

When Mr. O is used as a reference frame, the starting point is where his arms and body cross... and the set of directions is related to his body. Hold up the Mr. O and remind the children of a few of these directions.... Then write a list of all the directions (*above, below,* and so on) which the children say Mr. O could use. If no one thinks of a double direction (*in front and to my*

From Science Curriculum Improvement Study, *Relative Position and Motion,* Teacher's Guide (Chicago: Rand McNally & Company, 1972), pp. 39–43.

right), mention this as an example for the children to follow. You may also give an example of a three-fold direction (*in front, to my right, and above*). For each direction named, have one child hold a paper clip about a foot from Mr. O and in that direction from the starting point on his body. The other children should discuss the adequacy of the placement and suggest corrections if necessary.

Magnetic Compass

Undoubtedly some children mentioned compass directions in one of the earlier activities of this unit. Show them the demonstration compass base and let them read the inscriptions; point out that this object is a reference frame with a starting point at the center and a set of directions that have been identified by letters. Set the base on the table in an arbitrary orientation. The large arm is not yet on the cone. Now invite a child to describe the position of a classroom object (desk, flag, sink) relative to the compass rose on the base.

Some children may protest that north is not really in the direction indicated by the marker on the compass base. This is an excellent criticism and points out the difference between the personal directions relative to Mr. O (which move along with Mr. O) and the directions indicated by a magnetic compass (which are fixed relative to the earth). Invite the children to solve this problem. Some of them may happen to have compasses in their pockets; others may ask you for one. Let them work out the solution as best as they can with the materials they request. After they find a solution or become baffled, show them how the large compass arm can be used (by setting it on the base) to orient the demonstration compass accurately toward the magnetic north. During this activity, another question may arise: Which end of the compass arm points north? This also could be answered by the children or left unresolved.

If the children accept your use of the compass base without sensing the need to orient it with the compass arm or a known geographic direction, let them do so. They may become aware of the problem when they work in their manuals or later in the unit, and devise a procedure to solve it.

OPTIONAL ACTIVITIES

Direction Hunt

Illustrations in newspapers or magazines almost always include clear evidence about the up–down direction (trees, buildings, people) and sometimes evidence about the direction the camera was facing (shadow angles, landmarks). Invite children to identify the camera directions in photographs. They may wish to post their pictures and explanations on a bulletin board.

Even though up–down evidence is usually unmistakable, this is not true if you clip a small section from a larger photograph. The up-down direction of a section of a pine tree (showing neither the ground nor the tip) can be identified only by someone who knows the growth direction of the branches and/or recognizes the tapering of the trunk. By trimming a picture, therefore, you can make a more difficult subject for a direction hunt.

Equilibrium

If your pupils have studied the SCIS unit *Energy Sources* they may be interested in the compass needle (individual and/or demonstration compass) coming to equilibrium while interacting with the earth's magnetic field. The demonstration compass arm executes interesting vibrations if it is pushed lightly and then allowed to come to equilibrium.

North in the Classroom

Which way in the classroom is north? Invite a group of children to make a large arrow (two feet long or longer), mark the head "north" and the tail "south," and decide in what direction the arrow should point. The arrow should be suspended or supported to be easily visible and to prevent rotation.

The class could make an octagonal compass rose (with the four primary and four secondary compass directions) and suspend it parallel to the ceiling. This activity is trickly since the suspended compass rose is to be viewed from below but probably is made by children looking at it from above. They may have east and west reversed. Caution the children to first draw the compass rose in pencil, hang it up to check its accuracy, and only then color or ink the marks (with any necessary corrections)....

8. *SCIENCE—A PROCESS APPROACH LESSON: FORCE AND MOTION*

This exercise begins with the teacher holding two carts on a table, one of which has a rubber band attached to it and a box. A discussion ensues, the purpose of which is to analyze the forces which are acting on the carts.

The objectives are for the children to learn to:

1. Construct a force diagram to illustrate that an unbalanced force is acting on a body that is changing speed.

2. Construct a force diagram to illustrate that only balanced forces are acting on a body that is at rest.

3. Demonstrate that the greater the unbalanced force acting on a body, the greater the acceleration.

Force diagrams are drawn as a part of each activity. For the first activities the cart is not in motion, although rubber bands may be attached to it. In later activities the cart has a large force applied to it which results in acceleration.

The final activities are based on what happens when several rubber bands are attached to the cart. One case is when all of the rubber bands are pulling in the same direction. A second case is when two rubber bands are pulling on the cart in opposite directions.

From *Science—A Process Approach* (1968), Part E, Exercise R, p. 1. Reprinted by permission of the American Association for the Advancement of Science, Washington, D.C.

9. ELEMENTARY SCIENCE STUDY LESSON: INVESTIGATING THE PENDULUM

1. Introductory Problems

Can you get two pendulums to swing together?...for 10 swings?...for 20 swings? What about three pendulums?

Here you will find that the children may spend a great deal of time simply "messing about." They will swing things through a wide arc or start them with a push. Bobs will bang into supports or fall off. After a time, you will notice that the children's approach becomes more careful and the swinging is not so wide or wild. Their sheer enjoyment of motion and banging is being replaced by more discriminating interests.

What can you do to a pendulum to change the way it swings?

Children do, in fact, find many ways to change the way a pendulum swings. Some will shorten the string as the pendulum swings. Others will shorten the string after the pendulum stops swinging. Some will release the bob so that it travels in directions other than straight back and forth. Still others will put many bobs on one string to see if weight affects the swing.

In the process of adjusting two pendulums so that they will swing together, the children become familiar with the effect of varying the length of the string. Most children will soon show by their actions and will be able to tell you that the shorter pendulum "swings faster," "getting ahead" of the longer one. There may be other variables that children will be thinking of, too, such as the weight of the bob and the width of the swing. All of the variables will not be sorted out at once, and you shouldn't expect them to be.

2. Weight and Shape

If you pull the bob back and let it go, how far do you predict it will swing to the other side? Hold your hand where you think the bob will reach.

Which swings out farther, a heavy bob or a light bob?

Which swings for a longer amount of time, a heavy bob or a light bob?

Can you get two bobs of unequal weight to swing together for 10 swings?

Adjust two pendulums of equal weight, so that one swings 20 times in the amount of time that the other swings 10.

Substitute a very heavy bob for one of the bobs. Will the ratio still be 20 swings for 10?

Weight is one of the first factors that children want to look at more closely. They may start by putting several bobs on one hook or by finding something to use for a heavier or lighter bob.

Some children suppose that a heavy bob will swing much farther out on the other side than a light one will, when both are released from the same point.

Some children are quite sure that the strings must be of very different lengths if two bobs of different weights are to swing together—though they often disagree on whether the heavy bob should be on the shorter or the longer string!

It will take a lot of familiarity with bobs of different weights before the children come to any conclusions about the importance of weight. A steel bob swinging is different from a wooden one, and it is a difficult task to go beyond that impression to find that some important things are the same for both.

It is a most surprising fact that a substantial change in the weight of a bob does not substantially affect the time it takes to swing back and forth or the distance it will travel (assuming, in this case, that both heavy and light bobs are released from the same point).

One boy succeeded in getting two bobs of the same weight and size to swing together for 10 swings. He then substituted a heavy bob of the same size for one of the two bobs. To his amazement, within two trials he also succeeded in getting the bobs of unequal weight to swing together for 10 swings.

This seems opposed to what intuition leads the children to expect, and you will see them misread evidence, seem not to "register" their conclusions, or repeatedly forget or ignore what they see.

3. Round Trips

How else can you swing a bob besides straight back and forth? (Before trying this with a pendulum, have the children draw all the ways they think a bob can be swung.)

> With a pencil close to the bob, follow the bob as it swings, tracing a line on a piece of paper that will show how the bob swung.
>
> Can you make the bob go in a circle?...an egg shape?...a triangle?
>
> How many other shapes can the pendulum's swing describe?

Which pendulum do you think will win a race back to the starting point— a pendulum swinging in a straight line or one swinging in a circle?

> What about an oval versus a straight-line race?
>
> Release the bob so it swings in a big circle, and time how long it takes to go around. Timing can be done by counting aloud at a consistent rate or by watching the sweep-second hand of a clock. One person can do the activity while a partner keeps time.
>
> Release the bob so it swings in a little circle, and time how long it takes to go around. How do the big—and little—circle times compare? Try comparing them a second or third time to see how consistent your results are.
>
> Release a bob so it makes a long swing, and time how long it takes to return to the starting point.
>
> Release a bob so it makes a short swing, and time how long it takes to return to the starting point. How do the long- and short-swing times compare? Try comparing them a second or third time to see how consistent your results are.
>
> Compare the time it takes a pendulum to make a circular trip with the time involved in a straight back-and-forth trip. What do your results show? Can you think of reasons for this?

One class used the term "round-trip time" to refer to the time it took a pendulum to make one swing back to where it started from.

Children will be surprised that most kinds of round trips take about the same amount of time. However, let them find this out for themselves.

10. ILLINOIS ASTRONOMY PROJECT LESSON: FORCES AND SPEEDS

Tug a rope in one direction and have a partner pull just as hard in the opposite direction. What happens to the knot in the center of the rope? Is it changing its motion? Can you explain why?

When two forces are equal, but act in opposite directions, they are *balanced* forces. So the resulting force, the *net* force on the rope, is zero. The knot remains stationary.

Can balanced forces also act on a moving object?

Imagine you are riding in a jeep on a straight stretch of road. Not another car is in sight. The jeep is moving along at a constant speed of 35 miles an hour. It is neither gaining nor losing speed. Picture the forces acting on the car. There is the forward force driving it ahead and also the backward force of friction. Think of these two forces being equal, but acting in opposite directions. The forces are balanced. The result, the *net* force on the jeep, is zero. So the jeep moves along at constant speed.

Step on the gas. What happens? A net force acts on the jeep. It acts on you, too. You feel a push on your back. The forward force is now greater than the backward frictional forces. The forces on the jeep are no longer balanced. A net force is pushing in the direction of the jeep's motion, so you gain speed in the direction you are going. Finally you are traveling at 45 miles an hour.

Let up a little on the gas, and the jeep moves at a steady speed again. It rolls along at 45 miles an hour. Once again the forward force is balancing the backward frictional force. The net force is zero. Speed is constant. Stop sign ahead. Step on the brake, and the frictional forces become much greater. The forces are unbalanced again. In which direction is the net force acting? What happens to the jeep's motion?

Force and Motion

You don't have to ride in a jeep to understand how force affects the motions of objects. You can work in the classroom.

From the Illinois Astronomy Project, *Gravitation*, pp. 15–29, by permission of Harper & Row.

Stand about eight feet from the wall of your classroom. Place an empty can on the floor. Then give it one push so it rolls toward the wall. Watch what happens to the can the instant it strikes the wall.

Picture the forces at work in your experiment. When the can was motionless on the floor, there was no net force acting on it. But as you gave it a push, there was a net force on it. Which way did the force act? Which way did the can move?

If you watched the can roll toward the wall, you probably noticed that it moved at almost constant speed. As it rolled, there was practically no net force acting on the can. So it just keep moving steadily in a straight line. What happened when the can collided with the wall? In which direction was the net force applied? What happened to the motion of the can?

In the world of moving things we occasionally see a quick push or pull. But most forces act on objects for a longer time. Let's see what happens to an object when a *constant* force continues acting on it for a while.

Make a rubber-band scale to measure force. Place a paper clip at the edge of a thick piece of cardboard. Slip two rubber bands through the clip. Each rubber band should measure about three inches in length. Use rubber bands that are of the same thickness. Tie a five-foot piece of string to the rubber bands.

Hold your scale so the string and rubber bands hang toward the floor. Make a mark beside the bottom of the rubber bands. Make two or three more marks at one-inch intervals below the first mark.

Now tie the other end of the string to a small cart with a brick in it. Place the cart and its load on the floor at one end of a long hallway. Holding the rubber-band scale with both hands, take a position ahead of the cart. Make sure that the string is not too loose.

When you are ready, pull the loaded cart with the rubber-band scale. Try to keep the force steady. Keep the end of the rubber bands at mark #1 on the scale. In this way you will be pulling with the constant net force of mark #1. What happens to the speed of the cart? What must you do to keep pulling with a constant force?

Try this activity several times. How fast is the cart moving when you first start to pull it? Notice the speed after you've been pulling with a *constant* force for one second. For several seconds. The arrows in the sketch represent the distances traveled by the cart in each unit of time.

Can you see that the cart is constantly changing its motion? It is being accelerated. What is happening to its *speed* during each second? Can you imagine how fast it would be traveling after 10 seconds?

Measuring Acceleration

In the last activity you applied a constant force to the loaded cart. You found that the cart continued to gain speed, to *accelerate*. So a constant force seems to make an object keep changing its speed, keep accelerating. Let's see if acceleration can be measured.

Use the loaded cart and the scale again. Place a mark on the floor beside the front wheel. This will show the cart's starting point. Use the force scale to pull the cart just as you did before. Try your best to keep the rubber band at mark #1 on the scale so the net force on the cart will be constant. In this activity keep track of time, in seconds.

It may be difficult to keep the force constant and make precise measures of time. Practice before trying this activity. When you are confident that everything is ready, start the cart moving with a force of mark #1. Keep the force constant.

At the end of second #1, have an observer put a mark on the floor to show the position of the front wheel of the moving cart. Have other observers do the same at the end of seconds #2, #3, and #4. They will have to work quickly.

Let's try to find the acceleration of the cart. Stretch a string from the "start" mark to the position of the cart at the end of second #1. Call this length one *unit* of distance. Now find out how many units the cart traveled from the end of second #1 to the end of second #2.

How far does it move in the next second? The next? Make a record of your measures. Round off all measures to the nearest whole number.

To find the acceleration of the cart, arrange your data in a table like the one below. Enter the measures from your activity in the middle column. At the end of second #1, how far has the cart traveled? One unit of distance. It moved one distance unit in one second. So its speed was 1 unit/sec. How far did it move in the next second? What was the speed? Three units/sec. The cart traveled two distance units more in this second than in second #1. You can say the cart speeded up 2 units/sec during this second. Its acceleration was 2 units/sec in a second.

Time From Start	Distance Traveled Each Second (Average Speed)	Increase in Speed in One Second (Acceleration)
0 sec		
	1 unit/sec	
1 sec		2 units/sec each second
	3 units/sec	
2 sec		units/sec each second
	units/sec	
3 sec		units/sec each second
	units/sec	
4 sec		

Remember that the constant force of mark #1 was acting on the cart. ...What do you notice about the *speed* of the cart from second to second? Complete the acceleration column. What do you notice about the acceleration of the cart at different times?

You worked as carefully as possible to find data on the cart's motion. But no matter how hard you tried, some errors probably occurred. What are some reasons for errors in measurement? Why is it difficult to measure accurately?

If precise measures of time and distance could be made and the net force on the cart were constant, the table would look something like the one below.

Time From Start	Distance Traveled Each Second (Average Speed)	Increase in Speed in One Second (Acceleration)
0 sec		
	1 unit/sec	
1 sec		2 units/sec each second
	3 units/sec	
2 sec		2 units/sec each second
	5 units/sec	
3 sec		2 units/sec each second
	7 units/sec	
4 sec		

Notice that each second the cart travels a greater distance than the second before. So each second the average speed of the cart is increasing.

What was the acceleration of the cart? With a net force of mark #1, the cart gains speed at the rate of 2 units/sec in a second. The acceleration is constant—2 units/sec each second. A *constant force* seems to result in *constant acceleration*. Did you find similar results in your experiment?

Forces and Accelerations

You have observed the cart as it was accelerated by the constant force of mark #1. What will happen if the load remains the same, but the net force on the cart is greater? Can you guess something about the rate of acceleration? Test your hunch.

Work your experiment in exactly the same manner as before. This time, however, exert more force. Pull the cart with the rubber bands stretched to mark #2. Try to keep the force constant all the time.

Use the same distance unit as in the first experiment. Make measures as you did before. Round off all measures to the nearest whole number. Then enter the data in a new table to find the acceleration of the cart when the force is at mark #2.

Compare your acceleration data with those from the first experiment. Make comparisons of your findings for each second. How do the accelerations compare? From the results of this experiment, can you make a statement that tells how *force* affects acceleration?

In this experiment, as in the one before, measurement errors creep in. If you had been able to make precise measures of time and distance when the net force on the cart was doubled, the table would contain the data shown below.

Time From Start	Distance Traveled Each Second (Average Speed)	Increase in Speed in One Second (Acceleration)
0 sec		
	2 units/sec	
1 sec		4 units/sec
	6 units/sec	each second
2 sec		4 units/sec
	10 units/sec	each second
3 sec		4 units/sec
	14 units/sec	each second
4 sec		

Remember the load was the same but the force was doubled. What happened to the acceleration? Can you make a precise rule about force and acceleration?

Take a moment to compare the distance traveled in second #1 with the rate of acceleration. What do you notice? Now look back to the table on page 108 and make the same kind of comparison. Can you find the relationship between the distance traveled in second #1 and the rate of acceleration?

Acceleration and Mass

Suppose you repeat the experiment. This time, however, keep the force at mark #1 but double the mass. How will the acceleration be affected? Make a good guess and then experiment to find out if your guess is reasonable.

Place a second brick on top of the first and tie them both to the cart. Now the mass of the object is almost doubled. Accelerate this mass with the force of mark #1. Try to keep the force constant. Make distance measures with the same unit you used in previous activities.

With the mass doubled, what do you notice about the speed of the cart? How much distance does it move during each second?

Make a new table and find the acceleration of the cart when the mass is doubled. Compare your data with the data from the first activity. Make comparisons of your findings for each second. How do the accelerations compare? Can you make a statement that tells how acceleration is affected by *mass?*

With precise measures of time and distance when the mass of the cart is doubled, the table would contain data shown below.

Time From Start	Distance Traveled Each Second (Average Speed)	Increase in Speed in One Second (Acceleration)
0 sec		
	1/2 unit/sec	
1 sec		1 unit/sec
	1-1/2 units/sec	each second
2 sec		1 unit/sec
	2-1/2 units/sec	each second
3 sec		1 unit/sec
	3-1/2 units/sec	each second
4 sec		

In this activity the force remained at mark #1, but the mass was doubled. What happened to the acceleration? As mass increases, how is acceleration affected? Can you explain why? Try to invent a rule that tells how acceleration is related to mass.

Compare the distance traveled in second #1 to the rate of acceleration. Do you notice the same relationship you discovered before?

Force, Mass, and Acceleration

Now let's put together the two rules you invented. Each tells something about how objects accelerate.

From your experiments you learned that when force increases, acceleration increases. Do away with friction, make precise measures of forces and distances, and keep the mass constant. You find that when force is doubled, acceleration is doubled. If force is tripled, acceleration is three times as great. Look at the table. Notice what happens to acceleration when force is 500 times as great. You can see that the acceleration of any object depends *directly* on the force exerted on it.

Force	Acceleration
1	1
2	2
3	3
500	500

You have also learned that when mass increases, acceleration decreases. Keep the force constant and accelerate objects. Under ideal conditions you find that when mass is doubled, acceleration is halved. If mass is tripled, acceleration is just one third as great. What happens when mass is raised to 100,000? In each case, notice that the acceleration number is the *inverse* of the mass. So you can say that the acceleration of any object is *inversely related* to its mass.

Mass	Acceleration
1	1
2	1/2
3	1/3
100,000	1/100,000

From your experiments with forces and masses you found two rules that tell about the acceleration of objects. Long ago Isaac Newton put these same rules together in one statement, which we call a law of motion. Newton stated that the acceleration of an object depends *directly* on the net force exerted on it and *inversely* on the mass of the object.

Think of two objects of the same mass. Exert twice the force on one as on the other, and its acceleration will be twice as great. Think of an object with a small mass and another a million times as massive. Push each with the same force. The more massive body is accelerated only one millionth as much.

Try this problem. Imagine there is no friction and all your measures are precise.

Think about the acceleration if you double the mass and *also* double the force. How will the acceleration be affected?

What will happen if both force and mass are 100 times as great? A million times as great? Can you see what would happen if the force and mass are multiplied by the same number? Would the acceleration change?

In this chapter you have learned that an object accelerates when a force acts on it. And you have seen that the acceleration is in the direction of the net force. You have found that the acceleration of an object is directly related to the force exerted and inversely related to the mass of the object. And when force and mass are increased in the same proportion, the acceleration is unchanged.

Although your experiments have been with a loaded cart, perhaps you've already guessed that these same rules work for any object pushed or pulled on earth. How are objects accelerated when they are not touching the ground but are being pulled toward the earth by the force of gravitation? Do falling objects obey Newton's law?

In a variety of ways, children can be introduced to the concept of change as a part of their world. Skills in communicating these changes are likewise important to these learning tasks.

To take this posttest, you will need only this grid:

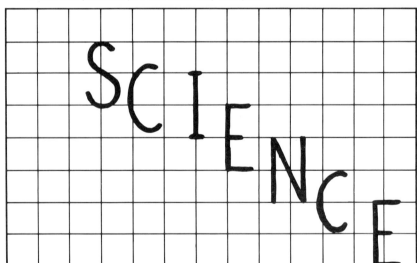

1. Before you show another person this grid, write out the directions he would need to know to locate the letter I in Science.

2. Two small bugs were having a race in the letter *S*. The results of this race were not completely clear as they tried to tell a third bug. Both bugs started in the middle of the letter *S* and the spotted bug went to the north end. The striped bug got as far south as the sixth horizontal line. Both bugs raced for the same time. Draw arrows that they could use to communicate their

displacement:

velocity:

3. A week later, the two bugs raced over the same course. The spotted bug went from the middle to the north end of the letter *S* in two minutes. The striped bug went about half way to the south end of the letter *S* in one minute. Draw arrows that they could use to communicate their

displacement:

velocity:

4. To show his devotion to being fit, Jack has been jogging. He finds that jogging on the escalator is a really fun experience.

  a. What is Jack's velocity relative to the rate of the escalator if he is jogging up on the up escalator at 2 meters per minute? (Note: This escalator is going up at 3 meters per minute.)

  Show how you could find out using arrows.

  b. What is Jack's velocity if he jogs down on the up escalator at 2 meters per minute?

Show how you could find out using arrows.

c. What is Jack's velocity if he jogs down on the up escalator at 3 meters per minute ?

Show how you could find out using arrows.

5. In which of the above situations is the rate of change involved ?

6. State the rule for finding the rate of change.

Acceptable Responses for the Posttest

1. To perform the first task, you need to number the coordinates of the graph, for example :

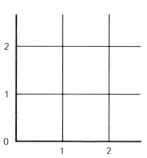

Using this system, the / is located as a straight line from (6, 5) to (6, 7).

2. The displacement of the spotted bug would be from about (3.5, 5.5) to (3.5, 7), whereas the displacement of the striped bug would be from (3.5, 5.5) to (3.5, 5). Displacement arrows would be

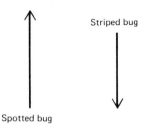

Since they went the same time, but the spotted bug went three times as far, his velocity would be three times larger.

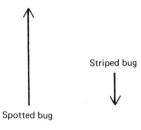

3. Note that their displacement arrows would be similar to #2, but their velocity arrows would be much more like each other.

4. Jack's velocity relative to the base would be

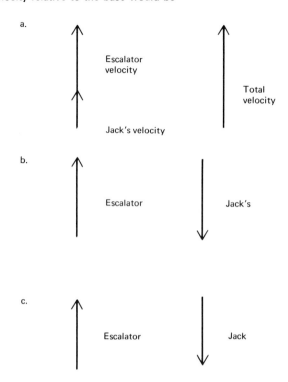

a.

Escalator velocity

Total velocity

Jack's velocity

b.

Escalator

Jack's

c.

Escalator

Jack

5. You are correct to say that rate of change is involved in #2, #3, and #4.

6. A rate of change is the amount of change divided by the time needed for that change.

6. Explaining
What You Observe

By the end of this chapter, you should be able to: (1) distinguish between statements that are based on observations and those that are based on inference; (2) identify which observations support a given inference and describe alternative inferences for same observations; (3) describe a suitable test for either an inference or a prediction; and (4) construct a prediction, given a set of observations recorded on a graph.

Check yourself now. If you can successfully perform these tasks, you should omit this part of the chapter and go to page 133.

To perform this task, you will need only a sheet of graph paper.

1. In the following cartoon, identify which frames are based on observation and which are based on inference.

Frame 1	Observation	Inference
Frame 2	Observation	Inference
Frame 3	Observation	Inference
Frame 4	Observation	Inference

2. Here are three pictures of the same birthday cake. Write three inferences and related observations about the situation in which the pictures were taken.

A. Inference

Supporting observations

B. Inference

Supporting observations

C. Inference

Supporting observations

Describe how you would test or find out if your first inference was correct.

3.   A group of students were beginning their lessons at the golf course. They were told by the golf coach that their golf clubs were useful in hitting the ball different distances. In their practice they found that for each club they could hit the ball these distances:

#1 Wood—Distance 125 yds.
#2 Wood—Distance 75 yds.
#3 Wood—Distance 50 yds.
#2 Iron—Distance 75 yds.
#5 Iron—Distance 50 yds.
#7 Iron—Distance 20 yds.
#9 Iron—Distance 5 yds.

A.   On a separate piece of paper, make a graph of these data .
B.   On your graph, the manipulated variable is _____

_____

C.   On your graph, the responding variable is _____

_____

D.   Suppose you have in your golf bag the following clubs. What distance do you think they would be useful for ? (Assuming of course that *you* can hit the ball !)

#3 Iron—Distance _____
#6 Iron—Distance _____

#8 Iron—Distance _____

Putter—Distance _____

E. What would you do to find out if your prediction for #6 Iron was accurate?

Following is a discussion of acceptable responses of this pretest. If you were successful with the pretest, go on to the next part of the chapter on page 133. If you were *not*
successful, carry out the activities suggested on page 121 as a way to help you develop
skills in explaining your observations.

Discussion of Acceptable Responses for Pretest

1. The first frame is primarily one of observation—the dog could both see and feel
the rain. The third frame is also observation as the dog could hear his master.
The second and fourth frames are both inferences. They illustrate the dog going
beyond direct observations to inferences about others not caring or really caring.

2. Your inferences might have included:
     Inference: The birthday candles had been burning.
     Supporting observations: In the pictures, they were progressively shorter.
                                         Or
     Inference: The birthday candle was for a three-year-old boy.
     Supporting observations: Candles had been burning and there were three of
     them. (Would have to ask parent if Robin is a boy or girl!)
                                         Or
     Inference: Robin blew out the candles in one blow.
     Supporting observations: In the last picture, the candles were out. (Would
     have to ask Robin's mother if he did it in one blow.)
     In testing and finding out if your inferences were correct, you would have
to secure more information by making new observations. For example, in the first
inference "The birthday candles had been burning," you might examine the wick
of the candles and smell to see if they had had a burning odor.

3. A. Your graph must include three items to be complete:
        1. A title.
        2. A label for the horizontal axis which should be the manipulated variable,
        the club.
        3. A label for the vertical axis which should be the responding variable, the
        distance.

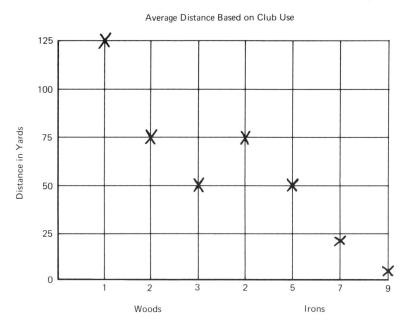

Average Distance Based on Club Use

B. The manipulated variable is the one that the user selects, in this case, the type of club.

C. The responding variable is the one that you measure or count, in this case, the distance the ball goes.

D. #3 Iron—Distance would be about $62^1/_2$ yards.

#6 Iron—Distance would be about 35 yards.

#8 Iron—Distance would be about $12^1/_2$ yards.

Putter—You really have no idea on this except it isn't supposed to be used for hitting the ball long distances!

E. To test the prediction, you need to gather more observations or go hit the ball with a #6 Iron and measure how far it goes.

Introduction

When we explain what we observe we do more than merely use our five senses. We have a basic belief that nature is not capricious. If we see water change to ice at a certain temperature today, we believe that water will change to ice at that same temperature tomorrow. This belief in nature's regularity is the basic assumption that makes all reasoning about the real world possible. With this assumption we can predict what we expect to see happen in a new situation, and we can construct explanations that help us to interpret patterns of events and interrelationships between observations.

In this chapter, which emphasizes inductive reasoning, the concept of graphing is used as a convenient way to record observations for subsequent mental operations.

Note: When we connect the points of a graph to form a line, we expect to find some sort of pattern. This expectation is justified only by our basic assumption that nature operates in a regular way.

Two types of mental operation are made possible by our assumption that nature is regular. We construct a prediction when we expect to see event X occur when conditions A and B are present. The logic of human thinking, however, is to go beyond prediction to ask the question, "Why?" What reasons connect these conditions to this event? The trial explanation is an inference, the second type of mental operation made possible by our basic assumption.

New observations may require us to modify both our expectations and explanations. Thus the tentative nature of the results of our reasoning must always be kept in mind. We must be open to new observations that seem not to fit our conclusion rather than change our observations to fit the expectations we have!

The art of investigation requires this open-mindedness—as well as the belief in the regularity of nature. It requires a mind prepared to look both for regular patterns and for observations that do not fit the expected pattern. This chapter is intended as a beginning in the preparation for these two tasks.

It may be relevant to indicate that it is possible to reason without observation. Such reasoning is called *guessing*. Making statements of what one expects to see without observational evidence upon which to base it or statements of how one explains events with no observations upon which to base them are guesses. This might be briefly pictured as:

	Statements Based on Observation	Statements Based on No Observation
What I Expect to See	Prediction	Guess
Why It Happened	Inference	Guess

Although intuitively the term "educated guess" may seem to be a useful way of communicating the idea of either prediction or inference, you are cautioned that it will help you to keep a consistent distinction between reasoning based on observation (inference or predictions) and reasoning based on no observation (guesses).

Enough about explaining what we observe, let's use our observations in these activities.

To do these activities, you will need only a sense of humor.

After each set of cartoons, you will find a set of questions. Check what you feel to be the appropriate category of the question.

Observation   Inference

1. The children hear a clicking noise.
2. They think the noise is a time bomb.
3. The noise is made by the dog.

For the first set, based on the information given you in the cartoon, you probably identified statements 1 and 3 as observations and 2 as an inference. Try this one.

Observation   Inference

1. The boy has a whistle.
2. The whistle is for dogs and cannot be heard by humans.
3. The dog hears the whistle.
4. He does not like the whistle.

Based on the information given you in the cartoon, statements 1 and 3 are observations, whereas statements 2 and 4 are interpretation or explanation types of statements; hence, they are inferences. Ready for another set?

Observation   Inference

1. The dog is cold.
2. He is sleepy.
3. He is asleep on the little boy's blanket.
4. The boy is not happy with the dog's behavior.

Again, if you base your answers on the information given you in the cartoon, statement 3 is the only statement of observation. Statements 1, 2, and 4 are interpretations of the evidence presented in this specific situation; hence, they are statements of inference.

Observation   Inference

1. It is a warm day.
2. The dog is looking for a drink.
3. He is thirsty.
4. The boy can see that the water dish is empty.

    In these cartoons, the evidence suggests that numbers 2 and 4 are statements of observation. Although quite likely true statements supported by the evidence in cartoons, numbers 1 and 3 are statements that go beyond the evidence and therefore are inferences. Here is the last set.

Observation   Inference

1. The dog can stand on his head.
2. Annie thinks the trick is clever.
3. The boy wants to teach Annie to stand on her head.
4. Teachers don't have to do what they teach.

From the cartoons, you have evidence to support numbers **1** and **2** as statements of observation. Although number 3 may be true, it is an interpretation of the evidence; hence, an inference. Statement 4 is almost a direct quote. But it is an inference, since it is an interpretation.

Statements of inferences are interpretations or explanations, but it is important to identify the observations on which they are based. (Explanations that are not based on observational inferences are *never inferences* but only guesses!)

Suppose you visited the office of a friend and while you were waiting for him to arrive, you saw these books on his shelf:

The Sea	*Water*
The Sea around Us	*The Road to Spindletop*
Geology	

Circle what you think might be the major interest of your friend:

1. He might be interested in water sports.
2. He might be an oceanographer.
3. He might be a petroleum engineer.
4. He might be a frustrated banker.

Of course, you could have selected any of the four inferences. Unless you knew more about the books, it would be less than likely that you could tell much about the occupation of your friend. It might help, for example, if you knew whether these books were for his use or merely for decoration. Suppose that he really used them. Number 3 might be the best choice, for petroleum engineers may be interested in the history of oil discovery (*The Road to Spindletop*). They carefully make their explorations based on the crust of the earth (*Geology*), and are certainly continuing their search for oil deposits under the ocean and coastal areas (*The Sea, The Sea around Us,* and *Water*).

On the other hand, your friend might be interested in these subjects but still be a frustrated banker.

The next time you visit the home of a friend, look at the magazines or books that are there. What inferences can you make about your friend's politics, hobbies, and so on based on these kinds of evidence?

To do the next activity, you will need three small boxes (shoe boxes with lids will do), a spoon, a pencil, and a ball.

Put these objects in the three boxes and tape the lids closed. Label one box Able, the other one Baker, and the third one Charlie.

For Able box:

1. What object is inside it?
2. What evidence do you have for your statement in #1?
   (Based only on your senses *after* the lid is closed!)

   A. _____

   B. _____

   C. _____

   D. _____

For Baker box:

3. What object is inside it?
4. What evidence do you have for your answer to #3?

   A. _____

   B. _____

C. _____

D. _____

For Charlie box:

5. What object is inside it?

6. What evidence do you have for your answer to #5?

A. _____

B. _____

C. _____

D. _____

Name two other objects that would give you the same evidence as the ones that you have listed in #2, #4, and #6.

1. _____

2. _____

1. _____

2. _____

1. _____

2. _____

A significant point in explaining what we observe is that for the same set of observations there are many times *equally useful inferences.*

To do the next activity, you will need a dishpan or bucket partially filled with water, a drinking glass, and a piece of paper.

First, stuff the paper into a wadded bunch and put it inside the glass. Push it as far as possible. Turn the glass upside down and make sure that the paper does not tend to fall out. Second, turn the open end of the glass upside down and push it into the water. Third, take the glass out of the water.

1. Describe the outside of the glass.

2. Describe the inside of the glass.

3. Describe the paper.

Your descriptions probably included the observations that the outside of the glass was wet and that both the inside of the glass and the paper were not wet.

Here are two inferences about why the inside of the glass was dry.

1.   The paper has a chemical substance that repels water and keeps it outside of the glass.

2.   The water did not go inside the glass because the glass was full of air.

Describe a way in which you could gather more evidence to support or not support both of these inferences.

Test for Inference 1 :

Test for Inference 2 :

In your test for Inference 1, you probably decided to repeat it with two glasses, one with paper used and the other without paper. If you did this, did your results support the inference?

In testing the second inference, you probably decided to use two glasses, both with paper, but one upside down and the other tilted halfway. Did your results support this inference?

In testing an inference or in gathering more observational evidence, you will find it helpful to systematically repeat the experiment but to change only one part of the system at a time.

To do the next activity, you will need a box of birthday candles, matches, a roll of modeling clay, a meterstick, and a table or surface which will not burn or mark easily.

With a bit of the clay, arrange a candle so that it is standing up straight. Light it. In how many ways can you extinguish the candle flame ?

1.   _____

2.   _____

3.   _____

4.   _____

5.   _____

6.   _____

Suppose you said that one of the ways you could extinguish the flame was to blow it out. Do you know how far away from the candle you could stand and still blow it out? If you have not measured your candle-blowing distance, your answer would really be a guess !

Let's have some fun. Set up five or six candles in a row. Stand 2 decimeters away from them and see how many you can blow out. Light them again. This time stand 5 decimeters away. Repeat this for 1 meter and 2 meters. Now make a graph of your results. What will the title of your graph be? What will be labeled on the X axis and Y axis?

Your labels should somehow indicate the title of candle blowing related to distance. The X axis would be the distance and the Y axis would be the number of candles blown out.

Now use your graph to predict how many candles you can blow out at

a.   One decimeter _____

b.   Four decimeters _____

c.   Eight decimeters _____

d. 1.5 meters _____

e. Four meters _____

In what way do predictions *a* and *e* differ from predictions *b*, *c*, and *d*?

Since your data started with 2 decimeters and went up to 2 meters, *b*, *c*, and *d* are all predictions within the range of what you know, or your observational evidence. Predictions within your known observations are called *interpolations*. Predictions *a* and *e* are outside your known observations and are called *extrapolations*.

How could you test your prediction for *a*?

Explaining what you observe involves considering the evidence and then searching in that evidence for useful patterns. Inferences and predictions are ways of describing your observation. These skills have been further developed by several of the current curriculum programs.

The writers of the *Science Curriculum Improvement Study* emphasize the importance of this skill as follows:

Certain basic assumptions are usually made in science. One assumption is that there is a real physical universe, that there is matter, and that matter is involved in natural phenomena. In the example, it is assumed that the ball, wood, metal, feather, balloon, and the earth actually exist. A second assumption is that natural phenomena are reproducible, that is, if the same set of conditions are set up, the same phenomena will occur. These assumptions are implicitly made by the members of the scientific community, and are a part of what might be called the "scientific point of view.". . .

In science, *the ultimate test of an idea is an empirical one*. Is the idea consistent with direct observations? Does it work when it is tried? Based on previous experiences and theory, it is possible to predict with some certainty what will happen when certain operations are carried out. For example, we can predict that, when a ball is released, it will fall to the ground. The ultimate test of this prediction is the empirical one of what actually happens when a ball is released. Sometimes, of course, the empirical evidence does not uphold the prediction. Then, the theoretical framework on which the prediction was based has to be reconstructed in light of the empirical evidence.

The empirical test of ideas is of central importance in science. Even in very theoretical discussions an attempt is usually made to suggest empirical tests for ideas. For example, as a check on one of his ideas associated with relativity, Albert Einstein suggested observations of starlight that could only be made during a total solar eclipse. The observations supported his ideas and were used to substantiate his theory.

Theoretical predictions can be checked in empirical tests. Again, ideas associated with the theory of relativity were used to predict that objects accelerated to velocities approaching the velocity of light would gain in mass. These predictions were made even though there were no ways of achieving such velocities at that time. Later, with the invention of the cyclotron, it became possible to accelerate particles to velocities approaching the velocity of light. The prediction was substantiated—the particles did gain in mass.

The significance of empirical evidence in science has important implications for elementary science programs. Certainly, it underscores the importance of children having direct firsthand experiences with science materials and equipment.[1]

The emphasis on this skill as part of logical thought has also been described by the writers of the *Science Curriculum Improvement Study*.

We need to learn much more about the ways in which individuals make the transition from the concrete operational level to formal operations. However, it is reasonable to assume that it is dependent upon the kinds of educational experiences that an individual has. The following are some of the hypotheses that are being suggested in the program of the Science Curriculum Improvement Study and the logical extensions of these hypotheses into educational experiences.

Regularities in the Physical Universe Provide a Base for Logical Operations. In some ways, the regularities of the physical environment provide a number of opportunities for hypothesizing, deducing, and experimenting that are within the grasp of elementary school children. For example, gases expand upon heating and contract upon cooling, and children can deduce consequences of this statement and set up experiments to check the consequences. Such physical regularities make science a particularly useful area of study to develop the ability to make logical deductions from abstract ideas and to check these ideas through observation and experimentation.

One of the most basic assumptions in science is that there is an order and regularity in the universe. The order and regularity are stated in physical laws, and these physical laws can be used to make predictions, and to plan observations and experiments to check on the predictions. However, the appreciation, understanding, and ability to use these regularities do not develop automatically; they must be nurtured through education.[2]

The developers of MINNEMAST suggest that a systematic organization of our observational evidence will assist in explaining. They say,

... an investigation of a phenomenon or problem can frequently be simplified by concentrating attention on certain objects and their interrelationships. A scientist is concerned with gathering his observations so that they will be meaningful and useful. When he notices a phenomenon, he focuses his attention on a limited set of objects involved in that phenomenon. This set of objects and the relationships that exist among them is the system on which he makes observations and tests his discoveries.

A mathematician also finds it useful to think in terms of systems. To him, a system is a set of elements (symbols or numbers) together with a set of statements relating these elements. Further relationships among the elements are discovered through formal logic. In contrast with a scientific system, a

---

1 Science Curriculum Improvement Study, *Elementary Science Source Book,* Trial Edition (Chicago: Rand McNally & Company, 1968), pp. 20–21.
2 Science Curriculum Improvement Study, *Elementary Science Source Book,* Trial Edition (Chicago: Rand McNally & Company, 1968), pp. 36–37.

mathematical system is not observable or testable in terms of physical phenomena.

The relationships among the elements in a scientific system are sometimes similar to those of a mathematical system. When this is the case, the mathematical system might be used as a model to explain or discover relationships within a scientific system. The observable relationships of the scientific system are tested to see if they do indeed correspond to the mathematical relationships. This way of looking at things can be a great help in understanding a complex situation or in solving a complicated problem. The systems concept helps one to focus his attention on those elements that are relevant to a particular problem.

The systems thread provides situations in which the children (1) select relevant elements to observe, (2) discover relationships among these elements, and (3) verify the relationships by testing.[3]

Strategies for helping children explain their observations have been developed by several of the recent curriculum programs. In these illustrations, children have many opportunities to collect evidence, search for their patterns, and then to make explicit what they think will happen based on the pattern of repeated events (predictions) or to explain their reasons for the pattern (inferences). Activities illustrating the prediction dimension of explaining your observations are found in *Science—A Process Approach, Science Curriculum Improvement Study*, and the *Elementary Science Study*.

1. SCIENCE—A PROCESS APPROACH LESSON: DESCRIBING THE MOTION OF A BOUNCING BALL

This exercise involves experimenting with various types of balls. The exercise begins with the children sitting in a semicircle with the teacher bouncing a ball on different surfaces while the children discuss their observations.

The objectives are for the children to learn to:

1. Construct a bar graph showing the relationship between the height from which a ball is dropped and the height to which it bounces.

2. State and apply a rule that a ball's bounce height is directly related to its drop height.

3. Construct a prediction of a bounce height, by interpolating on a graph, given two or more bounce heights, and two or more drop heights.

4. Demonstrate the test of a constructed prediction.

The class is then divided into groups of eight with each group having four different balls. The children drop the different balls from shoulder height and count the number of times the ball bounces. The data is then graphed by the children placing the number of

---

[3] MINNEMAST, *Conditions Affecting Life*, Unit 23 (1969), p. x. Copyright 1969 by the Regents of the University of Minnesota.

From *Science—A Process Approach* (1968), Part D, Exercise C, p. 1. Reprinted by permission of the American Association for the Advancement of Science, Washington, D.C.

bounces on the vertical axis and the kind of ball on the horizontal axis. Discussion of the results including an interpretation of the graph follows.

In the next activity, the children use lined paper attached to the walls of the classroom and drop the balls from different heights. Each group of children then collects the agreed upon data. If they have not done so, it is suggested that a graph may be helpful in recording the data. Through the class discussion one graph which is on the chalkboard is used as a basis for making predictions about what would happen if the ball will bounce when dropped from different heights.

The prediction skills that have been learned from bouncing balls from different heights is generalized by using two inclined planes which are facing each other and rolling a marble down one and observing how far up the other plane the marble will roll. A bar graph is then constructed of the findings from this experiment. Then the elevation of the inclined planes is changed and a new set of observations made.

2. SCIENCE CURRICULUM IMPROVEMENT STUDY LESSON: RESPONSES OF SNAILS TO BRIGHT LIGHT

SNAILS AND LIGHT

Ask the children if they think snails respond to light. Did they see any evidence in the terraria? Do they think snails would move to a dark place or a light place? Discuss the techniques for testing the snails and recording their responses.

SETTING UP THE EXPERIMENT

Distribute the equipment (except snails). The children can work in teams of three, with two teams sharing one heat/light source. They should position their overlays near the heat/light source so the zero mark on each overlay is nearest the bulb. Thus, the light intensity will be highest at 0 degrees and lowest at 180 degrees.

TESTING SNAILS

Each child should obtain a snail and place it near the center of his team's overlay. As the snail moves about the overlay, the child should record its path with a crayon. (As snails crawl, they leave behind a layer of mucus, making it sometimes difficult to mark their progress with crayons. If a child has trouble marking on an overlay, tell him to "follow" his snail with a paper towel to wipe up the mucus just before marking with the crayon.) When a snail stops or reaches the perimeter of the overlay, the child should gently slide it off the plastic and return it to the center for another test. If possible, each child should run two tests and mark two lines on the overlay—a total of six lines for each overlay. A period of ten to twenty minutes is usually sufficient for the snail testing, unless the animals are very slow.

From Science Curriculum Improvement Study, *Environments,* (Chicago: Rand McNally & Company, 1970), pp. 56–57.

After they have completed the experiment, the children should initial the overlays, give them to you, and return the snails to the classroom container.

DISCUSSION

The data from this experiment can be displayed better with an overhead projector than by holding all the overlays in your hand. Select one overlay and project it or hold it up for the class to see. You might suggest that the paths on this overlay represent all the snails' paths. This statement should produce some lively denials and lead to a discussion of the disadvantage of forming conclusions on only three snails' tracks. You might ask how many snails' tracks your pupils think are necessary in order to make a reliable judgment. There is no perfect number, but many are better than a few.

To provide more data for the discussion, place a second overlay over the one you showed the class, so that the numbers match. The children can now see through both overlays and observe twelve snail tracks. Continue to add overlays in this manner and encourage the children to discuss the general trend of the snails' direction of travel.

Ask the children whether the data indicate an optimum range of light for snails. Is this optimum range about the same as that for isopods, or is it different? Encourage the children to speculate about whether isopods and snails could live in the same environment.

"INVENTING" VARIATIONS

It will probably be obvious by now that all snails did not respond in exactly the same manner. Explain to the children that differences among organisms of the same kind are called *variations*. Snails' responses to light are examples of variation. Ask the children to suggest other examples of variation in organism response. They may want to refer to the data collected in Chapters 6 and 7 to provide additional examples of the concept. Tell the children that all kinds of organisms exhibit some variation. Someone may suggest examples of variation in humans, such as the differences in height and weight of his classmates.

IMPROVING THE EXPERIMENT

The children may suggest that testing a snail's response to a light that also produces heat is not a good experiment. This observation shows they have noted a weakness in the experimental design due to the presence of two environmental factors (light and temperature), where only one should be tested at a time.

Encourage your students to improve the experiment and to see if they can control the temperature variable. They may also suggest using "cold" light (as from a flashlight). They may also suggest other modifications, such as using soil or sand instead of plastic, or starting the snail in a certain direction when placing it in the center.

SNAILS AND TEMPERATURE

If the children mentioned that the bulb in the light experiment also produced heat, you can use that discussion to introduce the experiment with temperature. Or you might begin this activity by having the children recall whether terraria placed in areas of different temperature exhibited differences in organism survival. Ask them if they think snails respond to temperature.

Other activities illustrating children searching their evidence for explanations or inferences are:

3. SCIENCE—A PROCESS APPROACH LESSON:
LOSS OF WATER FROM PLANTS

A healthy plant serves as the topic for discussion in the introduction to this exercise. The class discussion is based around the things a plant needs to live and grow. As the discussion continues it focuses on the way water gets to the plant and how long a plant can live without water. Two growing bean plants are then placed before the class and a plan for systematically watering one plant and not watering the other is laid out. A simple record of the watering results are kept for a week.

The objectives are for the children to learn to:

1. Construct appropriate inferences about water loss from plants based on observations of investigations demonstrating water uptake and loss.

2. Construct situations to test such inferences.

3. Construct predictions from a graph about water loss from plants over a given period of time.

At the end of the week the children review the results of the week's observations. The discussion then focuses on what happened to the water which was given to the plants. A celery stalk is then placed in colored water and allowed to stand for awhile. The class is asked to make observations, writing them down on paper. They then cut across the celery stalk observing the tube like structures in the stem that carry the colored water from the stem toward the leaves of the stalk. This experiment serves as verification of the inference that the water moves into the celery plant.

Next by completely filling a tube with water and inserting a leafy shoot of a plant in the tube the children are able to make observations throughout the day and observe the amount of water which leaves the tube and moves into the plant shoot. As an outcome of their observations it becomes apparent that at different times of the day that the plant used different amounts of water.

Subsequently the class is able to break into groups working upon several alternate kinds of problems, especially related to whether stems or leaves lose more water. A possible follow up activity deals with examining the upper and lower surfaces of leaves to see if it is possible to identify holes where the water could pass out of the leaf.

From *Science—A Process Approach* (1968), Part D, Exercise 1, p. 1. Reprinted by permission of the American Association for the Advancement of Science, Washington, D.C.

4. SCIENCE CURRICULUM IMPROVEMENT STUDY LESSON: MIXING WARM AND COLD WATER

Preview the experiment before you distribute the equipment. The procedure includes the following three steps:

1. Each team fills one can with warm water and one with cold water.

2. The children measure and record the temperatures of the separate cans of water.

3. Each team pours both samples into the styrofoam cup and records the temperature of the mixture.

Suggest that interested teams who complete the experiment might repeat it, writing the second set of data under the first, or they might carry out other experiments and record their results on the lower part of the page.

After you answer any questions, distribute the equipment and invite your pupils to proceed. Watch their approach to observe improvement in their skill in using thermometers. . . .

COMPARING DATA

After all children have mixed their water samples and recorded the temperatures, ask them to put the equipment aside while several teams report their results. List the first two teams' data on the chalkboard in a tabular arrangement.

When you call on the third team, however, ask its members to state the cold and warm water temperatures only, and write these on the board in the next column. In order to focus your pupils' attention on the pattern of the results, ask the other children what temperature they would predict for the mixture, and their reasons. Then invite the reporting team to tell its result and record it on the board.

As you continue recording the data, occasionally ask your pupils to predict as above, or have a team report its cold and mixed water temperatures only, so the class may infer the warm water temperature. Each time invite the children who predict to explain how they arrived at the predictions. For variety, intersperse hypothetical problems (40°F and 80°F or 100°F and 160°F water being mixed), especially if you find your pupils' reason for predicting to be the similarity of all the data.

At the conclusion, ask the children to name variables that affect the temperature of the mixture and list these on the board or on a chart for future reference. Invite them also to describe the energy transfer, identifying energy sources and receivers.

OPTIONAL ACTIVITIES

Energy Chain

If an electric hearting tray is available to you, you can focus the activity on energy chains by using the tray to heat the water for some teams. Set up a station with the heating tray and cans filled with cold water.

From Science Curriculum Improvement Study, *Energy Sources,* Teacher's Guide (Chicago: Rand McNally & Company, 1971), pp. 66–69.

To begin the activity, show the tray to your pupils, select two or three children to measure the temperature of the water in several cans, and write their data on the chalkboard. Then plug in the tray and turn it to its highest setting. While the water is warming, invite the children to describe an energy chain for the process and diagram the chain on the board. Interrupt the discussion occasionally in order that a student may measure the temperature of the water on the tray. . . . When the temperature reaches approximately 120°F, the water is ready for the children's experiments.

How Fast Does the Water Get Warm?

Invite students who showed interest in the heating tray to investigate the temperature changes while the water is being warmed at various settings of the heat control. For each setting, they could measure and record the temperature of water samples at regular intervals; these may be one or five minutes, depending on the rate of heating, chosen so that the temperature rises several degrees between readings. They might also see how the temperature rise is affected by other variables, such as the location of the can on the tray, the material of the water container (aluminum, steel, copper, ceramic), the size and shape of the container, and the amount of water. The results may be stated variously as (1) the time needed to heat the water thirty or forty degrees; (2) the temperature rise in ten or twenty minutes; or (3) a line graph showing the water temperature in its relation to the warming time. . . .

Unequal Quantities of Water

Encourage interested children to consider mixing various quantities of hot and cold water. . . . Many children will know that if they use twice as much hot water as cold, the resulting mixture will be hotter than if equal quantities were used, and that if they use twice as much cold water, it will be colder.

Although few of your pupils may be able to come up with a mathematical equation for solving the problem, some will analyze it in a way that gives an accurate solution. For example, they might reason that the final temperature is found by simply averaging the temperatures of all the cans of water. In a mixing experiment using two cans of water at 108°F and one can of water at 52°F, for instance, the predicted temperature is 108 plus 108 plus 52 divided by 3, or about 89°F. By discussing this problem with groups of children, you can learn a great deal about their developing ability to reason abstractly.

Graphing Temperature Changes

Select two stations in the room for distribution of materials. Just before class, place a bucket of cold water (between 40° and 60°F) and a bucket of hot water (between 80° and 100°F) at each station. Place eight vials, eight plastic cups, and sixteen thermometers at each station.

From Science Curriculum Improvement Study, *Energy Sources* (1969), pp. 42–44.

TEACHING SUGGESTIONS

Introducing the Activity

Begin this chapter by letting the children review the outcomes of their experiments during the last session. If you do not feel that the children understand that they had to transfer energy to the water from the warming tray in order to achieve a change in temperature, review this idea with them now.

Demonstrate how to assemble the hot water–cold water system by pouring a vialful of cold water in the cup and filling this empty vial with hot water. Ask the class what they think will happen if you place the vial containing the hot water into the cup containing the cold water. Listen to their predictions, and encourage them to discuss each one. Emphasize the need to collect evidence in order to determine the validity of any prediction.

The Experiment

... Each team of two should put a vialful of cold water into a plastic cup, fill the vial with hot water, and take these and two thermometers to their desks. When the children have obtained their materials, ask them to turn to page 12 in their Student Manuals and discuss the recording for the experiment as outlined on that page. When everyone is ready, each team will record the beginning temperatures of the water in the vial and in the cup. On your signal, each vial is placed into a cup. Explain that you will give a signal every minute for ten minutes and that on your signal they are to read and record the temperature shown on each thermometer.

Plotting Data

... When the data collecting is completed, have the children return their materials to the work stations and call the teams together with their manuals for a discussion. Most of the children in your class will have studied the SCIS unit *Environments*, in which the technique of graphs is emphasized. If, however, your class seems unfamiliar with graphing procedures, you might prefer carrying this activity out at the chalkboard with one or two children as your assistants. In this case you will have to use the data from only one team. If other teams have collected data that differ significantly from the class graph, see if the children can discuss variables that might have caused this.

After you plot one set of data on the board, the children can then plot graphs of their own data in the student manual. Suggest that they use different colors or symbols for the hot water points and the cold water points on the graph. Remind them that each point needs two measurements—a time reading and temperature reading—to describe it and to locate it on the graph. Show them that the temperatures are read along the vertical axis and the time along the horizontal axis.

After the children have plotted the data, show them at the board how they can draw a smooth curve to average out any up and down fluctuation in the temperature readings. A sawtooth line connecting each point stresses small variations rather than the actual pattern of the results.

Discussion

Let the children discuss the graph. They will bring up the fact that the line for the hot water subsystem indicates it is cooling down while the line for the cold water subsystem indicates it is warming up. What is their evidence of energy transfer? Which subsystem was the energy source and which the energy receiver? This question may bring about controversy, but most children will probably agree that the hot water transferred energy to the cold water. Ask the children to mark on their graphs the point at which the temperature of the hot water and the temperature of the cold water subsystems came to be about equal with each other. Ask them if they think there was evidence of energy transfer at this point.

Further changes may be noticed after this point as both subsystems interact with the air in the room and finally come to the temperature of the room. If the graphs in your class show this additional change, let the children discuss this and see if they can come up with an explanation for it. Some children may realize that the energy source has now changed; the room or the water system (whichever starts out warmer) is the energy source and the other becomes the energy receiver. Any suggestions should be used for encouraging further experiments in order to gather further evidence. If the data did not reflect this change, ask the children to predict what would happen if the system were allowed to stand for some time.

OPTIONAL ACTIVITIES

General Suggestions

Using different amounts of hot and cold water, water at different starting temperatures, and carrying the experiments out under very different conditions (such as near a heating vent or even in the refrigerator or an ice chest) provide many opportunities for extending this activity.

In these individual experiments, the children should be allowed to do their own timing. Their experiment records should indicate the variables in their experiment, such as temperatures and amounts of water used. The way in which individuals carry out such experiments will provide feedback on their understanding of how to plan and carry out an experiment. Encourage the children to make interpretations of their data based on the concept of energy transfer. What was their evidence of energy transfer? Did the energy receiver become a source of energy to another subsystem?

More Cold Water

You could provide the opportunity for all the children or a small group to work on the following problem: What would the graph look like if they used twice as much cold water as they did in the class experiment? Encourage predictions based on the evidence from their earlier experiment before they begin investigating this question. Interested children can first draw a graph to represent what they predict will happen. Let them devise their own methods for timing and carrying out the experiment.

5. MINNEMAST LESSON: INTRODUCING THREE ENVIRONMENTAL CONDITIONS

Ask the children to look at the Set A cartoons.

Have them describe the differences between Pictures 1 and 2. (In Picture 1, it is raining and the children are dressed in rain clothes. In Picture 2, it is not raining and the children are dressed differently.)

What kinds of weather account for the differences in these two pictures?

Most children will probably say that it is raining in one picture and not raining in the other. Bring out and emphasize the fact that there is more water or *moisture* shown in one picture than in the other. Discuss with the children if the amount of moisture affects our behavior and what we do to protect ourselves from too much of it.

Next have the children look at Pictures 3 and 4.

Ask what is wrong with these pictures. During the discussion, emphasize the main idea again—that the amount of moisture affects the way we live. Also elicit from the children the things that man has devised to avoid the discomfort of too much moisture—the raincoat and rubbers, the waterproof homes, etc.

Write "moisture" on the chalkboard. Tell the class that *moisture* is only one of the things that affect the way we live. Have the children look at the pictures of Set B, and see if they can discover another thing that affects the way we live. The children will probably say that these are pictures of day and

Set A Cartoons: Pictures 1 and 2

From MINNEMAST, *Conditions Affecting Life* (1969), pp. 3–11. Copyright 1969 by the Regents of the University of Minnesota.

Set A Cartoons: Pictures 3 and 4

night. Lead them to realize that one difference between day and night is the amount of *light* that is present. Ask them to describe how behavior is changed by light or the absence of it. Then have them discuss some of the ways man has been able to overcome unwanted light (by means of shades, awnings, sunglasses, tinted windshields, beach umbrellas, etc.). And have them also

Set B Cartoons: Pictures 5 and 6

Pictures 7 and 8

discuss how man has managed to provide more light when he needs it (by means of house and street lamps, candles, flashlights, headlights, light for night ball games, etc.).

Tell the children that they have now talked about two things (condi-

Set C Cartoons: Pictures 9 and 10

Pictures 11 and 12

tions)—moisture and light—that affect the way we live. Now ask them to look at the pictures in Set C, to see if they can figure out a third thing (condition) that affects us.

Answers will probably vary. The most common answer may be that the pictures show winter and summer scenes. Lead the children to the generalization that during different seasons—or even during shorter periods, such as weeks or days—we usually have some differences in temperature. Hold a discussion of some of the ways the changes in temperature affect the way we live. Also bring out in the discussion some of the things man has done to overcome these differences in temperature—how he uses different kinds of clothing, heating systems for homes, air conditioners, car heaters, etc.

Remind the children that they have now discussed three of the conditions that affect the way we live—moisture, light, and temperature. Then ask:

> Do you think that moisture, light, and temperature affect what other living things do?

Let the children speculate about this. Then ask:

> If other living things react to these conditions, do you think they react in the same ways that we do?

This question, and others, could lead to a very enjoyable discussion, e.g.,

> Does a rabbit wear a raincoat when it rains?

> Does an earthworm turn on a heater or wear warmer clothing when it is cold?

Next ask:

> What do animals do to make themselves comfortable? Do they find places to live that have suitable amounts of moisture, light, and temperature?
>
> If they do, what could we call such places? (Animal homes.)

Now ask the children to tell about any animal homes they have seen. Urge them to be specific about describing the kind of place and the time they saw each of the homes. After these reports, ask:

> If we were to go to the woods, to the park, or to a vacant lot, where would we be likely to find several small animals living in one place? (Trees, holes in the ground—various answers.)
>
> Have any of you ever turned over a rock or a log on the ground? Did you find anything interesting beneath the rock or log? (Yes, animals.)
>
> What kinds of animals did you see?

Answers will include a few animals. List these on the board. Then lead the children to the idea that perhaps a film or photographs will suggest other animals that could be added to the list. Show the film, *Living Things Are Everywhere,* if you have it. Then have the children turn to the pictures of small animals in their Student Manuals. These include an earthworm, snail, slug, cricket, toad, beetle (with larva and pupa), sow bug, centipede, ant (with eggs, larva, and pupa), salamander, and millipede.

Ask the children why they think these animals might live under rocks.

> What conditions would you find under a rock? Would it be warm or cold, wet or dry, sunny or dark?

Let the children speculate freely, but keep the discussion rather short and limit it to just a few other animals. Ask the children to talk about only one animal and its home at a time. Children may suggest that earthworms live under rocks so that the birds can't eat them, or that toads live there because they eat insects that live there, or that ants may live there to get protection from the rain.

> Tomorrow we will go on a field trip to look under rocks, logs, and boards. We will observe carefully what kind of animals live there and what their homes are like. We will bring back a few small animals to study.

Emphasize the two purposes of the field trip: (1) to observe the conditions at each location where an animal is found and (2) to collect small animals for further observations in the classroom.

Note: Before teaching Lesson 2, make a preliminary survey of the site for the field trip. You will find many more animals in a wet, shady area than in a dry, sunny one. (However, some children should check out a drier area.) Select a site that has at least five places in it where you are sure animals will be found, so that the trip will be a success. Also, consult *Living Things in Field and Classroom* so that you will know how to keep most of the small animals alive in the classroom.

6. ILLINOIS ASTRONOMY PROJECT LESSON:
MODELS OF THE SOLAR SYSTEM

When objects are very large or very small, it is often useful to make a model that is human-sized. Then you can examine it and better understand what each part does. You have seen models of ships, models of rockets, and models of the earth. You may also have seen models of atoms, models of viruses, and models of tiny insects. Accurate models give you a clear idea of the structure of an object.

The group of objects we call the solar system includes the sun, planets, moons, asteroids, comets, and meteors. This system is so large that it is difficult to imagine what it would look like if a person could see it from far away. You already know about distances in the solar system. Perhaps you have built a scale model to help you picture these distances. Right now we'll be more concerned with motion than with distances. In this chapter you will be asked to imagine models that account for motion.

To help you think about motion models, here's one that isn't astronomical. Imagine you want to make a model showing your motion as you walk from your house to school. You stroll down the sidewalk, climb a fence, jump over a hedge, and dodge around a lamp post. . . .

MODELS OF DAY AND NIGHT

To start with motion models in astronomy, imagine one that includes earth and sun and accounts for day and night. Get a ball and a lighted bulb. A lamp without a shade works well. The ball represents the earth, and the lighted lamp represents the sun. Have one person hold the lamp while the other holds the ball.

For the first model to account for day and night, imagine the earth does not move. How can the lamp be moved to produce "day" and "night" on the ball? Try it. Now make a diagram of the model. Put the motionless earth on the model. Put it in the path of the sun.

In this activity you will make a different model that accounts for day and night. This time, keep the sun in one place. Can you make the ball move in such a way that you have day and night? Make a diagram of this motion.

Keeping the sun motionless, can you make still another model to account for day and night? Try it. Make a diagram of the new motion.

You have now made at least two models of the motion of the sun and the earth to account for day and night. You may have worked out three. Each model works. Each one explains the daily observed motion of the sun as seen from the earth. Which is best?

For the job of describing day and night, none of these models is better than any other. Each one fits the facts. You may know that for most of the history of mankind, people preferred the model in which the earth does not move. Such a model was developed very carefully by the Greeks and was ac-

Reprinted from *The Universe in Motion* by the Elementary Science Study. Copyright 1966 by Education Development Center, Inc., 55 Chapel Street, Newton, Massachusetts 02160.

cepted for thousands of years. In this model, the sun moves once around the earth in 24 hours. So do the stars.

However, the Greeks knew that the sun does not move in quite the same way as the stars. During the year the sun moves slowly eastward among the stars. For example, in July it is in the constellation of Gemini the Twins. In August, in Cancer the Crab. In September, Leo the Lion. To explain the sun's motion, the Greeks thought it moved on a circle that is closer to us than is the sphere of stars.

MODELS OF PLANETARY MOTION

In the last chapter you read about how the planets are seen from the earth. Their motions differ from those of moon, sun, and stars. Every once in a while, planets appear to go backward. And when they start to back up, they get brighter. The motions of the planets presented Greek astronomers with one of their toughest problems. How could they account for such motions in their earth-centered model?

Think about the earth and Mars. Review the Martian facts you learned in the last chapter, particularly that Mars seems to move backward, and that Mars seems brightest when in the middle of its reverse motion. Ptolemy, one of the outstanding ancient astronomers, thought that the earth was motionless. If you thought so too, could you figure out a path for Mars which accounts for these two facts? Try.

Have one person put his diagram on the chalkboard. Check it. Does it fit both facts? Try diagrams developed by other people. See what diagrams account for reverse motion and the fact that Mars is brightest during the middle of its reverse motion. Find out how Ptolemy solved the problem. See whether your answer is similar.

COPERNICUS

Ptolemy's theory fits the facts and was not seriously questioned until the early 1500s. Copernicus, a native of Poland and one of the great astronomers in history, preferred to think of the sphere of stars as being at rest, with the sun at rest in the center of the universe. Said he,

> In the midst of all, the sun reposes, unmoving. Who, indeed, in this most beautiful temple would place the lightgiver in any other part than whence it can illumine all other parts?

What did this choice mean? If the stars are fixed, it must mean that our *earth* is spinning or rotating once each day. The stars and sun and moon and planets only *appear* to go around us from east to west because our own globe is spinning the opposite way each day. To Copernicus it seemed much simpler to spin the earth instead of making all the stars whiz around us at high speeds every day.

Putting the sun at rest and at the center of things meant that the whole earth must do the moving, following a path around the sun once each year. The Copernican idea was that the sun seemed to move slowly through the stars because of our own motion around the sun.

To see the idea of Copernicus, walk in a circle around a flag pole. As you watch the flag pole, it appears to change its position smoothly against the background. First you see it against the corner of the schoolhouse, then against the snow pile, then against the store across the street, and then against the corner of the schoolhouse once again. But of course the flag pole doesn't really move at all.

Copernicus reasoned that all the planets move around the sun, too, rather than around the earth. In fact, in his model the earth becomes just one of the planets.

In his sun-centered model, Copernicus had to account for the same observed motions of the planets as Ptolemy did when he made his earth-centered model. In 1543, when Copernicus published his ideas, Mars was moving in the same pattern that had been known to the ancient Greeks. It was still moving in reverse every two years or so. And it continued to look brightest in the middle of its backward motion. Copernicus had to account for the same observations the Greeks did. But how? How can Mars appear to go backward and get brighter if the sun, not the earth, is at the center of the solar system?

Copernicus said that the earth moves forward in its orbit faster than Mars. Thus, every once in a while, we pass Mars.

Ask a friend to hold a flashlight and stand about five yards in front of you. Tell him to start walking away very slowly, pointing the flashlight toward you. Meanwhile you start walking quickly in the same direction so that you will pass near him. Notice what seems to happen as you pass your friend. You have to look backward to see the flashlight. It seems to be moving backward. And when you pass, the flashlight is brightest. Why?

Can you see why Mars sometimes appears to go backward and change brightness?

Who was right? Ptolemy's earth-centered system fit the facts. Copernicus's sun-centered system did, too. And Copernicus had no proof that his sun-centered universe was a better theory. In some ways it just sounded simpler to him; he preferred it. So both models explained the observations of astronomers equally well.

It took many years before additional facts were discovered which could only be explained by Copernicus's picture. But remember that even though he could not prove his theory correct, Copernicus took a very daring step. His bold choice was a new way of looking at the universe.

GALILEO, JUPITER, AND VENUS

It was not possible to prove the Copernican idea during the 1500's and 1600's. But some astronomers were collecting evidence that made it seem likely that smaller objects move around larger objects. Galileo, an Italian scientist, found some evidence that was particularly useful.

Galileo was the first man to look at the sky through a telescope. The year was 1609. When he looked at Jupiter, he saw certain objects nearby that looked like stars. But as he watched for these objects over the months, they changed position around Jupiter—sometimes even disappearing.

A model will help you understand the motions Galileo observed.

Bend a piece of wire until it forms a 90° angle. Put a small ball of aluminum foil on one end of the wire. Place a larger ball around the bend of the wire to represent Jupiter. Hold the wire upright at arm's length and slowly twist it. What do you observe about the motion of the small ball?

Galileo concluded that these objects were not stars, but moons—moons going around Jupiter in definite orbits. To Galileo it seemed that Jupiter and its moons might be a small version of the entire solar system, one large object with small ones revolving around it.

When Galileo observed Venus through a telescope, he discovered something that didn't fit one of the models. In Ptolemy's model, what changes should be seen in Venus as it moves through the sky? How should Venus change in Copernicus's model?

Ask a friend to hold a flashlight representing the sun. Another friend can hold a soccer ball above his head. This will be Venus. You be the observer on earth. Arrange the sun, Venus, and earth according to Ptolemy's model. Set the model in motion. Keep the light shining on Venus and watch the planet carefully.

Now set Venus in motion according to Copernicus's model and continue to observe the planet. Does Venus go through the same changes in both models?

Ptolemy's model predicts that Venus goes through some phases but never appears as a complete circle of light like the full moon. The Copernican model predicts that Venus should be seen going through all phases. Without a telescope none of these changes can be seen. But when Galileo observed Venus through a telescope, he found that it goes through all phases just like our own moon. Galileo saw that Venus sometimes appears as a full circle of light. If you saw the same thing, which model would you prefer?

Bouncing balls, burning candles, potato shoots, nails, pendulums, lights, balloons, plants, water, cartoons, tea bags, and the stars—these represent a diverse collection of experiences. They have a central theme—they are useful ways to guide children in explaining their observations.

Being able to search for patterns and to find evidence forms an important dimension of many science curricula. It is equally important to each of the lessons included in this chapter.

How do these lessons emphasize the various ways in which children should learn to explain their observations?

By now, your skill of explaining what you observe should be quite satisfactory. Check yourself before you go on.

Posttest

1. In this cartoon identify which frames are based on observation and which are based on inference.

Frame 1	Observation	Inference
Frame 2	Observation	Inference
Frame 3	Observation	Inference
Frame 4	Observation	Inference

2. Here are three pictures of plants. Write three inferences and related observations about the event.

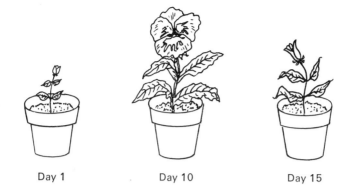

Day 1   Day 10   Day 15

A. Inference

   Supporting observations

B. Inference

   Supporting observations

C. Inference

   Supporting observations

Describe how you would test or find out if your first inference was correct.

3. A group of students had been having tutorial assistance with their mathematics problems. They were wondering if the extra work really helped them. To answer this question, they kept a record of how much extra time they spent on mathematics and how many problems they got right on their weekly test.

Week	Time Spent	Correct Problems
1	30 minutes	10
2	40 minutes	12
3	10 minutes	3
4	60 minutes	20
5	15 minutes	5
6	60 minutes	20

A.   On a separate piece of paper, make a graph of these data.

B.   On your graph the manipulated variable is _____.

C.   On your graph the responding variable is _____.

D.   Suppose in week 7 they studied fifty minutes. What would you expect their number of correct problems to be? _____

In week 8 they studied only twenty minutes. What would be the number of their correct test problems? _____

E.   What would you do to find out if your predictions in D are correct? _____

Now check the following discussion for acceptable responses. If you find that you are having difficulty, you may wish to discuss this with your instructor.

Discussion of Acceptable Responses for Posttest

1.   The first frame is primarily one of inference. The dog is describing what he thinks he would like to be. The third frame is also primarily that of inference, as his friends are discussing both what they think they heard and how it is probably explained by one's losing his mind. Observations are the keys to Frames 2 and 4. Frame 2 is observing with sense of hearing, and obviously Frame 4 is both hearing and sight.

2.   Your inferences might have included:

> *Inference:* Someone forgot to water the plant.
> *Supporting observations:* Plant seemed to grow better days 1 and 10. Plant looks wilted on day 15.

> *Inference:* They are pictures of three different plants.
> *Supporting observations:* There is no evidence to insure that they are of the same plant.

> *Inference:* The plant contracts a disease or pest.
> *Supporting observations:* If it is the same plant, it showed healthy growth between days 1 and 10. Then day 15 the healthy appearance changed.

In testing and finding out if your inferences were correct, you would have to secure more information by making new observations. For example, in the case of the first inference, "Someone forgot to water the plant," you might examine the soil to see if it was moist.

3.   A.   Your graph must include three items to be complete:

> 1.   A title.

> 2.   A label for the horizontal axis that should be the *manipulated variable*—the time spent on study.

> 3.   A label for the vertical axis that should be the *responding variable*—the number of correct test problems.

B. The manipulated variable is the one you select—in this case, the amount of study time.

C. The responding variable is the one that you measure or count—in this case, the number of correct test problems.

D. For fifty minutes, it would be about seventeen problems correct. For twenty minutes, it would be about seven problems correct.

E. To test your predictions, you need to gather more observations or have students study fifty minutes and then give them a test.

7. Conducting An Experiment

By the end of this chapter, you should be able to: (1) Identify or name relevant variables in an event; (2) When given a systematic analysis of an event, including the variables, construct a question that could be investigated; (3) When given a question for investigation, identify or describe a plan for securing data needed to construct an answer for that question.

Check Yourself Now. If you can successfully do these tasks you should omit this part of the chapter and go to page 167.

For these tasks you will need either your good imagination or a collection of balls, such as a baseball, a ping-pong ball, a sponge-rubber ball, a tennis ball, a basketball, and a golf ball, plus an inclined plane.

1.   Begin by messing around with the balls and watching as they roll down the inclined plane—which one seemed to be in the winner's circle? Are your results similar to ours, in which we found that the baseball, the sponge-rubber ball, and the golf ball consistently won over the ping-pong ball, the tennis ball, and the basketball?

Which variables do you think are relevant in this event?

_____   a.   Size of inclined plane.
_____   b.   Weight of ball.
_____   c.   Diameter of ball.
_____   d.   Roughness or smoothness of surface texture of ball.
_____   e.   Color of ball.
_____   f.   Amount of empty space inside of ball.
_____   g.   Kind of material ball is made of.
_____   h.   Outside temperature.
_____   i.   Barometric pressure of air.
_____   j.   Day of the week that you are doing the experiment.

2.   Write down a question that you think would be helpful in finding an explanation of the winner.

3. Suppose you wanted to investigate the question, "Does the size of the ball make a difference in any way?" What would you do to find an answer to your question?

Check the following acceptable responses for this pretest. If you were successful with the pretest, go on to the next part of the chapter, page 167. If you were not successful, do the suggested activities as a way of helping you to develop skills in conducting an experiment.

Acceptable Responses for the Pretest

1. There are several variables that you may have selected as relevant. Unless you conduct an experiment to test each one, you really don't know which ones are or are not relevant. However, numbers a, e, h, i, and j are variables that are probably *not* related to the event, as you can rather easily decide.

2. This leaves you with variables b, c, d, f, and g as variables that might be related. Your question should include any one of these as the explanation for the winner. For example, does the weight of the ball make a difference? Or, does the amount of empty space inside of the ball make a difference?

3. To investigate the relationship between the size of the ball and its winning the race, you should keep all the other variables the same, except size. So to answer this question you would need four–six rubber balls that are hollow and then systematically race them in pairs to see if one size wins more frequently. You should have included in your answer:

      which variables you would change;
      which variables you would keep constant;
      what data you would collect;
      how you would record your results.

Conducting an Experiment

Is everyone a scientist?

Before you answer that question, you may wish to recognize that though the individual is given an array of observational data about an event, it does not necessarily follow that he will automatically spring into a meaningful investigation. The creative minds of the past 100 years have been so characterized because they saw new combinations in old events. They saw the unusual in the very usual that their colleagues had passed by.

In *The Art of Scientific Investigation,* Beveridge (in the preface) supports his purpose for training "would-be" investigators:

Research is one of those highly complex and subtle activities that usually remain quite unformulated in the minds of those who practice them. This is probably why most scientists think that it is not possible to give any formal instruction in how to do research. Admittedly, training in research must be largely self-training, preferably with the guidance of an experienced scientist in the handling of the actual investigation. Nevertheless, I believe that some lessons and general principles can be learnt from the experience of others. As the old adage goes, "the wise man learns from the experience of others, the fool only from his own." Any training, of course, involves much more than merely being "told how." Practice is required for one to learn to put the precepts into effect and to develop a habit of using them, but it is some help to be told what are the skills one should acquire. Too often I have been able to do little more than indicate the difficulties likely to be met—difficulties which we all have to face and overcome as best we can when the occasion arises. Yet merely to be forewarned is often a help.

Scientific research, which is simply the search for new knowledge, appeals especially to people who are individualists and their methods vary from one person to another. A policy followed by one scientist may not be suitable for another, and different methods are required in different branches of science. However, there are some basic principles and mental techniques that are commonly used in most types of investigation, at least in the biological sphere. Claude Bernard, the great French physiologist, said:

> Good methods can teach us to develop and use to better purpose the faculties with which nature has endowed us, while poor methods may prevent us from turning them to good account. Thus the genius of inventiveness, so precious in the sciences, may be diminished or even smothered by a poor method, while a good method may increase and develop it. . . . In biological sciences, the role of method is even more important than in the other sciences because of the complexity of the phenomena and countless sources of error.[1]

Beveridge continues:

The rare genius with a flair for research will not benefit from instruction in the methods of research, but most would-be research workers are not geniuses, and some guidance as to how to go about research should help them to become productive earlier than they would if left to find these things out for themselves by the wasteful method of personal experience. A well-known scientist told me once that he purposely leaves his research students alone for some time to give them an opportunity to find their own feet. Such a policy may have its advantages in selecting those that are worthwhile, on a sink or swim principle, but today there are better methods of teaching swimming than the primitive one of throwing the child into the water.

There is a widely held opinion that most people's powers of originality begin to decline at an early age. The most creative years may have already passed by the time the scientist, if he is left to find out for himself, understands how best to conduct research, assuming that he will do so eventually. Therefore, if in fact it is possible by instruction in research methods to reduce his non-productive probationary period, not only will that amount of time be saved, but he may become a more productive worker than he would ever have become by the slower method. This is only a conjecture but its potential

---

1 Claude Bernard, *An Introduction to the Study of Experimental Medicine* (New York: The Macmillan Company, 1927).

importance makes it worth considering. Another consideration is the risk that the increasing amount of formal education regarded as necessary for the intending research worker may curtail his most creative years. Possibly any such adverse effect could be offset by instruction along the lines proposed.[2]

Beveridge suggests that a typical sequence for investigating a problem would be:

1. review related literature in a critical manner, for possible fresh approaches;

2. assemble complete data from field and laboratory testing;

3. organize the information so that specific questions are identified as components of the problem;

4. make as many educated guesses as possible to answer the questions;

5. design experiments to test the questions, beginning with the most probable guess concerning the most critical questions.

Though hypotheses, which indicate the need for additional observing and testing, serve as the primary tools of the intellect in research, curiosity and imagination also participate in the evaluation of problem solutions, according to Beveridge.

Moreover, the importance of chance as a contributor to discovery cannot be over-appreciated. For example:

It was not a physicist but a physiologist, Luigi Galvani, who discovered current electricity. He had dissected a frog and left it on a table near an electrical machine. When Galvani left it for a moment someone else touched the nerves of the leg with a scalpel and noticed this caused the leg muscles to contract. A third person noticed that the action was excited when there was a spark from the electric machine. When Galvani's attention was drawn to this strange phenomenon, he excitedly investigated it and followed it up to discover current electricity.

But let's not spend our time with second-hand information about other people conducting experiments. Now be prepared to conduct some experiments yourself.

For this activity you will need four birthday candles and some matches.

Suppose you were to place the four candles in four different locations in the house or room. If you were to light them, what would happen?

Suppose you wrote that they would eventually burn down. Would they all burn totally down? In the same amount of time? Try it and see. What were the results that you expected or predicted?

What happened that you did not predict?

[2] Reprinted from, *The Art of Scientific Thinking* by W. I. B. Beveridge, pp. x-xii. Revised Edition, 1957. By permission of W. W. Norton & Company, Inc. Copyright, All Rights Reserved, 1950 by W. W. Norton & Company, Inc.

In one situation, a person found that three of the candles burned for $1\frac{1}{2}$ minutes longer than the fourth candle. Make a list of three reasons why that might have happened.

1. _____

2. _____

3. _____

You may have included many different reasons in your list, such as: the person lit the fourth candle first; it was in a draft; or, the fourth candle was shorter than the other three candles.

To investigate this situation, or one that you did not expect, it helps to organize your information. Here is one way to do this:

What is your question?

What variables do you think may be related to this question?

Why did the fourth candle burn down in a shorter time?

1. Length of candle.
2. Kind of candle.
3. Time they were lit.
4. Drafts in room or location in room.

If, for example, you thought the location in the room was the most likely variable, how could you investigate this?

Your answer probably included using similar candles—two or three at a location—and measuring the height and burning time. A graph here would be helpful.

Burning Time

Location in Room

Suppose you found that the results of your experiment were very similar to those in the first event. Can you now say that all candles will burn faster when placed in a certain location in the room? _____

What would you need to do in order to have more confidence in your conclusion?

Let's try another situation. Think about exams that you have taken as a student. Do you recall one that you did rather poorly on (maybe even a complete bust)?

With this question, "Why did you flunk the exam?" list the possible reasons or variables.

What is your question	What variable do I think may be related to that question?
Why did I flunk the exam?	1. I had a headache.
	2. I had not studied.
	3. I didn't like the subject.
	4. I didn't sleep all the night before.
	5. I didn't have enough background information on the subject.
	6. The teacher was boring.
	7. The test was unfair.

Select one of the variables and write down how you can investigate it.

For example, if you had selected reason #6, the boring teacher, you might have started with this question: "Did I do poorly on the test because he was a poor teacher?" Procedure: You would need to first decide what a poor teacher is. Maybe he is boring because he has such a dull, monotonous tone.

To keep all the other variables the same, you would need to have several teachers all teaching the same subject and giving the same exam. Maybe you could rate the teachers as to your judgment of "poor" and "good" and then compare their ratings with your exam results. By the way, you will have to do the same amount of studying for each one.

Conducting an experiment requires that we recognize the variables, define them carefully, and systematically investigate their effect on the system.

For fun try this one.

Fill a glass half full of water. *How cold can you get the water?*

What are the variables you will need to change?

How can you know when you have finished your experiment, that is, how will you know that you have the water at its coldest?

Which variables in the system did you keep the same?

Which variables in the system did you change?

Which variables in the system did you measure?

When you think about conducting an experiment, what are the essential tasks?

In the more recently developed curricula, several useful dimensions of experimenting are suggested. Investigating phenomena is a logical interest of children, according to the developers of MINNEMAST.

During the kindergarten and first-grade years the children observe individual objects. Now they are introduced to the study of sets of interrelated objects or substances which are looked upon together as systems. Emphasis is placed on having the children investigate the relationships among the components of the different systems through experimentation. They work with magnets and with flashlight cells and bulbs. Their study of seed dispersal systems includes a field trip and classroom experiments. They mix colors and they observe simple chemical reactions. The children use themselves as subjects in studying eating systems.

To understand a system, the children observe some phenomenon. Then they determine experimentally which components of the system are necessary by eliminating one at a time and observing whether the phenomenon still occurs.

Common to all the activities is the basic objective of developing a rudimentary understanding of the systems concept, which will be broadened in later grades. The systems concept is important because it simplifies investigations by focusing attention on limited portions of a complex environment.

The children learn that many questions can be answered through experimentation, and they gain experience in recording and interpreting data.[3]

They use systems as logical tools in helping children to investigate.

The systems concept is introduced through six sets of lessons, beginning with very simple situations. The structure of each section follows a general pattern:

1. The children observe a phenomenon.

2. They identify the objects involved and observe their properties.

3. They experiment to determine whether each component is essential to the system. They do this by eliminating objects or substances from the system one at a time and observing whether the phenomenon still occurs.

The children repeat this pattern of observation and experimentation in biological, chemical, and physical situations. Through these activities it is hoped they will begin to develop an intuitive sense of the meaning of the

---

[3] MINNEMAST, *Overview* (1968), p. 28. Copyright 1968 by the Regents of the University of Minnesota.

term "system" and, more important, a sense of the usefulness of the concept. The children are not expected to make a formal definition of the term at present. The systems concept will be developed further in later units.

What Is a System?

A system actually exists only in the mind. It is no more than a convenient way a person chooses to isolate and look at things in order to make them easier to study and understand. A system may be delimited in many different ways.

One type of system consists of those objects, substances, or phenomena we decide to group together because of their similarity. We define such a system in terms of those characteristics its members have in common. As we study the system, we may decide to enlarge it or to reduce it still further, in order to understand it better. An example of this kind of system is found in Section 2 of this unit—the system of colors the children are able to produce by mixing pigments. The system includes any color that turns up in their paintings. This is a large group of similar components—similar in that all are colors. In studying the system, the children discover that it can be reduced to three basic components—red, yellow, and blue.

Another type of system is a group of components that interest us particularly because they interact in some way. For example, sunlight and droplets of water in the air interact to produce a rainbow. Several such systems of interacting or reacting components are studied in this unit. In one, a number of substances are combined, and a chemical reaction occurs. The children note what substances were combined. Then they determine, by the process of elimination, which of the substances are actually necessary for the reaction to take place. As long as the phenomenon continues to occur, no essential part of the system has been eliminated. Thus, by elimination of nonessentials, the system is reduced to its basic ingredients. Other systems of this type are based on the attraction between a magnet and a paper clip, and the rolling of a ball down an inclined ruler.

A third type of system is a group of elements that all work together to do a particular job. For example, the children study the eating system. The purpose of this system is to take in food. The children determine the parts of the body that are involved in the process, and they are able to see the relation between the structure and the function of the parts. Some parts of the body that are components of the eating system may also serve other purposes, but that is of no concern in this particular study, because the system has been defined in terms of eating.

Why Systems?

Why is this way of looking at things so useful? Suppose an astronomer wants to study the universe. Its complexity is staggering to the human mind. But when he looks at one portion at a time, he can begin to understand it. First, he might look at the solar system as a subdivision of the universe. But the motion of all the planets, satellites, comets, etc. is still very complex. So he may select just two objects, the earth and the sun, and the gravitational force between them. The study of this simpler system, isolated from the larger one, helps him understand the more complex system as well.

Another example of a complex system is the human body. For the purpose of study it can be reduced to a number of simpler systems, such as the circulatory system, the nervous system, or the system of locomotion. These, in turn, can be narrowed further, according to need. Today, much attention is focused on what goes on in just one cell of living tissue. The study of each of these more and more narrowly delimited systems contributes to the understanding of the larger system, the human body.[4]

The writers of the SCIS emphasized the place of systems in scientific study.

The sun is a part of the solar system, but it can also be a part of other systems: The sun is one of one hundred billion or more stars in the Milky Way Galaxy. In other words, whether an object is included in this or that system depends on the interests of the individual studying the phenomena associated with the object. An object does not have a predetermined place in any system. The scientist considers it as a part of a system for his own convenience. In fact, a system does not exist until it is imagined by man, for a specific purpose, usually as an aid in analyzing and interpreting observations. Any one object, therefore, may be included in different systems depending on a person's intent and frame of reference. The brain, while it usually is studied as part of the nervous system, might also be considered part of the circulatory system or the respiratory system, or any other system of the body, since it is vitally related to all the other organs. A system, then, is a group of objects mentally or physically isolated for a specific purpose. Any one object may be considered to be part of more than one system.

The systems concept aids one in analyzing and interpreting his observations of natural phenomena. Since matter is conserved (is not created or destroyed under ordinary conditions), a system retains its identify if nothing is added or taken away, despite changes in appearance or form. If the appearance or form of objects in a system changes, this is evidence of some interaction —between objects within the system, or between this system and other systems. When we notice that the relative positions of the planets change with time, we may infer that the differences in relative positions resulted from interactions between members of the solar system, or perhaps even with other systems. To give another example: If we add a little sugar to a glass of water, we may say that the sugar interacts with the water, as evidenced by its apparent disappearance (change in form and appearance). We can only say this, however, if we accept the idea that the water–sugar system before adding the sugar to the water is the same system that you have after the sugar has been poured into the water. We also assume that the sugar was not "destroyed into nothingness." In other words, physical systems have an identity which is preserved through changes in form and appearance. On the other hand, if the sugar is removed or another substance is added to it, we no longer have the same system, and the disappearance of the sugar would be very difficult to analyze.

---

4 MINNEMAST, *Investigating Systems,* Unit 15 (1969), pp. 1–4. Copyright 1969 by the Regents of the University of Minnesota.

Subsystems

While a system is a whole made up of interrelated parts, a subsystem is a system which is part of another, more comprehensive system. The heart, considered by itself, is a system (it has various parts which are essential for it to work). The heart, therefore, may be considered a subsystem of the circulatory system.

Since subsystems are systems in themselves, everything that has been said for systems, including the conservation properties, also applies to subsystems. The identity of the subsystem is retained if nothing is lost or gained even if the appearance or form of the subsystem changes. However, if an object is added to or taken away from a subsystem, the result is not the same subsystem; its identity has been changed.

At this point, let us consider a common occurrence in terms of systems and subsystems. In preparing a fine soup, a cook might be concerned with adding the right amount of salt to the broth. We can call the broth and the salt together the soup system. The broth and the salt separately then become subsystems of the soup system and will be called the broth subsystem and the salt subsystem, respectively. The cook adds the salt to the broth a little at a time, tasting as he does this.

Is a grain of added salt a subsystem of the soup systems? Is it a subsystem of the salt subsystem? The answer to both questions is "yes," since the grain of salt is a part of the final mixture of salt and broth, which together is the soup system, and also, it is a part of the original salt subsystem.

When all the salt has been added to the broth, is the content of the pot the soup system? Is the final spoonful that the cook tastes a subsystem of the soup system? "Yes" to both because the soup system was defined as both broth and salt together, and while you no longer see the salt, it is all there with the broth (you can taste it); therefore, any portion of the final soup becomes a subsystem of the soup system.

Is a single grain of salt added a subsystem of the broth subsystem? Is the final spoonful that the cook tastes a subsystem of the broth subsystem? of the salt subsystem? The answer to these questions is "no" because the salt is not part of the original broth subsystem. The final spoonful of the soup contains salt, which was not part of the broth subsystem. This spoonful also contains broth, which was not part of the salt subsystem.

The subsystems concept allows us to identify variable factors which determine the action of a system or the relative action of similar systems. For example, if your car does not start even if the motor "turns over," a good mechanic does not randomly try different solutions to the problem—like checking the tires, hitting out the bumps in the fender, or charging the battery. Instead, he realizes that the subsystems of the car system, like the tires, fenders, or battery, have nothing to do with the problem. He may, however, check the fuel subsystem for such variable factors as the amount of gasoline, or the degree of clogging in the fuel lines. In other words, he attends to the relevant subsystems in analyzing his observations relative to the working of the car system. In his training he has learned (though probably not in these terms) that the car system is made up of many interrelated subsystems—the fuel subsystem, the gear subsystem, the electrical subsystem, the exhaust subsystem, etc.—and he knows which subsystems are most likely defective when a car does not start. Upon a few preliminary tests, he may even determine which variable (for example, amount of gasoline) leads to difficulty in starting the car.

To focus his attention on these relevant variables, however, the mechanic had to learn about the subsystems of the car system, and not just individual, unrelated facts concerning the tremendous number of variables involved in running a car. When the system is studied in terms of the interrelationship among subsystems, it is more likely that attention will be focused on the relevant subsystems.

Science is not the only area in which the systems–subsystems concept can be utilized. For example, a "school system" can be considered to be made up of many separate but interrelated entities: the school board, the district administrators, the school administrators (principals), the teachers, the students, the curricula, and the custodial force. Each part of the organization assumes and discharges specific functions as its contribution to the total system. The organization operates efficiently to the extent that the roles and responsibilities of each part are clearly defined, accepted, and carried out.

It is usually helpful to think of various combinations of these entities in order to study the functioning of the entire system. The student–teacher, teacher–principal, and student–curriculum subsystems within the school system are probably the immediate and most important concerns of teachers. The interactions that take place within each subsystem may affect the behavior of the entire system or other subsystems of the system. For example, the school board's decision to accept a certain program may have a marked effect on the interaction of the teacher–student subsystem; or the subsystem of teachers may decide to strike and thereby affect the entire system.[5]

Experimenting is basic to science according to the developers of *Science—A Process Approach.*

There is joy in the search for knowledge; there is excitement in seeing, however limited, into the workings of the physical and biological world; there is intellectual power to be gained in learning the scientist's approach to the solution of human problems. The first task and central purpose of science education is to awaken in the child, whether or not he will become a professional scientist, a sense of the joy, the excitement, and the intellectual power of science. Education in science, like education in letters and the arts, will enlarge the child's appreciation of his world; it will also lead him to a better understanding of the range and limits of man's control over nature.

Science as Enquiry

Science is best taught as a procedure of enquiry. Just as reading is a fundamental instrument for exploring whatever may be written, so science is a fundamental instrument for exploring whatever may be tested by observation and experiment. Science is more than a body of facts, a collection of principles,

---

5 From Science Curriculum Improvement Study, *Elementary Science Source Book* (Chicago: Rand McNally & Company, 1968), pp. 70–72.

and a set of machines for measurement; it is a structured and directed way of asking and answering questions. It is no mean pedagogical feat to teach a child the facts of science and technology; it is a pedagogical triumph to teach him these facts in their relation to the procedures of scientific enquiry. And the intellectual gain is far greater than the child's ability to conduct a chemical experiment or to discover some of the characteristics of static electricity. The procedures of scientific enquiry, learned not as a canon of rules but as ways of finding answers, can be applied without limit. The well-taught child will approach human behavior and social structure and the claims of authority with the same spirit of alert skepticism that he adopts toward scientific theories. It is here that the future citizen who will not become a scientist will learn that science is not memory or magic but rather a disciplined form of human curiosity.

The Scientific Attitude

The willingness to wait for a conclusive answer—the skepticism that requires intellectual restraint and the maintenance of doubt—is oftentimes difficult for adult and child alike. The discipline of scientific enquiry demands respect for the work of the past together with a willingness to question the claims of authority. The attitude of intelligent caution, the restraint of commitment, the belief that difficult problems are always susceptible to scientific analysis, and the courage to maintain doubt will be learned best by the child who is given an honest opportunity to try his hand at scientific enquiry. With his successes will come an optimistic appreciation of the strength of enquiry; with his failures will come an understanding of the variety and challenge of our ignorance. For the scientist, child and adult, novelty is permanent; scientific enquiry continually builds novelty into a coherent design, full of promise, always tentative, that tames our terror and satisfies for a while the human desire for simplicity.

The Procedures of Science

Scientific problems arise in the life of children just as they arise in the guided exploration of scientists. Astonishment in the presence of natural beauty, surprise—even frustration—at the failure of a prediction, and the demand for sense in the face of confusion are the beginnings of scientific enquiry. But how do we then proceed?

Among the most demanding of scientific tasks and certainly among the most difficult to teach is the *statement* of a problem. Is there a meaningful question to be asked? What techniques should be used to answer it? How does one go about making a prediction or developing a hypothesis? As he asks these questions, the student begins to learn how active enquiry can lead to testable questions and eventually to the solution of problems. He is introduced also to the pleasures and problems of inventive thought—of considering what might be as well as what is.

There are many ways to answer a provocative question in science and the child should come to recognize that he must adapt his method to the problem in hand. As he runs against different problems, the child will learn to use several *sources of reliable information*—observation, experiment, books, museums, and informed adults.

Whatever the problem, the child's *ability to observe* should be extended so that he understands the wide range of observations possible even when simple phenomena are under study. He must learn to order the evidence of all his senses.

Attention to the complex activity of *comparison of phenomena* will introduce the child to an essential task in science—the perception of differences and similarities among events.

The child will use his ability to observe and to compare in building *systems of classification* and in recognizing their usefulness and their limitations in science.

The child should learn to use the *instruments of science*. As he studies these instruments, the teacher is given an opportunity to instruct the child in *measurement*. He will learn when it is wise to estimate a measurement and when precision is required; he will learn the importance of agreement among observers and the relations among different systems of measurement.

The use of laboratory techniques—especially the *experiment*—deserves special attention. The experiment is the sharpest tool of science and in devising an experiment the child exercises his ability to pose a question, to consider possible answers, to select appropriate instruments, to make careful measurements, and to be aware of sources of error. It is unlikely that children in the first years of school will manage all aspects of sound laboratory procedure, but the best lessons of the experiment can be taught only to the child who is actively engaged with the equipment and procedures of the laboratory. The teacher must adapt his desire for precision to the child's excitement in the search; a premature demand for exactness in experimental manipulation may blunt the student's commitment and pleasure.

After the problem is posed, the data gathered, and a hypothesis developed, the science student must *evaluate evidence and draw conclusions*. Sometimes this is a simple step; sometimes it involves the review and modification of the entire plan with renewed attention to problem, to hypothesis, and to data-protocols. The goal is to make sense of the data and the pursuit of this goal will, on occasion, lead to the detection of an error or to the design of another study. It may also lead to the *invention of a model or theory* through which we can comprehend data.

Throughout the course of science education the need to communicate is present. Describing a bird to his class, graphing a mathematical function, writing an experimental paper—experience with each mode of report is essential to the development of the science student.

The child's ability to communicate in science will both depend on and contribute to the solution of this most general problem of the curriculum—accurate and effective communication.

The procedures of science described here in the context of early science education are recognizably the procedures of science at all levels of sophistication. Scientific enquiry is a seamless fabric. The content will change, the demand for precision will vary, the generality of conclusion will be different, the interrelation of studies will be understood in different ways; but the procedures and attitudes of scientific study remain remarkably the same from the time the kindergarten child wonders about color to the time the graduate physicist wonders about particle emission.

Scientific Knowledge

The facts and principles of science change with each advance in our understanding of the world. For this reason, it is difficult to forecast with precision what scientific content the child should know. Nonetheless, it is possible to sketch in outline the scientific knowledge that the properly educated child will possess within the first years of school. A knowledge of the basic findings of centuries of scientific enquiry gives boundaries and direction to the child's active exploration of his world.[6]. . .

Systematically searching for answers to our questions is important to science and to each of our decisions. We learn to do this by practice in real situations. Helping children practice in making decisions, or systematically conducting experiments, is equally important. Taken from different curriculum programs, the following are illustrations of activities in which the child is provided with opportunities to conduct experiments.

1. THE SCIENCE CURRICULUM IMPROVEMENT STUDY LESSON: MAKING PAPER AIRPLANES

ADVANCE PREPARATION

Select a suitable area for testing the airplanes. The playground, a gymnasium, or a multipurpose room are preferable to the classroom, where the flight distance is limited by room size and furniture. Plan to use an indoor area on a windy day, however. It is important that all sheets of paper be of the same size and weight. Sheets of duplicator or mimeograph paper are suitable.

TEACHING SUGGESTIONS

Making the Airplanes

Show your pupils the paper they will use to construct airplanes and explain that they will have a contest to see whose plane flies the greatest distance. Tell them to write their names on the planes and to follow two rules: (1) each plane must be made from one sheet of paper; (2) no other objects may be added to the paper (no tape, glue, or paper clips).

Encourage a child who has no design ideas of his own to team up with

---

6 *Science—A Process Approach Commentary* (1970), pp. 3–6. Reprinted by permission of the American Association for the Advancement of Science, Washington, D.C.

From Science Curriculum Improvement Study, *Energy Sources* (Chicago: Rand McNally & Company, 1971), pp. 32–33.

another pupil for assistance. The pair will have two sheets and can therefore try out two designs in the contest.

Flying the Planes

Take the extra sheets of paper to the launch area for use after the first contest. Your students should launch all planes in the contest in the same direction from one starting point. The activity will proceed quickly if the children line up behind the starting point and take turns. Allow the planes to remain where they land so everyone can see how far they went.

Give rcognition to the designer of the winning plane after everyone has participated. Have your pupils point out which planes traveled the greatest distance and which the least, so they can infer which were the most successful designs.

Invite them to modify their designs or to build another airplane if they have new ideas they would like to try. Allow a few minutes for the necessary construction work, and then hold a second contest so your pupils may determine the value of the changes they made. Let them recognize the winner of this contest, but postpone discussing the results until after your return to the classroom. Winning planes might be saved for further examination.

Discussion of Variables

To open the discussion, write the heading *Variables that Affect the Flight Distance* on the chalkboard. Ask your pupils to identify the variables that affected the flight distance of their airplanes in the contest. If necessary, explain that a *variable* is something that can be changed from one experiment to the next or that is different for one airplane compared to another. Invite children to furnish examples and write these under the title on the board, but be prepared to provide one or two yourself in case they need these to get started. You might, for instance, mention the height from which a plane was thrown, the launching speed, and/or the wing spread of the plane.

2. THE SCIENCE CURRICULUM IMPROVEMENT STUDY LESSON: COMPARING PULLEY SYSTEMS

Show the children each of the covered pulley systems while you turn the handles to make the propellers rotate. Then ask them to name the interacting objects, seen and unseen, that they think are in each system. Encourage them to speculate by asking, "What other objects might there be in this system?" They should state their reasons and explain how a handle is able to interact with a propeller, so that one turns along with the other, but not necessarily at the same rate or in the same direction.

From Science Curriculum Improvement Study, *Interaction and Systems,* Teacher's Guide (Chicago: Rand McNally & Company, 1970), pp. 68–69.

Because of their earlier experiences, they will probably say that your system contains wheels connected by a rubber band even though they have no visible evidence to support this hypothesis. You might ask them for evidence that the connection is a rubber band and not a string. Or, you might challenge them to use something other than a rubber band to connect the pulleys when they experiment. Make available the string and ribbons you have collected for this purpose.

Children's Experiments

Distribute the pulley sets so the children can investigate these further. Leave the covered systems in a place where the children can compare these with their own. As you talk with individuals, ask them to describe how they might experiment to find out more about the sizes of the pulleys in the two covered systems. Assist them with questions such as: Is your propeller turning faster or slower than the handle? What happens if you exchange the handle and propeller? Their ideas will enable you to determine whether they use quantitative (number or fractions of turns) or only qualitative (faster-slower) information about the turning rates. Also notice whether your pupils connect their observations of turning rates to the relative sizes of the pulleys.

Listen to the children's explanations of how the demonstration systems operate. In these conversations you might also encourage children to invent ways to make the propeller turn much faster or slower than the handle. A large system of two or more pulley bases (use spares in your kit or pool supplies from two or three pairs of children) gives additional latitude to these investigations. You might point out that a clock has two or three hands that turn at very different rates (the second hand completes a revolution once a minute, the minute hand once an hour, the hour hand once in one-half a day), as do the children's pulleys.

Leave a few of the pulley sets on the science table so that children can experiment with these at unscheduled times. We do not suggest a class discussion of the children's findings, because children usually discuss their observations and ideas informally while they experiment.

OPTIONAL ACTIVITIES

Scales

How much use you make of the printed scales on the pulley bases for quantitative experiments will depend on the ability and interest of your pupils. Although experiments with scales may be difficult for most second-grade children, some are able to meet the challenge and enjoy it. If older children study this unit, more of them will appreciate these activities. The basic question is: How far does the propeller turn when the handles is turned around once (or more times)? This question can be asked about all possible pulley combinations. It is answered by stating the number of whole turns plus the number of small intervals (indicated on the scale) that the propeller moves. Since there are ten small intervals in a turn, the answers can be expressed in decimals or fractions. For instance, 1 turn plus 4 spaces is 1 4/10 or 1.4 turns. If you wish to give the children practice with common fractions, you or they can prepare paper scales that slip over a pulley base and on which one full turn is divided into two, three, or four equal intervals.

3. MINNEMAST LESSON: SIMPLE SYSTEMS WITH MAGNETS

ACTIVITY A

1. Arrange the folders at random on the table, and have a magnet ready. In your discussion, do not use the word "magnet" until this first part of the demonstration is completed.

Who would like to come up and touch one of these papers with this rod?

If the volunteer touches a paper that sticks to the rod, appear perplexed. Take the paper from him and ask him to touch another paper. Look perplexed again at the result, whether it sticks or not. Call on another child to try it with a few papers. You may have several children try, as long as they continue to be puzzled.

How can we find out why this rod picks up some papers and doesn't pick up others?

Follow through suggestions for investigation until the children discover the reason. After the reason has been discovered, be sure that all see the slip inside the folded paper. At this point, you may begin to call the rod a magnet.

2. The next part of the demonstration confirms the explanation of the mystery by showing that a magnet and a paper clip can indeed support a sheet of paper between them.

Hold up a magnet with a large clip hanging from it.

What is the magnet doing to the clip? (It is holding it up.)

Have a child hold the magnet in one hand and a clip in the other, and bring the two slowly together.

What are the clip and the magnet doing to each other? (They are pulling or attracting each other.)

Now have the child hold the clip and magnet apart while you insert a sheet of paper between them. Then have the child let the clip and magnet come together again.

Are the magnet and clip still attracting each other? (Yes.)

What is keeping the paper from falling? (The attraction between the magnet and the clip.)

Pick up one of the folded papers with the magnet and hold it up.

Why doesn't the paper fall? (It is held between the clip and the magnet.)

Now, using two magnets, two paper clips, and a sheet of paper, make

---

From MINNEMAST, *Investigating Systems,* pp. 7–11. Copyright 1944 by the Regents of the University of Minnesota.

a tray.... Lift the tray, using the magnets as handles. Show how it can carry a pencil, a rubber band, etc.

Next, place a large metal clip against one of the magnets, to which it will cling.

Is this clip a necessary part of our tray?

Does it help hold the tray together?

Ask those who say "Yes" to raise their hands, and then those who say "No."

How can we find out? (We can remove the metal clip and see if the tray still works.)

Have a child remove the clip and let the class see that the tray is still a tray. Then ask the same question about the clips under the paper. Have a child remove one. One side of the paper will bend down and you will no longer have a tray. The conclusion, therefore, is that the clips under the paper are necessary parts of the tray.

Now ask whether other objects can be made part of the tray. Children may find it difficult to understand what you mean by making an object part of the tray. Explain that you do not want these objects to change the way the tray is made, but that you want to add some objects to make it better. If suggestions are slow in coming, give the following hint:

To carry this tray I need to use both hands. Could I add an object to make a handle so that I can carry it with one hand?

Hold up a ruler.

Can we make this part of our tray? Who will try?

Have volunteers try with the ruler, with a pencil, and then with a pair of scissors. The scissors should make a good handle lying across the tops of the two upright magnets.

Why can the scissors be made part of the tray, but not the ruler or pencil? (The scissors stick to the magnet; the ruler and pencil do not.)

What other things would you like to try? (Let the children try their suggestions.)

Place all the objects that can be made into a handle—a spoon, a pair of scissors, an iron rod—in one pile. In another pile put those objects that can't be made into a handle—a wooden ruler, a plastic spoon, a pencil, a strip of cardboard. Challenge the children to say which property the objects in one pile have that the objects in the other pile do not have. This is intended to elicit a generalization. It may be made in the form of "These stick to a magnet and those don't." Or a child may say, "These are metal and those are not." (Accept this statement without complicating matters by saying that some metals, such as copper and lead, are not attracted to a magnet.)

ACTIVITY B

Provide each child with 2 magnets, 2 jumbo paper clips, 4 rubber bands, and 3 sheets of construction paper, 4″ × 5″ each. (It saves time to have these on trays for small groups of children.)

See if you can put some of these objects together to make something interesting. You may use all the objects or just some of them. See how many things you can make.

During the exploration period, if you see that a child has made what he feels is an exciting discovery, have him report it and demonstrate it to the class.

After the children have had time to complete some systems, have them shown to the class, and have the class analyze how each object in the system relates to and affects the other objects.

What does each object in the system do to the others?

To display some of the children's systems, suspend them from spring clips.

You may want to prepare some of the additional systems for the children to see and manipulate:

A sheet of glass or transparent plastic has a nail underneath. The magnet is moved above the glass and the nail follows it below.

Two rulers and a magnet are stuck into clay. Challenge the youngsters to get the second magnet to stay up in the air.

4. MINNEMAST LESSON: SIMPLE SYSTEMS WITH BALLS

ACTIVITY A

1. Set up the rolling ball system as shown. Have the children gather around and identify the familiar objects assembled on the table. Then have them describe the relations of the objects to one another. Positional relations can be determined by observation. The child can see that one end of the ruler is resting on the pencil. But if he should say that the pencil is holding the ruler up, ask, "How can we be sure?" and have him test his statement by seeing what happens if he removes the pencil.

Lead the children to think of these objects not as a mere collection, but as a system of related objects. If they need help in making observations, you might ask questions such as the following:

Under what number on the ruler is the pencil that is on the table?

What effect does the pencil under the ruler have on the ruler? (It is holding it up.)

How can we be sure? (Take the pencil away and see what happens.) Have a child do so.

What is the other pencil doing? (It is keeping the ball from rolling down.)

How can you show you are right? (Test it.) Have a child do so.

What is the effect of the grooved ruler on the ball when the ball rolls down? (It makes the ball roll down in a straight line.)

From MINNEMAST, *Investigating Systems,* pp. 12–16. Copyright 1944 by the Regents of the University of Minnesota.

How can you test it? (Take the ruler away and see what happens when you let the ball roll off the pencil that was under the ruler.)

2. Now direct the children's attention to the properties of the assembled objects and how they relate to the system.

If, instead of the ruler, we used a strip of paper of the same length and width, would the ball roll down in a straight line?

How can we find out? (Try it.)

What properties of the ruler help the ball roll down in a straight line? (It is stiff; it has a straight groove along its length.)

Does the ruler have to be this color for the ball to roll down in a straight line?

How can we find out? (Try a ruler of another color.) Have a child do so.

Rearrange the assemblage so that the pencil tilts the ruler.

Will the ball roll the same way now?

How can we find out?

What properties must the object under the ruler have if the ball is to roll down in a straight line? (It must be able to hold up the ruler so that one end is higher than the other and so that the ruler is not tilted to one side.)

Now look at the pencil on the ruler.

Is the eraser on the pencil necessary to keep the ball from rolling?

How can we find out? (Try using a pencil from which the eraser has been removed.)

3. The children have now observed the relations among the objects in the assemblage, and they have noted the significance of particular properties of the objects. Next they will observe the system in action and consider how to modify the system so that it can serve particular purposes.

Have a paper cup, a marble, and a ping-pong ball ready. Set up the system just as it was at the start of the lesson. Place a paper cup on its side with its opening about 6″ away and facing the lower end of the ruler.

Have a child remove the pencil on the ruler so that the ping-pong ball can roll into the cup.

Then ask if the marble would do the same thing. Have a child come up and "work the system" with a marble.

Now place the cup a little to one side so that the rolling ball will miss it. Ask a child to work the system (without moving the ruler) and let the children see that the marble does not roll into the cup.

Can anyone think how we could add an object to the system to make the marble roll into the cup?

Tell the children that they will have a chance to try their suggestions out for themselves.

ACTIVITY B

Give each child at least two grooved rulers, three pencils, a marble, a ping-pong ball and a paper cup. With these they may devise any systems they choose. Give them the following suggestions one by one, when appropriate.

Can they discover how to make a ball roll into a cup that is off to one side of the ruler? Have the children try to use the same objects to make a different rolling-ball system from the one they made before. Ask them to find out what happens when one kind of ball hits another kind.

Have the children demonstrate their discoveries. Help them analyze the interactions of the different objects. For example, in connection with the last suggestion above, you may want to ask them what happened to the ping-pong ball after the marble hit it, what happened to the marble after it hit the ping-pong ball, and how the marble would have moved if the ping-pong ball were not in the way.

After the children have finished their own explorations you may set up systems like those below for them to observe and work with in their free time. Systems invented by the children that are different from the one used in the lesson may also be displayed.

5. SCIENCE—A PROCESS APPROACH: GROWTH OF MOLD ON BREAD

This exercise begins by dividing the class into groups of four and providing each group with three different containers in which there is a piece of bread. In one container there is a larger area of mold growth, in the second container there is a smaller area of mold growth, and in the third container there is no mold growth on the bread. The children are asked to observe the containers and then to ask questions which can be answered by yes or no which would help them to learn more about the contents of the containers.

The objectives are for the children to learn to:

1. Identify the variables held constant and the manipulated variable from the description of a test in which mold is grown.

2. Identify the responding variable from the description of a test in which mold is grown.

3. Describe the qualitative observations that differentiate between growth responses of mold to manipulations of an environmental factor.

The children are to design an experiment in which they identify and control the variables for studying the growth of mold on bread. The children are divided into small groups or pairs to plan a test that will answer a specific question which they have identified. They are to control the variables keeping most of the variables constant but manipulating one variable, and then observing how the other variables respond.

Some questions which could be investigated deal with variables such as: the effect of temperature on the mold, effects of various kinds of bread on mold growth, the amount of light, the kind of mold, whether squashing or flattening the bread will make any difference, and how much moisture is available.

Once the experiments are designed, the children proceed with carrying out their

---

From *Science—A Process Approach* (1968), Part E, Exercise P, p. 1. Reprinted by permission of the American Association for the Advancement of Science, Washington, D.C.

experiments, making sure to make as definitive observations as possible and keeping usable records of their observations. The teacher is free to move about the group, aiding students in formulating their questions and in setting up techniques necessary for carrying out their experiments.

At the finish of the experiments each group is permitted to interpret the data they have collected, and they then report their findings so that all the members of the class can become knowledgeable in the results of all the investigations. Where possible, the children are encouraged to use graphs and tables for organization of their data as well as having a summary conclusion of their findings.

As a generalizing experience the children are asked to review all the experiments which were conducted and decide upon what they would do to have the greatest amount of mold growth in the shortest amount of time, and what they might do to prevent mold from growing at all. These questions may then lead to side investigations by some groups of children who are interested in following up their ideas with an experimental investigation.

Slippery surfaces, paper airplanes, pulleys, magnets, balls, bread mold, and potatoes—they all represent contexts for generating questions and conducting experiments.

To what extent is conducting an experiment of the same importance in these seven units?

In what ways do the units emphasize that children should learn how to be systematic?

By now your skill of conducting an experiment should be quite satisfactory. Check yourself before you go on.

Posttest

To perform these tasks, you will need only your sharp thinking strategies.

1. A teacher in the third grade observed that her students were doing very poorly on their spelling test. She decided to try an approach different from the usual assigning of spelling unit, providing studying time, and then giving a test on the unit. In her new approach, she had students make up stories using the words they missed on the pretest. They would exchange the stories and check the spelling of all words. Then she gave them a posttest on the unit. The class's grades averaged near 95 in two months. She wondered why.

Which variables do you think are relevant to the event?

_____   a.   the teacher.

　　　　　　_____   b.   the principal.

　　　　　　_____   c.   the pretest.

　　　　　　_____   d.   the posttest.

　　　　　　_____   e.   the spelling unit.

　　　　　　_____   f.   the creative writing.

　　　　　　_____   g.   the study time.

　　　　　　_____   h.   the checking of another's paper.

2.   Write down a question that you think would be helpful in finding an explanation for the improved spelling scores.

3.   Suppose you wanted to investigate the question "Does children's checking each other's papers help spelling scores?". What would you do to find an answer to that question?

　　Following, you will find acceptable answers. If you find that you are having difficulty you may wish to discuss this with your instructor.

Acceptable Answers for Posttest

1.   There are several variables that are quite relevant to this event. Others may be relevant, but probably to a smaller degree—such as a, b, d, and e, for they were constant both before and after the new approach for spelling was tried.

2.   This leaves you with c, f, g, and h as variables that might be relevant. Your question should include any one of them if they are to be used as an explanation for the improved spelling performance by the students. For example, does taking a pretest help students to do better on their spelling? Or, does using missed words in creative-writing stories help children to do better in their spelling?

3.   To investigate the relationship between one variable and the results on spelling scores, you should keep all variables the same except the one that you are questioning. The problem was that the teacher in this situation changed four variables at the same time and therefore was unable to tell which one was the most important.

　　So your answer should have included:

　　1.   Changing only one variable.

　　2.   Keeping all the other variables the same.

　　3.   Defining the variables.

　　4.   Keeping a record of the results.

---

8. Causes
and Effects

By the end of this chapter, you should be able to identify (1) at least three controlled variables; (2) the manipulated variable; (3) the responding variable when given the description of an experiment.

Check Yourself Now. If you can successfully perform this task, you may omit this part of the chapter and go to page 187.

For this task, you will need two full soda bottles and a bottle opener or two cans of soda.

For this pretest, take the two soda bottles or cans from the storeroom or refrigerator.

Place the bottles in front of you. Observe the bottles, noting various of the characteristics of the two soda bottles.

1. Shake one of the bottles vigorously for ten seconds, then open both bottles. List five observations that you made when you opened the bottles.

    1. _____

    2. _____

    3. _____

    4. _____

    5. _____

2. Name three variables that were held constant for both soda bottles.

    1. _____

    2. _____

    3. _____

3. What was the manipulated or independent variable?

_____

4. What was the responding or dependent variable?

_____

Acceptable Responses for the Pretest

1. Your observations were probably many more than five, especially since you could get five observations by just reporting one observation for each of the five senses. The one observation that you should make is that the bottle that was shaken overflowed.

   1. Overflow of one bottle.

   2. Fizzy sound.

   3. Red color.

   4. Sticky liquid.

   5. Sweet taste.

2. Some variables that were held constant were:

   Temperature of soda bottles.

   Size of bottle.

   Kind of soda.

   Time of day.

   Amount of soda in the bottles.

3. The manipulated or independent variable was:

   whether or not the bottle was shaken.

4. The responding or dependent variable was:

   overflow of the bottle or perhaps the loudness of the fizzy sound.

If your answers are the same or similar to the above, you may go directly to page 187. If your answers are dissimilar (which is unacceptable), or if you wish to do further work with the topic of variables, then do the activities that follow. Perform as many of the activities as you wish, read whatever you want, and then take the posttest beginning on page 201.

In doing an experiment, the scientist is interested in finding out which properties or factors of a situation cause another factor to change. In other words, what is the effect upon one characteristic of an event when another characteristic is altered? Not only scientists but everyone is involved in considering the cause and effects of events and situations.

For example, what will be the effect on a cake if the temperature at which it is baked is changed or if baking soda is substituted for baking powder? Or, how will the sogginess of cornflakes be affected by the amount of milk that is added or by the speed with which you eat them?

In any situation where something can change, there are factors or *variables* that change, resulting in occurrence of the event. In most cases there is more than one variable that affects the happening of the event. This causes great problems in determining to what extent any one variable will affect the event. In studying an event, the scientist will go through the process of controlling variables. He will attempt to keep all the variables unchanging (constant) except for two. The scientist will systematically change one of these two variables (manipulated variable), and he will then observe how the other variable is affected (responding variable).

For example, if in eating your cornflakes you want to avoid their becoming soggy, you have to find out how the amount of added milk affects the rate of sogginess of the cornflakes. In order to do this, you would have to control the following variables:

the amount of cornflakes in the bowl;

the size of the bowl;

the shape of the bowl;

the way the milk is poured in,

and so on.

Then you would add varying amounts of milk to the cornflakes (manipulated variable) and would observe how fast the cornflakes became soggy (responding variable).

A similar experiment could then be made based on eating time. What variables would you then have to control?

1. _____

2. _____

3. _____

4. _____

You would have to control:

the size of the bowl;

the shape of the bowl;

the amount of cornflakes;

the amount of milk;

the time at which you begin eating.

What would the responding and manipulated variables be?

Manipulated variable

_____

Responding variable

_____

When trying to identify the manipulated and responding variables it might help to think of the question you are asking. In this case the question was: How does the amount of time taken to eat the cornflakes affect their rate of sogginess?

The manipulated variable, that is the one *you* change, was eating time. In this case, the responding variable—that is the one that changed *as a result* of what you did and about which you wonder as to what affects it—was the sogginess of the cornflakes.

The Pendulum

Let's take a look at another activity that will give you practice in distinguishing between constant, manipulated, and responding variables.

For this activity you will need string, at least four equal weights such as washers, and a stopwatch or a watch with a second hand.

A pendulum can loosely be defined as an object at the end of an arm which is free to swing. In our case the pendulum will be one or more washers tied to the end of a string.

The period of the pendulum is the time it takes the pendulum to make a complete cycle, that is to swing over and then back to the starting point.

There are many variables which you think might affect the period of a pendulum. Without putting together a pendulum, list three of those variables.

1. _____
2. _____
3. _____

Some variables that you may have thought of are thickness of the string, length of the string, amount of weight at the end of the string, distance between the center line and the weight at the time of release, and steadiness in holding the string.

Your task is to determine which of the following variables has the most effect on the period of the pendulum.

1. The distance of the weight from the center line when it is released.
2. The length of the string.
3. The amount of weight on the end of the string.

Technical hints that may be helpful are: (a) attach your pendulum to a door, ceiling, or tabletop so that the mounting point does not move; (b) count the number of round-trip swings or periods in thirty seconds in order to get a better approximation of the interval for one complete swing (one period).

$$\text{Period} = \frac{\text{number of swings}}{30 \text{ seconds}}$$

Go to it:

What did you find out? Of the above-listed variables, which one affects the period most?

1. Does it affect the period if the release point is farther out from the center?

Perhaps a little if you take really far-out release points; however, when held fairly close to the center there is no effect.

2. What effect did the length of string have?

That's right, the longer the string, the longer the period.

3. Did the amount of weight on the end of the string have any effect?

You probably really looked hard to find the period change when you added more weight but kept the length of the string the same. However, if you were good at controlling variables and objective in observing, then you probably concluded that the amount of weight didn't make any difference.

In order to find answers for each of the above questions, you had to utilize the process of controlling variables. What were the manipulated and responding variables for the first question, which asked about the distance from which the weight was released?

Manipulated variable

_____

Responding variable

_____

The manipulated variable (the one *you* manipulated or changed) was the distance of the weight from vertical when it was released. The responding variable was the period of the pendulum, which in this case, except for relatively great distances, was unaffected.

What were three variables that were held constant in experimenting to find an answer to the second question?

1. _____

2. _____

3. _____

The amount of weight at the end of the string should have been kept the same, since you did not know the results of the third experiment; the distance from the center for release should have been kept the same; and the number of cycles counted should have been kept the same, since changes here would have introduced variation in your precision in measuring the period.

What were the manipulated and responding variables in the third experiment?
Manipulated variable

_____

Responding variable

_____

The manipulated variable was the amount of weight and the responding variable was the period.

TWO-SECOND PERIOD

You now know which variable affects the period of pendulum most. Now construct a pendulum that has a period of *two seconds*.
How long is the string? _____ Did the number of weights make any difference? _____
You may have had to cut several strings before you got one that was long enough. It takes around 100 cm of string in order for a pendulum to have a two-second period.
What were the manipulated and responding variables here?

Manipulated variable

_____

Responding variable

_____

What was the one controlled variable?

_____

The manipulated variable (cause) was the length of string; *you* varied this. The responding variable (effect) was the period of the pendulum. One variable that you should have controlled was the release point. Far-out release points can affect the period slightly. Therefore you should keep the weight 10–15 cm. from the center line.

Cups and Water

For this activity you will need: a source of water; two eight-ounce or larger paper cups; a ruler; a razor blade.

Cut a one-cm square hole in the bottom of one paper cup. Cut four square holes in the bottom of the other cup, with each hole being one-half cm by one-half cm, that is one-quarter of a square centimeter in area. The amount of area that is cut out of the bottom is the same for both cups. One cup has one big hole, whereas the other cup has four little holes.

Will eight ounces of water flow from the cup with the big hole in the bottom faster, slower, or at the same speed as eight ounces of water would from the cup with the four little holes in it?

What is your reason?

How could you find out?

In this case, what would three constant variables be?

What are the manipulated and the responding variables?

Manipulated variable

_____

Responding variable

_____

Some controlled variables are : both cups have the same size and shape; the amount of water put in the cups is the same; the holes in the bottom were made in the same way (for example, with your fingers); the timing procedures are the same. If you have someone else pour the water in each cup, you can hold your fingers over the bottom of the cups so that both cups will begin emptying at the same time. Oh, yes, the total number of square centimeters of holes in the two cups is the same.

The manipulated variable consists of the number of holes and the responding variable of the speed with which the cups empty.

Go ahead and make the experiment:

What did you find out?

As long as the holes are reasonably large, as in the specifications given you, the size of the hole does not make any difference. Both cups empty at the same rate.

How must the skill of identifying factors that cause an effect ᵤe presented to children in the elementary school? Developers of recent science curricula for the elementary school have taken varied approaches to presenting the concept of causes and effect to children.

In the *Science Curriculum Improvement Study* the identification of causes is dealt with in the unit, *Systems and Subsystems,* whereas causes and effects are studied in the unit *Interaction.*

INTERACTIONS

Interactions lead to changes in systems. If two rolling balls collide, their movements will momentarily stop, and they may start moving in other directions. If a lump of sugar is held in front of a friendly horse, the horse may come to get the sugar. Two roller skates with strong magnets attached to them that are rolled toward each other may reverse their direction of roll, rather than collide. When two liquids (or other materials) are brought into contact with each other, the color may change. When the switch on an electric motor is closed, the motor begins to turn. All of these are examples of interactions; they lead to changes in systems.

The changes that take place as a result of interactions are the evidences for interaction. If we exhale through a straw into water that contains a little of the indicator bromothymol blue, we will see a change in color take place. The air we exhale contains carbon dioxide. The carbon dioxide and water form carbonic acid, a weak acid. In the presence of this weak acid, the bromothymol blue changes color. This is evidence that an interaction has taken place. As they study interactions, children will see a variety of evidences of interactions.[1]

The MINNEMAST developers integrated mathematics and variables.

In previous MINNEMAST units the children have had experience in observing and describing some changing and unchanging properties. In this unit we want them to focus their attention on the way two changing properties in a system are related to each other. The children are guided to discover the relation between two changes by setting up a number of experiments. In an early experiment the children plant corn. They observe that there is a change in the height of their plants that is related to the change in the number of days since planting. Similarly, as they drop marbles into a container of water, they see that with each change in the number of marbles, there is a change in the height of the water, and that there is a relation (or rule that operates) between the two changes.

Relations between changes like these are called functional relations. If measurements of the changes can be made, the relation can be vividly shown on a graph. Therefore the children are given experience with several different methods of graphing the changes. (The stages in the development of graphing skills are outlined on the next page of this introduction.)

But even where measurement is difficult or impossible, the relation between changes can still be investigated by observation and/or experimentation. For example, the children do an experiment where they let one potato sprout in the light and another in the dark. It would not be difficult for them to measure and compare the longest sprout on each potato, but it would be impossible for them to measure precisely how much light (or heat) each potato received during the growing period. In such a case, the children can still observe the rule (the functional relation) that operated. They can make a fairly accurate statement saying that the potato that had less light had the longer sprout, or that there is a relation between darkness and the rate of growth.

The concept of functional relations is emphasized at this point in the

---

1 Science Curriculum Improvement Study, *Elementary Science Sourcebook* (Chicago: Rand McNally & Company, 1944), pp. 65–66.

curriculum because it is basic to man's attempt to understand the world around him. Ability to recognize and interpret the relation of one change to another and to express that relation in concise form is an important aspect of scientific and mathematical investigation. The limited understanding which the child acquires now will aid him in his attempts to explain his environment. His understanding will gradually be extended as his studies continue.

To bring out the advantage of graphing in helping to visualize functional relations and to record and communicate data, the children are given many opportunities to plot their measurements on grids.[2]

One of the integrated process skills of *Science—A Process Approach* is *controlling variables.*

You have probably heard a housewife remark, following a baking fiasco in the kitchen, "I can't understand why the cake didn't turn out. I did everything exactly as I always have." It is reasonable to suspect that something was different, even though the cook did not know what it was—perhaps an unnoticed change in the ingredients, the time the eggs were beaten, the temperature of the butter, the age of the eggs, or any one of a great number of factors. Each of these "factors" is a *variable,* a variable which may have influenced the quality of the cake.[3]

The word *variable* is used to describe any factor that may vary or change.

In science and in many other areas investigators try to determine what variables or factors influence the behavior of a system and how they influence it. The best way to determine this is to hold constant all except two of the variables, to manipulate one of these two variables in some way, and to make observations or measurements to find out how the remaining variable responds. In this way, all the variables are controlled: all but two are held constant; one of these is manipulated, and the other responds.[4]

The developers of the *Elementary Science Study* also have activities in which children must consider causes and effects.

The children's proposed experiments to determine the influence of water on the growth of molds will be varied and usually naive. Yet in this activity the children soon begin to grasp the need for experiments that are controlled. In controlled experiments all but one of the various factors that might influence growth are kept constant and only the one factor to be tested is varied to determine whether it does indeed have a causal effect.

2 MINNEMAST, *Comparing Changes,* Unit 19, pp. 1–2. Copyright 1944 by the Regents of the University of Minnesota.

3 *Science—A Process Approach,* Commentary for Teachers, p. 193. Reprinted by permission of the American Association for the Adavncement of Science, Washington, D.C.

4 *Science—A Process Approach,* Part E—Controlling Variables 1, Rolling Cylinders, p. 2. Reprinted by permission of the American Association for the Advancement of Science, Washington, D.C.

Here they are attempting to discover to what extent water, temperature, and light may influence the growth of molds. If they wish to test the effect of water, they soon grasp the necessity for having two pieces of bread, one moist and the other dry, subjected to the same conditions of light and temperature.

Some teachers have found it advantageous to let each child carry out his proposed experiment, and afterwards, as class discussion brings out the need for a more controlled experiment, to discover how to improve his procedure. Other teachers prefer to have the class discuss the proposed experiments in advance and thus modify the plans before the actual experiments are set up.

A child may suggest an experiment such as the following:

Take two pieces of bread. Add water to one and leave the other as it is. Observe.

Of course, if the bread is left uncovered, this child will discover that the bread will dry out. Perhaps a more sophisticated experiment will suggest itself. He may decide to put two pieces of bread in plastic boxes and then add water to one and cover the boxes tightly.

After four or five days he observes mold on both pieces of bread. Now the question in his mind is: Why did he get mold on both pieces? If it is suggested that there could be water in the bread already, an easy way to find out is to place a piece of fresh bread in a closed plastic container and put it in a sunny place. A piece of dried bread can be placed in a similar container next to it. After a day or so, a great deal of moisture from the fresh bread should condense on the inside of its container, while a small amount of moisture or none at all should condense in the other.

One way to avoid the problem of the moisture already present in bread is to use two pieces of dried-out bread and add water to one piece. A further refinement is to add increasing amounts of water to a series of pieces of dried bread.... The development of mold on these pieces of bread is observed and the children note whether there are differences in amount or diversity of mold growth in relation to the degree of wetness.

Through the interplay and gradual refinement of their own experiments, the children eventually grasp the idea of controlling particular variables, so that they can test each one independently. The children themselves should come to this realization through their own errors, discussions, and doubts, with your subtle but definite leadership and encouragement.[5]

The skill of analyzing causes and effects is common to scientists and students alike. One of its important aspects is the person's effectiveness at identifying all variables that have an effect.

The following activities are taken from several of the recently developed science curricula. They illustrate some approaches that have been successful for children to develop skill in analyzing causes and effects.

---

[5] Reprinted from *Microgardening,* p. 31, by the Elementary Science Study. Copyright 1944 by Education Development Center, Inc., 55 Chapel Street, Newton, Massachusetts 02160.

1. ELEMENTARY SCIENCE STUDY LESSON:
INVESTIGATIONS

After several weeks of looking at pond water animals and plants and drawing them, your class may want to do some experimenting. The best experiments will be those the children devise themselves. They may work singly or in groups. Discussions within the group about an experiment can be very fruitful. Some children may want to describe their experiments to the whole class. Others may experiment at home and then report to the class. What criticisms do the other children have of a particular experiment? Has the child shown what he set out to show? Should he repeat the experiment to be sure of the results? Perhaps he has chosen too complicated a problem and should narrow it down before proceeding.

The clearest kind of experimental results is usually obtained when a particular treatment is given to some animals while others are kept untreated. Results are then taken directly from a comparison of the two groups of animals —the treated group and the control group.

The concept of controls in experimentation is not easy for young children to understand. For instance, why do you need two snails if you want to find out whether snails will live in tap water? Isn't one enough? Encourage the children to think about this problem. In each trial class, at least one child has eventually seen the importance, for example, of raising one snail in pond water and another in tap water under otherwise identical conditions. In one instance, the children pointed out that if you didn't have one snail living in pond water, you couldn't be sure that it was the tap water that killed the other one. It might have been killed by heat, or sun, or handling, or lack of food. Other children argued that the pond water had food in it (in the form of small animals and plants) so maybe that was why the pond water snail didn't die. They suggested doing the experiment again and adding some food to the tap water or filtering the pond water.

Children often fall into a trap, however; they assume that pond water animals (and many others) have much more in common with humans than is actually the case. It will be your job to keep asking them if they are sure that the pond water animals breathe, that they have four legs, that they have two eyes, that they can see at all. Can the children devise experiments that will prove conclusively that a certain kind of animal can see? It should become clear to them after trial that this type of experiment is very difficult to carry out. Usually it will have to be modified into something a bit less ambitious; for instance, whether an animal is attracted to or repelled by light. Some very clear experiments can be carried out, for example, to show whether planaria like the dark better than the light. Cover one-half of the container with dark paper. Where are the animals five or ten minutes later? Try this again several times. (Why?) Do the planaria always end up on the same side? If you cut off

Reprinted from *Pond Water*, pp. 29–35, by the Elementary Science Study. Copyright 1964 by Education Development Center, Inc., 55 Chapel Street, Newton, Massachusetts 02160.

a planaria's head—you can do this without killing the animal—will it still respond to light? How does the head respond without the tail?

The first experiments that the children do will probably be very inconclusive. They will probably not write down what they have done and so won't be able to remember what has happened. Almost without exception, they will want to add four or five different substances at a time to their water, to see how the animals will react or whether they will feed on these substances. If an animal dies, they won't have any idea of what has really killed it. You can, of course, warn the children about this beforehand, but no amount of warning will eliminate the problem if the children are really allowed to direct their own experiments. Even so, it is better for them to do their own experiments than to carry out your directions. They'll improve their experiments as they go along, in any case.

You may want to ask the children to write up their first experiments as a homework assignment. In class, have them exchange notebooks and read someone else's experiment. Can each tell what the other child did? It may help also to have several of the children read out loud reports that they think are particularly good and then give the rest of the class a chance to talk about these. Can they tell exactly what a child did from his report? Can they tell what happened? Was it a good experiment? Did it really prove anything? How might the experiment be improved? If the experiment should work perfectly, an unlikely possibility, the class can suggest further experiments to be done along the same lines.

After a class period spent in this way, it should be much clearer to most of your students what a good experiment is, as well as what a good report should contain. They should come to realize that the report must be understandable to someone unconnected with the experiment. You may want to discuss with them the difference between a report and their own notes of the experiment. A personal notebook may contain abbreviations, incomplete sentences, secret codes, and other types of shorthand. The only requirement is that the notes allow the researcher to reconstruct his experiment completely and accurately without relying on memory. A report should be a complete record that anyone can read and understand.

Children commonly feed their animals far too much or, when experimenting, completely overwhelm their animals with a huge amount of the substance they are testing as a possible food. One teacher helped his class to understand the problem by drawing a simple stick-figure of a boy on the chalkboard. He asked one of the children to draw a sandwich of an appropriate size in the boy's hand. He suggested next that the boy might be starving so he would need a bigger sandwich. The children agreed that one twice as big would probably fill the boy. Then the teacher drew a dot on the board the size of the largest of the pond water animals that the children had seen. How big should this animal's food be? The class quickly realized that they had been feeding their animals much too much.

Similarly, one teacher pointed out that people eat bread, but a person might very well die if he were suddenly covered up with a roomful of bread crumbs. People eat beef, but if you tried to prove this by putting a person in a room with a living cow and watching them for a few minutes (or even a month), you probably wouldn't learn that people eat beef! Perhaps too much food clogs the water and suffocates the animals. Perhaps the food is not in a form in which the animals can eat it. In addition, the food may rot, and the mold or bacteria growing on it may deprive the other pond water organisms of air.

It might be interesting to ask the children what they think the animals ate when they lived in the pond. This is a tough question. Don't expect your class to have any very precise answers, but by watching their animals, they should at least begin to understand the complex relationships that make up the life of a pond. Large animals usually eat smaller ones; small ones eat yet smaller ones; and the tiniest animals eat tiny plants (algae). Of course many of the larger animals eat living plants, too, and a great many of the animals eat dead and decaying plants and animals. Where do the children think plants get their food?

In spite of such difficult questions, children are remarkably able and inventive at designing and redesigning experiments to prove a point. Here is a situation that took place in a trial class: the children wanted to find out whether a pond snail can move when it is out of water. One girl, Susan, said she had tried it. She put the snail on a dry slide and it went slowly—slower than on a wet slide. Joe said he had also tried an experiment. He had put a snail on a paper towel and had found that it went faster than on something wet. How could they find out which was right? Someone suggested that the snail moved faster on the paper towel because it had something to grab onto. Tom objected that snails don't have hands, so this one couldn't grab; but several others in the class countered this objection with their own observations: it didn't have hands, but it did have suction cups or some such thing that allowed it to stick to things.

Soon someone suggested that they measure the speed of the snail—they would need some kind of timer. There was also the problem of space. Maybe Susan's snail didn't go very fast because it didn't have enough room. Ray suggested that they make a line a foot long and time the snail as it went along the line. Then they could put water along the line and time the snail again. Would the snail go in a straight line? Dick thought it wouldn't, but you could measure the track it made to see how far it went. Tony made elaborate plans for constructing a track which would force the snail to go in a straight line, but he had forgotten one thing—the snail could go up, too. Linda suggested a tube, but this met the same objections—the snail could still crawl around inside the tube. Tom's proposed track seemed to take care of all the objections: he would take a narrow piece of cardboard, just wider than the snail, and coat the edges with some kind of slippery stuff so the snail couldn't go off it. He'd put the snail on this track and time it. Then he'd put water on the track and time the snail again.

All the children felt that to be really sure, you'd have to time the same snail on the same kind of surface, first wet and then dry. There was some feeling that maybe Susan's original snail was different from Joe's and that was why they went at different speeds. Several children were dissatisfied with the original experiments and kept saying throughout the discussion that the whole thing should be tried again before there was any more talk. About half the class volunteered to do the experiments at home during the next week. These are just the kinds of discussions you should encourage, for they can lead the children to design better experiments.

Some other children became interested in what a snail eats besides dead leaves and animals that it finds naturally in the pond. One little girl, Diane, undertook some experiments and then reported her results to the class. She said she had tried bread crumbs, but the snail didn't eat them, so she didn't think it liked bread crumbs. Enrique was not satisfied with this report, however. He asked Diane how many bread crumbs she had tried. He thought that she should try feeding it just one bread crumb, place the crumb right in the snail's path, and then see if it was there after the snail had gone over it. If it wasn't there and it wasn't sticking to the snail anywhere, she could conclude that it had eaten the crumb. Diane had also tried feeding the snail instant cocoa. She said she thought it ate it, since it left a clear path in the cocoa where it had passed. Other children objected, however, that the snail might just have pushed the cocoa out of the way, or the cocoa might be sticking to the snail and not have been eaten at all. They agreed that they couldn't really tell, because the cocoa was about the same color as the snail.

No one in the class suggested leaving the snail in a container with something like bread crumbs for several hours. Everyone expected the snail to eat immediately when given food. If it didn't, the children supposed that the snail didn't like the particular food. They seemed to forget about their own variable appetites.

During the course of the unit, the children will probably notice the change in number of different kinds of animals from one week to the next. Why should the ostracods, which were present in all the jars in one class by the "millions" during the third week become so rare that nobody can find any by the end of the fifth week? Where did all the worms come from that were first noticed in the fourth week? You should encourage the children to discuss these changes and their relation to the changes that occur in natural ponds. Ask them if they think the pond has changed since they collected their water and animals. If they become interested in this question, encourage them to go back to the same pond (possibly on a week-end) and get some more water, and then to compare what they can find in both collections. Perhaps you will want to arrange a class field trip again.

Do the children realize that some animals eat others? In the children's small containers it is possible for one kind of animal to wipe out another kind completely in a very short time. Try to get the children to understand what the life of a small animal is like. Could the changes in the containers be caused by animals running out of food, or being eaten by another animal, or getting sick and dying? Everything has to eat. What happens if the food spoils? What if the water is too hot for the animals to live in? What happens in the natural pond? It is essential that the children begin to wonder about the answers to these questions, since they are basic to a broader perception of the natural lives of each of the pond water creatures they are observing.

Some of the children may want to try experiments to see what will happen to their small aquariums if they are not kept cool or left in a light place. If they do such experiments, they will probably kill many of their animals, but they will learn a lot about the conditions necessary for healthy pond life. They may want to investigate why it is important for their aquariums to be placed out of direct sunlight. Why must the tops be left off the containers whenever possible? Why is a dark closet a bad place in which to keep an aquarium? Some children may want to put some pond water in different places around the room. They can try placing aquariums on the window sill, in sunlight, on a radiator, in a closet, and on a table in a cool, but bright part of the room. It might be interesting to take two containers of pond water from the same pond and leave them both in the same place, sealing only one tightly with a cover and leaving the other open. What differences can be observed in the two aquariums?

What other experiments can your class devise? Some of the questions that have been asked by children are listed below:

Can snails live in tap water?

Can a pond water animal live in a mixture of pond water and tap water?

Are green "porcupines" (ostracods) green because they eat plants?

Can pond water animals live alone?

How do pond water animals react if you put mold in with them?

Do pond water animals sleep?

Can pond water animals live in ocean water?

Can different-sized animals of the same kind survive the same conditions?

How do the animals react when orange juice, chocolate, Kool Aid, bread, grass, or milk is added to a child's aquarium?

Can the animals live in water containing soap, detergent, or DDT?

How do the animals breathe?

What happens to the animals when they die?

Do pond water animals like heat? How much can they stand?

Can pond water animals live in ice? If not, how do they survive the winter?

Do snail eggs hatch sooner in the cold or heat?

Can Cyclops see?

Do pond water animals change as they grow older?

Do these animals have blood?

Do pond water animals have bones?

Do the animals communicate with each other? If so, how?

How can we tell if something is a plant or an animal?

How can we group the animals?

Who are the friends and enemies of a particular animal? Of all the pond animals?

How fast can a snail walk?

Can any pond water animals live without water?

Would a pond water animal eat mold if it had no other food?

Do pond water animals need to be uncovered?

Can the animals live in other gases than air?

How do the animals multiply?

Can pond water animals live if you take all the dirt and plants out of the water by filtering?

2. SCIENCE—A PROCESS APPROACH LESSON: LOSS OF MOISTURE FROM POTATOES

Pieces of potato which have been placed in different environments serve as the interest arouser for this exercise. Working in groups the children are given three different containers each of which has a piece of potato in it. The children are to observe the three containers, to ask questions which may be answered by "yes" or "no," and to formulate some ideas about what they have seen.

The objectives are for the children to:

1. Identify the variables held constant and the manipulated variable from the description of a test in which moisture evaporates from fruits or vegetables.

2. Identify the responding variable from the description of a test in which moisture evaporates from fruits or vegetables.

3. Describe data in response to questions about the loss of moisture from fruits or vegetables.

Referring back to the previous exercise as well as to the observations and inferences they have just made, the children are asked to identify possible variables which might affect the amount of moisture lost by the potatoes. The possible factors are listed on the chalkboard, and the children working in groups are asked to identify which variables they would decide to include in an environment for their investigation. The groups then plan an exact test of one of the questions which have been listed on the board. The questions have come out of the earlier discussion; however, each group will need to identify which variables they will control.

The children then carry out the investigations making the necessary recording of their observations. At the end of approximately one week, the investigations can be concluded and each group is then asked to interpret the data it has collected.

Based on the conclusions which are on the board, the children are then asked to decide what they would do to a potato in order to have the greatest loss of moisture in the shortest time and what they would do to completely prevent the loss of moisture from the potato.

Both a group and individual competency measures are provided as a means for assessing student ability to demonstrate the desired performances for the exercise. In both cases the learner(s) are asked to consider an investigation which has been done and then to identify the manipulated, constant, and responding variables as well as to interpret some of the data.

From *Science—A Process Approach* (1968), Part E, Exercise q, p. 1. Reprinted by permission of the American Association for the Advancement of Science, Washington, D.C.

3. SCIENCE CURRICULUM IMPROVEMENT STUDY LESSON: INTERACTION

"Inventing" the Interaction Concept

A brief review of the children's earlier experiments sets the stage for the invention. You then introduce and illustrate the concept that objects interact when they do something to each other. Children observe and describe changes that occur during the demonstration experiments. They also interpret pictures of interacting objects in the student manual and later draw their own pictures. Plan to use one or two class periods. Optional activities by individuals or small groups may take extra time. . . .

For Demonstration Purposes:

1 spring

1 support stand

2 carts
vinegar in squeeze bottle
concentrated bromothymol blue solution (BTB) in squeeze bottle

1 large magnet

3 tumblers

1 pitcher (to be filled with water)

1 pail

1 tray of objects
paper towel (provided by the teacher)

ADVANCE PREPARATION

Prepare some materials. . . for review domonstrations. You might use the light bulb, wire, and a tested battery; water and an unused "mystery picture"; and a 3″×5″ card and scissors. For the first new demonstration, you will need one cart, the spring, and the support stand. Set up the support stand and hang the spring from the screw eye.

Another demonstration employs the large magnet and the second cart. Remove the keeper bar from the magnet by twisting it. Put the cart on a level surface. Practice attracting the cart with the magnet by holding the magnet above and in front of either end of the cart. Keep withdrawing the magnet so the cart does not catch up with it as it rolls forward. You may also use the magnet to pick the cart up by its axles.

The last experiment is demonstrated after the interaction concept has been introduced. It employs separate, dilute solutions of bromothymol blue dye (BTB) and vinegar. The dilute solutions are prepared by squeezing three or four drops of each liquid into separate tumblers, each about one-third full of water. When these solutions are poured into a third container, the dye turns

From Science Curriculum Improvement Study, *Interaction and Systems,* Teacher's Guide (Chicago: Rand McNally & Company, 1970), pp. 34–38.

yellow. Try it. The BTB solution should be blue, but if your tap water is slightly acid, the BTB solution will appear green. In that case use distilled water for the experiment.

TEACHING SUGGESTIONS

Review and Demonstrations

To establish a familiar context for the invention that follows, use a group of objects from Chapter 4 to demonstrate an experiment. Or, a child might demonstrate his experiment, using page 1 in his manual to remind him of the objects needed. Hold up the objects and ask the children what changes are occurring during the experiment. If they seem not to understand the question, describe the change yourself—for example, "The bulb is now lit." Then proceed to one or two other experiments and ask again about the changes that occur.

New demonstrations

Next, you may perform one or two of the new demonstrations you have prepared. First, identify one cart and the spring as the objects to which the children should pay special attention. Ask the children to watch closely as you hang the cart from the spring. Remove and reattach the cart two or three times, so everyone has a chance to notice that the spring stretches. Briefly discuss the changes that occur and then set the objects aside, after taking the cart off the spring.

Second, pick out the magnet and the other cart and use the magnet to attract the cart several times as you did before. Again, ask the children what changes they notice.

Invention

By now, you and the class have observed and discussed the changes that took place during several experiments. Tell the children, while indicating one set of objects with your hand, that you will use the word interact whenever objects do something to each other, as in the case of the cart and the spring. Write interact on the chalkboard and let the children pronounce it.

Illustrate the meaning of the word interact by repeating some of the earlier demonstrations. Ask the children to identify moments when the objects are interacting and also moments when they are not interacting. Finally, invite them to describe their evidence. As an example of objects that interact, firmly hold the cart and the magnet so close to one another that you can feel the attraction even though you do not let them come together. Let the children see you "straining" to keep them apart as you ask them about interaction. (This example illustrates interaction-at-a-distance, which will be introduced by name in Part Six.)

After this explanation, tell the children that you will show them another system of objects that can interact. Display three tumblers on a paper towel and prepare separate dilute solutions of BTB and of vinegar in two of them. Ask the children to watch carefully as you mix the liquids by pouring them into the third tumbler. Let them describe the changes they observe. Do they interpret these to mean that the liquids interacted while you poured them together?

Follop-up Experiments

Encourage all the children to experiment with the support stand, the spring, a plastic tumbler with a string handle taped on (to serve as a container for weighing crayons and other objects at the end of the spring), the magnet, and the cart. You may leave these on the class science table for a few days. (See the "Optional Activities" section for suggested experiments.) . . .

The children may draw pictures. . . . As you review the pictures, look for understanding of the interaction concept. If you find that some children draw objects after (or before), rather than while the objects interact, ask them to describe the evidence that the objects interacted and add "after" (or "before") to their drawings. Children who make this kind of error apparently find it difficult to focus their attention on one instant of time in a quickly changing phenomenon, as when a bat hits a ball. They may need additional explanations emphasizing the time aspect by your calling attention to the "before" phase (the ball comes to the bat), the "during" phase (the bat hits the ball), and the "after" phase (the ball flies away).

OPTIONAL ACTIVITIES

Interaction Bulletin Board

We encounter interacting objects on all sides: our feet and the floor interact when we walk, our hands, pencils, and paper interact when we write; our teeth and food interact when we eat. Have the children find and clip magazine illustrations that show objects interacting or after they have interacted. They can display their clippings on a bulletin board titled "Objects Interact." Either you or your pupils should write the names of the interacting objects under each picture, or the objects may be circled. Some of the children should identify the evidence that the pictured objects interacted.

Feed back

Invite individuals or small groups of children to identify interacting objects in a magazine picture. How many different groups do they pick out? And how do they respond when you ask them to explain why they think these objects are interacting?

Bromothymol Blue Interaction with Vinegar.

Your pupils will probably want to know more about BTB and vinegar. Show them the squeeze bottles and let them smell the vinegar. Repeat the experiments with variations the children suggest and allow them to participate. Pour waste solutions into the plastic pail. The children may want to use various ratios of the solutions such as much or little vinegar, or water without vinegar.

Note: A very small amount of vinegar will change the color of the BTB. Mix the dye with water, therefore, in tumblers that have been washed carefully or have never contained vinegar. You may even find it useful to label the tumbler you reserve for the bromothymol blue. If the blue color unexpectedly turns to green or yellow, the change is evidence that the container was contaminated with vinegar. You might purposely "stage" such a surprise and challenge the children to explain it.

Testing with Bromothymol Blue

Ask the children to bring samples from home to test with the BTB. Salt, sugar, baking powder, lemon juice, milk, pickle juice, detergents, liquid fertilizer, ammonia, and other materials can be grouped or listed according to how they interact with the dye. Children may also test two or more of these materials, one after another, with the same sample of BTB. They should use a dilute solution of the dye, perhaps from a storage jar you provide. If you need additional BTB, you may be able to obtain it from a local high school chemistry teacher or from a swimming-pool supply dealer.

Caution: Supervise these experiments to insure that the materials are properly handled. Be sure to dispense the concentrated BTB yourself. If the dye is spilled, rinse the spot with water or alcohol. It may stain some materials.

Spring Scale

The spring suspended from the support stand can be used to "weigh" objects that are held by it directly or in a hanging plastic tumbler. Encourage the children to invent a way to compare the weights of various objects.

4. SCIENCE CURRICULUM IMPROVEMENT STUDY LESSON: SYSTEMS TO INVESTIGATE

"Inventing" the Subsystems Concept

Through a demonstration using the sifting mixture in one container and also in separate parts, you introduce the subsystems concept. Then you gather feedback as your pupils identify subsystems in your demonstration and in the classroom. In the first discovery activity your pupils work further with the powdered mixture, which interacts with yellow BTB solution, turning it blue. The children then experiment to determine whether all or only part of the mixture is responsible for the color change. This chapter should take one class period.

For Each Team of Three Children

3 sets of sifting equipment

3 plastic cups

2 tumblers

1 magnifier

3 cardboard trays

For the Class

1 jar containing sifting mixture

1 squeeze bottle of bromothymol blue solution

From Science Curriculum Improvement Study, *Subsystems and Variables,* Teacher's Guide (Chicago: Rand McNally & Company, 1970), pp. 40–43.

1 bottle of vinegar

1 pitcher to be filled with water

1 plastic spoon

1 vial

1 tumbler

2 cardboard trays

ADVANCE PREPARATION

Clean the sifting equipment and supply replacements for items that have been consumed. Assemble the equipment for convenient distribution to the teams. Pour some sifting mixture into the tumbler for your demonstration.

TEACHING SUGGESTIONS

Invention

Show your pupils the tumbler with the sifting mixture and invite them to identify the materials contained in it. Then put a vial into the tumbler in your hand and designate the tumbler, the mixture in it, and the vial as System Mix (or a name proposed by your pupils). Now pour a little of the solid mixture into the vial and set it and the tumbler on a tray you can hold up. Remind the children that all the objects on the tray together make up System Mix, but point out that they might now think of them as two systems, and let them suggest names for these. Finally, explain that these two systems are parts of System Mix and that they are called subsystems. Write the word on the chalkboard.

Feedback

Invite the children to find other subsystems of System Mix. They may refer to one of the materials in the mixture (the salt alone, the sand alone), they may select the two containers (the vial alone and tumbler), or they may make other choices. Ask them also to name systems of interacting objects that are not subsystems of System Mix. One of these might consist of your hand and the tray, another of the tumbler and the tray. The children's ideas here will let you know how well they understand the subsystems concept. If they have difficulty selecting subsystems, give another example. For instance, designate a bulletin board as the system; point out one display as a subsystem and invite students to find other subsystems. Then ask them to find systems that are not subsystems of the bulletin board. Or suggest the Subsystems and Variables equipment kit as the system, with each drawer being a subsystem.

Powdered Mixture and Yellow BTB

With the children watching and some of them assisting, prepare yellow BTB solution. To do so, put two or three squirts of concentrated BTB into the pitcher of water, stir, then add a very small amount of vinegar, and stir again. Pour a little of this yellow liquid into the vial with the solid mixture. The color of the liquid will change to blue. Ask the children to describe briefly the evidence of interaction and to speculate about the interacting objects.

The problem now is this: Does the entire mixture interact to produce the color change, or do only some subsystems interact with the solution and turn it blue? Let your pupils suggest experiments to find subsystems that leave the liquid yellow. . . .

To prepare for later comparison of the children's findings, write the question "Which subsystems leave the BTB yellow?" on the board, and make three columns labeled sand, salt, and soda. Eventually, you may either total the number of children finding various results, or each child may write yes or no as his answer in each column as soon as he finds out.

Children's Experiment

Show your pupils one set of the prepared equipment and explain how it will be used by the team. The three children on each team will share a magnifier, a supply of yellow BTB solution in a tumbler, and an empty tumbler for disposing of waste liquid after the test. Each team member will have his own tray, a vial with mixture, cloth screens, construction-paper squares, and a plastic cup into which he will put the BTB. You may encourage each team to test a different subsystem, or the members may prefer to work individually. Warn them to rinse their cups between tests so there is no material left over to confuse their observations.

Then distribute the trays to the teams. While they are sifting the mixture, pour the yellow BTB solution into one tumbler for each team. As you walk among your pupils, encourage them to record the names of the materials and their findings in their manuals and on the board. You may have to supply additional yellow BTB solution occasionally—it may be used up, or a team may contaminate it.

Discussion

Begin a discussion after all children have completed their tests. Ask the children to raise their hands so you may count and record the yes and no indications for each column on the board, or merely count the children's reports if they have written their findings on the board already. A clear consensus may or may not emerge from the data. The findings for soda and sand are usually quite clear (changes BTB to blue and leaves it yellow, respectively), but the salt findings are often ambiguous. Let some children explain how their procedures might have led to disagreement. At the conclusion of the discussion, ask your pupils to think carefully about all the findings and to write. . .what they now believe about the subsystems that leave the BTB yellow.

OPTIONAL ACTIVITIES

Subsystems Hunt

A Subsystems Hunt can be carried out with many variations. For instance, you can designate an aquarium or terrarium in your classroom a system and have the children identify objects and subsystems in that system. Illustrations in the children's textbooks can be used similarly.

Subsystems Mural

Perhaps the class could plan to draw a mural on a well-defined theme such as the school playground or the circus. Then all the objects together can form a system, and the children can draw them to constitute various subsystems. It is important that the mural be formed around a single theme so all the objects can logically be grouped as one system.

Vinegar and the Powdered Mixture

If your pupils enjoyed the investigation to determine which part of the powdered mixture interacted with yellow BTB to turn it blue, they may be interested in a similar study in which the same mixture interacts with large quantities of vinegar. To demonstrate what happens, put two teaspoons of the powdered mixture and an uncapped vial full of vinegar into a small plastic bag. Be careful that the vial does not tip and spill prematurely. Then squeeze the air out of the bag and close it with a wire tie about an inch from the vial. Now tip the vial to pour the vinegar into the bag. It will interact with the mixture to produce a froth of bubbles and will slowly inflate the bag.

The children's problem now is to determine whether the entire mixture or only one subsystem interacted with the vinegar to produce the bubbles. They may again experiment in teams sharing a common supply of vinegar. We suggest that when they conduct their tests they use a medicine dropper to put a few drops of vinegar on the material to be tested while it is on the construction paper. For record keeping, supply a student page similar to page 9 but adapted to the new problem.

5. MINNEMAST LESSON: PLANTS

Planting Corn

Conduct this lesson on a Thursday. Prepare for it by soaking overnight sweet corn kernels (three per child and a few spares) and a few kernels of other kinds of corn, such as popcorn, calico corn or field corn.

In Activity A each child will plant three pre-soaked sweet corn kernels in a small container of sand or soil in order to have at least one healthily growing plant to tend, observe, describe and measure during the next two weeks. Soaking the corn kernels speeds up germination, so that by Monday each child should have one measurable plant.

The diversity of Activity B depends on what materials you can provide. It is desirable that the children experiment by planting some unsoaked kernels of sweet corn, by planting a few other kinds of corn for comparison, by testing growth in soil against that in sand, and by seeing how a corn plant grows (1) in the dark, (2) in extreme heat and (3) in drought.

Rather full discussions precede and follow the plantings. Suggestions are given in the activities for the direction of these discussions, but the children should contribute as much as they can to each. You may also wish to have

From MINNEMAST, *Comparing Changes*, pp. 8–14. Copyright 1944 by the Regents of the University of Minnesota.

them draw pictures of what they think their seeds will become, and later of the plants as they see them.

Corn is a very important American crop. It is processed in many ways, some of which are familiar to children (corn bread, corn flakes, corn syrup, popcorn). Corn has an interesting history, too; and it has sometimes been used as a decoration in North and South American architecture. You may wish to take advantage of the children's interest in their corn plants by having them investigate some of these areas in their social studies (Optional Activity C) during the weeks they are observing and measuring their corn plants....

ACTIVITY A

Have the children speculate about what will grow from a sweet corn kernel, how large it will get, how long it will take to reach a certain size, and so on. Let them do most of the talking, but focus their attention on several ideas:

1. Many things change from day to day.

2. Living things change in a way we call growing—which means to become larger in some way.

3. Plants are alive and grow.

Then ask the children how they could find out how much the seeds will grow and how they will change. They should suggest planting the corn and observing the growing plants.

When the children have suggested planting, ask them to think about what would make up a plant-growing system. They should be able to say that sand or soil, water, and light or warmth are necessary parts of such a system.

Now give the children a container of sand or soil and a label. Have each child print his name or initials on the label and paste it on the container.

Show the children how to plant their seeds by pushing the seeds down about one-quarter to one-half inch below the surface of the sand, then smoothing the sand over the top. (If the seeds are buried too deeply, the seedling may take longer to reach the surface. A good depth for planting is about equal to the thickness of the seed.)

After the seeds have been planted, ask the children how they could keep the sand moist over the weekend. Then have each child place plastic wrap loosely over the top of the container so that the sand will not dry out.

On the chalkboard, make a record: Soaked sweet corn kernels planted by all students, Thursday, Jan. 5.

Now ask the children where the containers should be placed. (Lead them to choose a shelf or table out of the sun.)

Finally, ask the children to make predictions about what will happen to the seeds they planted. Have them speculate how quickly the plants may grow in the different pots and suggest factors (water, sunlight, warmth, the quality of the seeds themselves) which might affect the rate of growth.

ACTIVITY B

In this activity you want the children in each group to use as much ingenuity as they can in thinking of an experiment to do with the seeds. If the children have trouble thinking of plant experiments by themselves, ask them why you soaked the sweet corn kernels which they planted. If the children have no theories, suggest that one group plant some unsoaked seeds as an experiment. Elicit that all the other conditions of the planting must be the same.

Other Suggestions

Ask the children to speculate about how popcorn might look as it grows. Will it be as large a plant as the sweet corn? How can they find out? Have them plant some.

Many plants grow in the desert. What is a desert like? (It is hot and dry.) Do you think popcorn would grow there? How can we find out? Guide the children to plant some popcorn and place it on a radiator.

When you planted your sweet corn kernels, why did I ask you to keep them out of the direct sunlight at first? Does too much heat from the sunlight prevent the kernels from sprouting as quickly? Does it prevent them from sprouting at all? Have the children set up an experiment to find out.

How will darkness affect a seedling's growth? Have the children do some plantings and cover each container with a paper bag. They may be astonished at what happens. The corn seedling may grow very fast at first, especially if it is warm under the bags, but later—though they may continue to grow tall— they will become pale and sickly from the lack of light. Do not tell the children this; let them find out by observing their experiments. No record sheets are provided for the experiments of this activity, but you can help the children keep track of what they have done by marking the containers and by writing the data on the chalkboard.

ACTIVITY C (OPTIONAL)

Reading, writing and art lessons may be used to take advantage of the children's interest in their plants. . . . The children might like to talk about their own experiences with house and garden plants, or try some plant experiments at home. . . .

The preceding are some ways of approaching the teaching of cause and effect to children. By now you should have an understanding of the difference between manipulated, responding, and constant variables, as well as some ideas on how to aid children in acquiring this understanding.

At this time check your own skill of identifying the various kinds of variables.

Posttest

For this test you will need a supply of baking powder, an eyedropper, and something to clean up with, for instance paper towels.

Begin by making observations of the baking powder, including what happens to it when water is added.

Observations:

1. _____

2. _____

3. _____

4. _____

5. _____

Your observations could have included white, powder, no sound, tastes bitter, bubbles when water is added.

If you were going to study the effect of the addition of water on bubbling, what would be three controlled variables, the manipulated variable, and the responding variable?

Controlled variables

_____

_____

_____

Manipulated variable

_____

Responding variable

_____

Acceptable Responses for Posttest

Three controlled variables are: (1) the amount of baking powder used, (2) the source of water (such as distilled), and (3) the distance from which the water is dropped in to the baking powder. The manipulated variable is the number of drops of water added and the responding variable is the amount of bubbling that occurrs.

If you find that you are having difficulty, either discuss this with your instructor or recycle yourself through this chapter.

9. Defining Terms

By the end of this chapter you should be able to construct operational definitions for terms and objects employed in doing an experiment or in your everyday life.

Check Yourself Now. If you can successfully perform this task, you should omit this part of the chapter and go to page 212.

No additional materials will be needed for this task.

Write an operational definition for the term *pencil sharpener.*

Now look at the discussion of acceptable responses for this pretest.

Acceptable Responses for the Pretest

Your definition of pencil sharpener should have included a description of (a) what would be done and (b) what would be observed. One definition of pencil sharpener is:

Place a pencil in the hole, turn the crank several turns, then pull the pencil out. The pencil will be sharpened.

Language is the basis for communication between men. Both printed and spoken language can be very precise or very vague in communicating a message. Precision in the use of words is often quite difficult. Government leaders have experts to check every word of a speech to insure that the ideas being communicated are those the author intends.

Scientists, as well as politicians, have to be careful in their use of words. In many instances both will define a term before they use it. The resulting definition is generally referred to as an *operational definition.*

Operational definitions have two basic components. The first component is a description of what is done to the subject or thing being defined and the second component is a description of what is observed or what happens as a result of what is done.

The following activities will help you in developing the skill of defining terms using operational definitions.

Activity 1 :   Detergent, cereal, and cooking oil.

For this activity you will need a cereal box, a detergent box or liquid-detergent container, and a cooking-oil container. You do not need the cereal, detergent, and cooking oil. What you do need are the labels on the containers.

One group in our society that has specialized in avoiding the use of operational definitions is the advertising world. Observe the labels on the three containers that you have and write down a total of ten terms that you find on the labels that leave plenty of room for interpretation or that are downright vague.

Detergent label	Cereal box	Cooking-oil container
_____	_____	_____
_____	_____	_____
_____	_____	_____
_____		

The following are some likely terms to be found on these containers.

Detergent label	Cereal box	Cooking-oil container
New	Bite size	High in polyunsaturates
Spotless	Family size	Pure
5¢ off	Economy size	Artificially flavored
Approved by leading manufacturers		

Think about the kind of meaning that each of these terms gives to the product buyer as compared to what the term *really* tells the buyer. For example, take the term "5¢ off." The product buyer immediately thinks that the price has been reduced 5 cents below the normal retail price. However, it is just as likely that the 5 cents off price *is* the normal retail price. What is not clear is what is the 5¢ off?

The same problem arises with a term like "pure." Pure what? Pure cereal, pure brand X soap, including its various ingredients? Even the quantified term "99-94/100% pure" does not tell you *what* it is that is pure.

Each of these terms needs to be operationally defined. Perhaps the advertising agencies should be required to publish a dictionary in which terms of this type are operationally defined.

An operational definition has two parts generally, indicating (1) what is done to the object and (2) what is observed as a result. It is not easy to operationally define terms; however, with practice the skill can be developed. You may find the ability to operationally define terms very helpful in your attempts to communicate to others.

Here is one possible operational definition of the term "new."

Any product which is packaged on or after January 1, 1975, will be labeled "new" and the package will have the date of packaging clearly stamped on it.

The definition might appeal to you as a consumer but the manufacturer probably would prefer the following definition.

For the first three years of production of a newly developed product the package labeling shall include the term "new." If dates are to be included on the package, they should be in code which defies interpretation.

Now construct operational definitions of the terms you found on your packages.

1. Detergent

_____ : _____
_____
_____
_____ : _____
_____
_____
_____ : _____
_____
_____
_____ : _____
_____
_____

2. Cereal

_____ : _____
_____
_____
_____ : _____
_____
_____
_____ : _____
_____
_____
_____ : _____
_____

3. Cooking Oil

_____ : _____
                 _____
                 _____
                 _____

_____ : _____
                 _____
                 _____
                 _____

_____ : _____
                 _____
                 _____
                 _____

_____ : _____
                 _____
                 _____
                 _____

The following are possible definitions for the sample terms listed on page 204.

1. Detergent

Spotless: When a clean dish is quickly dipped into three gallons of water at 93°C in which five millimeters of detergent have been evenly distributed, then no spots will form on the surface of the dish as the water-detergent solution on the dish evaporates.

Approved by leading manufacturers: From the list of manufacturers of washing machines compiled by the League of Small Businesses, the manufacturers who were willing to put a sample of Brand X detergent in their washing machines were considered as those who approved of Brand X detergent.

2. Cereal

Bite Size: One of the pieces just covers the surface of a teaspoon and can be passed without breaking through a circular hole of six-centimeter diameter.

Family Size: One of the pieces provides the equivalent amount of nutrition that would normally be eaten by a family of parakeets, consisting of one adult male, one adult female and one two-week baby during a twenty-four hour period.

Economy Size: One of the pieces provides the equivalent amount of nutrition consumption for a twenty-four hour period that would normally be eaten by one two-week old parakeet.

3. Cooking Oil

High in polyunsaturates: By quantitative analysis there is a larger percentage (51%) of polyunsaturates than there is of saturates.

Artificially flavored: For each gallon of banana juice, five gallons of hyperexol, which tastes exactly like banana juice, are added.

The above shows one way in which the terms could be operationally defined. Your definitions will probably be different. Anyway, in each case there should be a description of what was done and what could be observed.

Activity 2 : **Boiling Water**

You will not need any additional materials for this activity.

In science experiments, many terms need to be operationally defined. Once an experiment has been done, another person should be able to replicate the experiment exactly. In order to make this possible, there has to be clarity in communication.

Which terms in this hypothesis do you think would need to be operationally defined ?

Hypothesis: Salted water boils faster than unsalted water.

_____ _____ _____

_____ _____ _____

Your list should have included salted water, boils, and unsalted water. Some questions that need answers are : How much salt ? What kind of salt ? When exactly is water boiling ? What is unsalted water ?

How would you operationally define these terms ?

Salted water: _____

_____

_____

Boils: _____

_____

_____

Unsalted water: _____

_____

_____

The following is one way to define each of the terms :

Salted Water: One quart of water from the tap to which have been added three teaspoons of table salt.

Boils: The point at which the total surface of the water is no longer smooth but has bubbles.

Unsalted Water: Water taken directly from the tap in the kitchen of my house.

Activity 3 (Optional) : **Magazine Advertising**

For this activity you will need a "nonprofessional" magazine.

Magazine advertisements form another rich area for terms that need defining. Randomly pick up a nonprofessional magazine and read over the advertisements. You should be able to readily make a list of ten terms that are vague. Then operationally define the terms. You can define them in humorous ways if you wish ; just remember the necessary components of an operational definition.

_____ : _____

_____

_____

_____ : _____
                 _____
                 _____
_____ : _____
                 _____
                 _____
_____ : _____
                 _____
                 _____
_____ : _____
                 _____
                 _____
_____ : _____
                 _____
                 _____
_____ : _____
                 _____
                 _____
_____ : _____
                 _____
                 _____
_____ : _____
                 _____
                 _____
_____ : _____
                 _____
                 _____

For a check, read over your definition to see (1) what you would do and (2) what you would observe. The following are a couple of additional samples taken from some of the same journals.

Tastes tremendous: In the first five seconds after tasting, the tongue burns and then becomes numb, your mouth stops secreting additional saliva (it becomes dry), the carbon monoxide count in the bloodstream goes up, brain cells start having oxygen deficiency, the eyes dilate, and the lungs burn.

Lower in tar and nicotine: In comparison to the amount of tar and nicotine found in one three-inch long, half-inch diameter cigar, one of these cigarettes has one quarter less tar and nicotine.

Note: The following term was found in an advertisement for an automobile engine-oil additive and also for a perfume.

High performance additive   (engine oil) : One 4-cylinder engine was found to gain

3 DIN horsepower at 4,735 rpm when six ounces of this product are added to ten gallons of 96-octane gasoline.

The operational definition when referring to a perfume is left to you.

High performance additive: (perfume)

Developers of many of the new science curricula have given considerable thought to precision in the child's use of terms. The curriculum developers did not come up with a unanimous decision. Some of the curricula make practically no reference to operational definitions, whereas others place heavy emphasis on aiding students to develop skill in operationally defining terms.

The developers of *Science—A Process Approach* have established "defining operationally" as one of the integrated process skills for the curriculum. The following reading is a description of the process of "defining operationally" as defined by them.

Words are the currency of much human communication, and it is through verbal exchange, either written or oral, that much of our teaching and learning occurs. Our basic philosophy is that effective learning takes place when the student is actively involved in developing the process skills that form the central theme of the material he is studying. In all the processes, teacher-pupil and pupil-pupil interaction are vitally dependent on the precise use of terms. Competence in defining operationally is of critical importance in the precise use of terms in communication about investigations and experiments.

A measure of the cultural level of a society lies in the sophistication of its vocabulary; the extent of the application of that vocabulary contributes to the continuation and advancement of that society. In fact, as the complexity of societal operations increases, so does the use of more and more specialized words and terms. In our own society, we find that specialized groups—whether they be nuclear physicists or hippies—develop their own "jargon." The meanings of existing words may be changed by such groups to express entirely different ideas. It is in this context of communication and change, then, that defining operationally takes on its significance as a process skill. In *Defining Operationally*, the pupils will be expected to define terms in the context of their own experiences.

A definition that limits the number of things to be considered, and, at the same time, specifies the essential experimental evidence to be gathered is more useful than a definition that encompasss all the conceivable variations that might be encountered. More than one operational definition may be in a particular situation; you should encourage children to propose and use alternative definitions.[1]

---

[1] *Science—A Process Approach,* Commentary For Teachers (1968), p. 163. Reprinted by permission of the American Association for the Advancement of Science, Washington, D.C.

The developers of the Science Curriculum Improvement Study also considered the problem of defining terms and its relevance to science for the elementary school child.

Precision of definition and expression are important to science. When terms are defined precisely, scientists can communicate with each other. Of perhaps greater importance, precise statements make it possible for scientists to check each other's findings and to build upon the work of others. Operational definitions are a means for more precise communication in science.

It is important that children begin to use terms more precisely. Throughout the SCIS elementary science program, they will be asked to define terms operationally. In this chapter the nature of operational definitions and how they are used in science is described, and some specific examples of how operational definitions are used in the SCIS program are discussed.

THE NATURE OF OPERATIONAL DEFINITIONS

An operational definition includes instructions for the operations carried out in the process of defining. Terms are defined through the performing of operations. Let us see how two terms, "right angle" and "yellow," can be defined operationally.

We can operationally define a right angle by saying: "A right angle is the angle made when we first fold a piece of paper in half one way, and then, keeping it still folded, double it over the other way. We then open up the paper and lay it flat. The intersecting creases in the middle of the page form four right angles." By holding this piece of paper against angles in the room formed by corners, table legs, etc., we can determine which ones are right angles.

We can define yellow as "the color of a ripe lemon." In this instance we assume you know what "ripe" means. It should be mentioned, however, that if we were to operationally define "ripe lemon," we would have to use a gauge other than color (taste, for example) to avoid having a circular rather than an operational definition.

Nearby objects can be held against this ripe lemon until we find something whose color resembles that of the lemon. In this way we use a concrete example of something yellow as the standard of "yellowness" and measure other objects against it.

Operational Measurement Systems

Operational measurement systems are based upon such arbitrarily defined quantities as length, mass, and time. A standard unit of length is the *meter* which was once based on the length of a metal bar kept in the International Bureau of Weights and Measures in France. The standard is now based on the wavelength of the orange red light emitted by a krypton 86 lamp. The *kilogram* is a standard unit of mass and it is a platinum-iridium cylinder carefully kept in the International Bureau of Weights and Measures. A standard unit of time is the *second,* once operationally defined as 1/86, 400 of a mean solar day. Recently, it has been more precisely defined in terms of a transition of the cesium 133 atom. These units are independent of each other, and a change in the size of one will not affect the size of the others.

From these basic units, units for other physical quantities can be derived. For example, the quantity density is equal to the mass divided by the volume (density = mass/volume). Mass is a basic quantity. However, volume is a derived quantity based upon measurements of length. The volume of a brick, for example, would be equal to its length times its width times its height (volume = length × width × height). All of these are measurements of length. When the mass has been measured and the volume compared from measurements of length, the density can be calculated. Thus, the quantity, density, is derived from measurements of mass and length. Similarly, the measurements of other properties and the performance characteristics of devices ranging from vacuum tubes to airplanes can be derived from the basis quantities.

Operational measurement systems are an excellent example of how a complex system of interrelationships is developed from a relatively few arbitrary units or statements. The basic units are kept static, although there is a constant effort to define these units with greater and greater precision. Other units are defined operationally by comparing them with the basic units. By a system of definitions and stated relationships, a wide range of properties and performance characteristics can be described with precision.

Operational Definitions and SCIS

Operational definitions are present in many forms in the SCIS program. First, the program operationally defines such concepts as temperature, length, area, and interaction-at-a-distance. They are defined in a broad sense in the teachers' and students' manuals and in a more specific sense in the invention and discovery lessons. The invention and discovery lessons, in turn, are tied in with the logical development of the children being taught.

In an invention lesson, a teacher will begin by taking the operational definition as given her, and carrying out its explicit instructions as a demonstration in front of the children. In this way the children are shown the definition rather than told it. The teacher may say, "Yellow is the color of this ripe lemon," and hold up the lemon. (She must also, in this case, operationally define "ripe lemon," perhaps by having a child or two taste it.) In this way the children are given a concrete example of operational definition, as well as the definition itself, in the same lesson.

The operational definitions are reinforced by the discovery lessons, where the children are asked to apply the operational definition demonstrated in the invention lesson. They use the operational definitions in experiments and other science activities.[2]

The following activities illustrate some of the ways in which developers of the recent science curricula approached definition of terms with children.

---

[2] Science Curriculum Improvement Study, *Elementary Sourcebook* (Chicago: Rand McNally & Company, 1944), pp. 58–59.

1. ELEMENTARY SCIENCE STUDY LESSON: SINK OR FLOAT

The developers of Elementary Science Study did not define processes of sequence as such and did not organize the curricula for systematic instruction and learner acquisition of predefined process skills. However, as in the following illustration, children doing ESS activities are verbalizing and refining operational definitions as normal part of their activity.

This group of activities covers a very wide range. In addition to the basic equipment, the children will probably want to draw on school and home supplies. They will want other items to sink or float (erasers, sponge, bar soap, paraffin, crayons, candles, and corks), other liquids in which to float objects (vinegar, corn syrup, pancake syrup, motor oil, linseed oil, and solutions of sugar, baking soda, or any other powder they may choose to try), and rubber cement for gluing cubes together.

Things That Sink and Things That Float

After every child has a container of water and a set of objects, you can usually start the children working by saying only, "See what you can find out."

The shapes and sizes of the objects in the kit lend themselves to stacking, so frequently the children's first activity is building towers. This is a good method for establishing the ways in which certain objects resemble or differ from others. Some children begin the work of each day by building a tower, while other children spend considerable time doing this during the initial lessons and then drop the activity.

Once they have begun to put the objects into water, children generally divide the materials into two categories—things that sink and things that float.

"These things don't float in water."
"I haven't gotten this to float."
"Only two things sank."

The greater the variety of objects available to the children, the greater will be their interest. In their explorations of things that sink and things that float, children will use all the materials at hand. Some children find they can get a great many objects to float at once—by using the plastic cups as boats.

Sinking Floaters

If a child needs some direction, you might ask if he can get the things that float to sink. After a short period of time, most children find a number of ways to do this:

"Put something that sinks on something that floats, and see if it sinks."
"Hey, look! With the clay on, the wood sinks. Maybe it's more weight."
"Everybody knows marbles sink."

In one class, a boy inverted a glass over a floating object to get it to sink. Two girls tried pressing on the top of a vial to get a wooden sphere to sink. This

---

Reprinted from Teachers Guide for the unit *Sink or Float,* *pp.* 11–15, by the Elementary Science Study. Copyright 1944 by Education Development Center, Inc., 55 Chapel Street, Newton, Massachusetts 02160.

was an outgrowth of previous work done on air pressure. This same group later became interested in Cartesian divers.

Floating Sinkers

Asked if they can get the objects that sink to float, children usually require some time and thought. You might ask, "Can you find a way to get the clay to float?"

"If the clay is flat, it floats."
"My clay floats till it gets all wet."
"I'm going to cut my clay into smaller pieces to see if it floats."
"When I tried to make it float, I first tried it in the shape of a snake, then like an ashtray, then like a canoe, then like a tall sort of glass, and it floated because I made it as light as I could in all parts."

You can ask the children a further question: "Can you put anything on the clay and still have it float?" Most children made a boat of clay and put into it objects that sink—some called the objects "passengers."

Aluminum foil will float under certain conditions and sink under others.

"Roll it up in a ball and it floats. Make a boat and it floats. Make it flat and it sinks."
"Mine floated when it was flat."
"Not if you push it all under or make holes in it for the water to come in."

Children have also used the foil to wrap together objects that sink or float.

"I put three balls that sank and one ball that floated and wrapped aluminum foil around it all, and it started floating."

2. SCIENCE CURRICULUM IMPROVEMENT STUDY LESSON: POPULATIONS

Populations of plants and animals exist in and around the schoolyard. Whether you have a "nature area" or park near your school, or simply trees and weeds at the edge of the playground, there should be some place where the children can find populations of plants and animals. Survey the schoolyard and nearby areas to find a spot you consider suitable for the children's trip.

FIELD TRIP

Each child should take a notebook or paper on which he can record each kind of plant or animal and the number of each kind he observes. It is usually best to guide the children's observation by giving them specific questions to be answered on the trip. You may wish to provide dittoed pages with questions such as: What kinds of plants do you see? How many of each kind are there?

From Science Curriculum Improvement Study, *Populations* (Chicago: Rand Mc-Nally & Company, 1944), pp. 23–24.

Exact identification of the plants and animals is not necessary. When an organism is observed that neither you nor the children can identify, simply give it a descriptive name (little blue flower; large brown bird). Some children may want to identify the unknown organisms. Encourage them to do so when back in the classroom if reference books are available. Plan to allow only about half an hour for observing and recording organisms. Return to the classroom while the children are still interested in their explorations.

RECORDING THE DATA

The children's records should be compiled into a class record within a day or two after the field trip. The total number of each kind of organism should be determined and recorded on a chart or bar graph. Do not be overly concerned about arriving at precise totals.

INVENTION OF POPULATION

Point out that the class record shows that several groups or organisms were observed on the field trip. Tell the children that a group of organisms of the same kind living in a particular place is called a population. Refer to a certain kind of organism observed on the trip. For example, "all the bullfrogs in Walden Pond are a population of bullfrogs." Write the word "population" on the chalkboard.

POPULATIONS PICTURE

Give each child a populations picture, and have him identify the populations shown. Which are animal populations? Which are plant populations? Which population is the largest? Which is the smallest?

Have the children identify the populations in the aquaria. Encourage them to report the populations they notice on the way to school. As you discuss different populations with the children, use the populations pictures and the records of the field trip to help emphasize the following points:

1. A population is two or more organisms of the same kind. It includes individuals in all stages of that organism's life cycle and individuals differing in sex and age.

2. There are plant and animal populations.

3. The populations we are considering are composed of living individuals that are born, reproduce, and die.

4. The size of a population is determined by the number of individuals, not by the physical size of an individual. Ask the children which population is larger, a population of ten elephants or a population of 100 ants. Point out that even though an ant is smaller than an elephant, in this case the number of ants is larger than the number of elephants. For this reason we say the ant population is the larger population.

It is not necessary to cover all these points in one discussion. In fact, a particular point might be most profitably discussed when children raise a question related to it.[3]

---

[3] Science Curriculum Improvement Study, *Populations*, pp. 23–24.

3. SCIENCE—A PROCESS APPROACH LESSON: ELECTRIC CIRCUITS AND THEIR PARTS

This exercise is built upon an earlier exercise where the children learned to construct a complete circuit and infer the wiring patterns hidden within circuit boards. This exercise begins with the class divided into groups of three or four children per group, and each group having a flashlight battery, bulb, switch, and three lengths of wire. The class is asked to connect the various pieces of materials together in such a way that the switch can be used to cut the bulb on and off. While the children are constructing their circuits the teacher writes several possible definitions for a switch on the board. Once the circuits are constructed a class discussion is undertaken to identify which of the listed definitions of a switch is most useful. At this time the concept of an operational definition is introduced.

The objectives are for the children to learn to:

1. Identify an object, a situation, or an event which is related to simple electric circuits and is described by an operational definition.

2. Distinguish between an operational and non-operational definition of an object, a situation, or an event related to simple electric circuits.

3. Construct a simple electric circuit from an operational definition.

For the first activity the children are given five operational definitions of various kinds of circuits. Around the classroom are placed circuits which are connected in various ways with each circuit being identified only by a letter. The children are to match the list of operational definitions of circuits with the letter for the real circuit. A class discussion of the findings follows the completion of the check list.

In the next activity the children are given a data sheet which has several definitions on it. The children are to identify which definitions are most useful and then construct a circuit to use to find out which materials are conductors and which are non-conductors. Additional data sheets are handed out and other tasks are done as the exercise unfolds.

As a generalizing experience the children are given an electric motor, several wires, and a copy of a circuit diagram. Their task is to wire the motor so that it will run.

Posttest

In order to take this test you should have watched at least one television advertisement for each of the following products: aspirin, deodorant, toothpaste, and mouthwash.

The advertisements surely have employed the following terms. Operationally define each of the terms.

Ho-hum breath:

Faster relief:

From *Science—A Process Approach*, Part E, Exercise i, p. 1. Reprinted by permission of the American Association for the Advancement of Science, Washington, D.C.

Lasts twenty-four hours:

Check the acceptable responses that follow.

Acceptable Responses for the Posttest

For each definition check to see if you have included (1) what should be done and (2) what should be observed.

Ho-hum breath: Once a person has made the suggested application, any person who comes within one meter's distance and deeply inhales will feel drowsy and in some cases fall asleep.

Faster relief: A person who takes the prescribed dosage will have a decrease in temperature of two degrees within five minutes.

Lasts twenty-four hours: If a person who has taken the prescribed dosage for faster relief comes within a one meter distance of a person with ho-hum breath and breathes deeply, he will sleep for twenty-four hours.

If you find that you are having difficulty, either discuss this with your instructor or recycle yourself through this chapter.

10. Searching for Patterns

By the end this chapter, you should be able to: (1) name the axis of a graph that is used for the manipulated variable and the axis that is used for the responding variable; and (2) study a graph and make a summary statement of the interaction of the manipulated and responding variables as reflected by the data pattern.

Check yourself now. If you can successfully perform these tasks, you may omit this part of the chapter and go to page 227.

For this task, you will not need any additional materials.

The following experiment was conducted by a fifth-grade class. The class planted bean seeds in five cups that were the same size and contained the same kind of dirt. All of the cups had the same volume of dirt and were placed at the same place in the classroom. The amount of water that each cup received was different.

The children observed the cups for a two-week period. They kept many records including in which cup plants grew first and the height of the plants. At the end of the two-week period the class constructed the following graph.

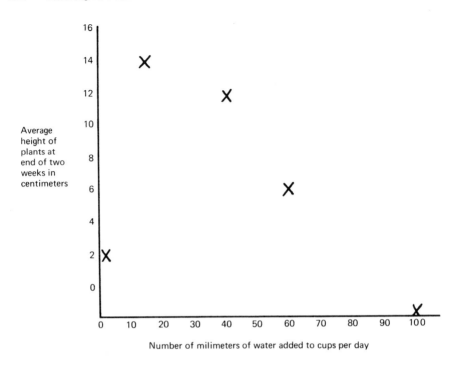

Number of milimeters of water added to cups per day

By referring to the graph answer the following :
1. For this experiment, what was the manipulated variable ?_____
    _____

2. What was the responding variable ?_____
    _____

3. Write a short description of the findings of the experiment as reflected in the graph.

Now look at page 219 for a discussion of acceptable responses for this pretest.

Acceptable Responses for Pretest

1. The manipulated variable was the amount of water each cup received.
2. The responding variable was the average height of the plants in each container.
3. One descriptive statement of the findings would be: The average height of the plants varied depending on the amount of water received. Minimum growth occurred when either no water whatsoever or 100 millimeters of water were added per day, whereas maximum growth took place when 20 millimeters of water were added daily.

    If you were successful with the pretest, go to the next part of the chapter, page 227. If you were *not* successful, carry out the activities suggested below as a way to further develop your skill in searching for and describing patterns in data.

In their work, scientists are always looking for patterns. They continually look for regularities in the interactions of events. In general, scientists believe that once something is understood well enough, the pattern of interactions will be quite simple and relatively easy to describe. During the search many of the proposed patterns to explain a phenomenon may be very complicated, since they have to account for what is known—which may be a very small part of the total picture. However, just because there are missing pieces, the job of finding the right pattern is very exciting.

In order to facilitate the study of the relationship among variables, diagrammatic charts and models are sometimes constructed to aid in visualizing the interactions. For this purpose, graphs are very handy tools. They are easy to construct and they also make it much easier for the experimenter to picture the relationship between variables.

When constructing a graph it is customary to place the data for the manipulated variables on the horizontal or *x* axis and the data for the responding variable on the vertical or *y* axis.

Once the data have been put in graphical form, experience is needed to figure out patterns. Nothing has to be learned. Just look at the data and try to see if there is some simple relationship or pattern. *Don't* forget to move the arrangement of the data around either mentally or on paper. This may help make sense out of it.

Activity 1:   Height of Boys and Girls

For this activity you will not need additional materials.

The following graph was constructed from data collected by a third-grade class. The class measured the height of children at each grade level and then plotted the grade average.

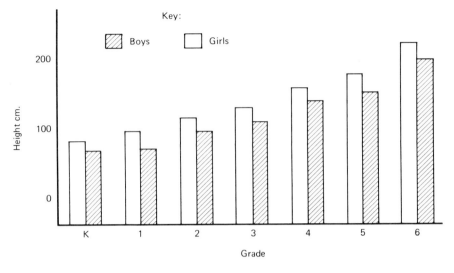

What was the manipulated variable? _____
_____ What was the responding variable? _____
_____ (The manipulated variable was the grade level and the responding variable was the height of the boys and girls.)

What are two patterns in these data?

1.

2.

You will not always be able to readily find two patterns in one set of data; however, in this case there are at least two patterns which might be of interest.

1. As the grade level increases, the average height of both the boys and girls increases.

2. At each grade level the average height of the girls is greater than the average height of the boys.

In describing data patterns, be careful that you do not talk about *all* first grades or *all* boys and girls. The class found the average height of only the boys and girls in their school, not all boys and girls in the universe.

Activity 2 :   Ball Bounce

For this activity you will need at least five different balls.

Number your balls in the order in which you found them, letting the first ball found be number 1, the second ball found be number 2, and so on. Drop each of the balls from the same height, say one meter. Count the number of times that each ball bounces before it comes to rest. Don't forget that more than one trial should be made with each ball.

	Ball	Number of Bounces		
1.	_____	_____	_____	_____
2.	_____	_____	_____	_____
3.	_____	_____	_____	_____
4.	_____	_____	_____	_____
5.	_____	_____	_____	_____

Next, plot the average number of bounces each ball made.

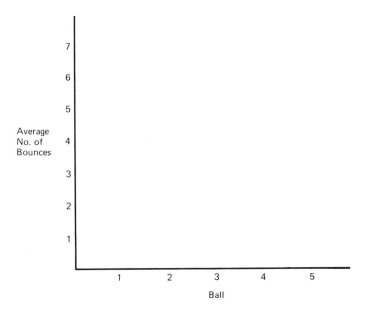

What pattern is there in your data ?

Chances are that your graph is irregular, that is, it has no readily identifiable pattern. The following graph may be quite similar to yours.

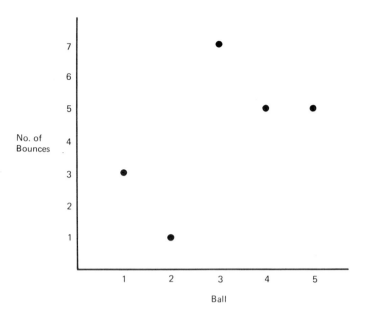

In order to get a different perspective in your search for a pattern, rearrange the balls on the graph so that the balls are in order from least to greatest number of bounces or from greatest to least number of bounces. The following shows how the sample data would look:

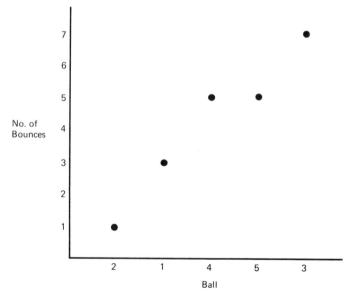

Do the same for your data.

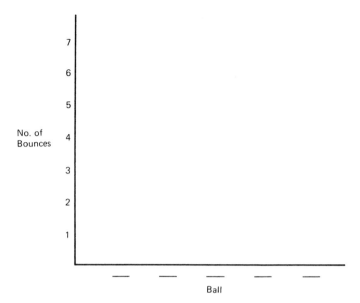

At this point the data are arranged in a pattern but we do not know for sure what the cause is, if any.

Next, place the balls in the same order as they are on this second graph. Observe the balls. Is there anything about the balls that changes systematically, either increasing or decreasing? Some possible variables are diameter, hollowness or solidity, hardness, and weight.

All you can do is look through the data and attempt to find a relationship. You may not find one. Perhaps there are several variables contributing and compounding the effects. For this activity, the fun is in the searching.

Activity 3: Cars and Spotlights

For this activity you should spend a day gathering observations. If some of your friends are doing this activity as well, split the time up with them.

On a weekday, select a traffic intersection with a traffic light. Pick the northernmost street from which traffic enters the intersection and for fifteen minutes—beginning at the following times—record the number of cars that have to wait for the red light.

Number of cars waiting for each red light

Time	1	2	3	4	5	6	7	8	9	10	average
7:30 A.M.	___	___	___	___	___	___	___	___	___	___	___
8:30 A.M.	___	___	___	___	___	___	___	___	___	___	___
9:30 A.M.	___	___	___	___	___	___	___	___	___	___	___
10:30 A.M.	___	___	___	___	___	___	___	___	___	___	___
11:30 A.M.	___	___	___	___	___	___	___	___	___	___	___
12:30 P.M.	___	___	___	___	___	___	___	___	___	___	___
1:30 P.M.	___	___	___	___	___	___	___	___	___	___	___
2:30 P.M.	___	___	___	___	___	___	___	___	___	___	___
3:30 P.M.	___	___	___	___	___	___	___	___	___	___	___
4:30 P.M.	___	___	___	___	___	___	___	___	___	___	___
5:30 P.M.	___	___	___	___	___	___	___	___	___	___	___
6:30 P.M.	___	___	___	___	___	___	___	___	___	___	___
7:30 P.M.	___	___	___	___	___	___	___	___	___	___	___

For each of the fifteen-minute intervals, find the average number of cars per red light. Then plot the average number of cars per red light against the time of day.

Of course you remembered to put the manipulated variable on the horizontal axis and the responding variable on the vertical axis. Yes, the manipulated variable was the time of day (*you* decided that) and the responding variable was the average number of cars per red light (you did not decide how many cars would back up at the light).

What kind of pattern do you find in your data?

It probably would not make sense to reshuffle the times so that the average would be shown in an increasing or decreasing order. However, there might be a pattern that has to do with variables you did not measure, such as the time of day called rush hour, change of shifts in a large factory, or a football game. Each of these events would result in increases and decreases in the average number of cars waiting for the light. You can make some inferences about the pattern of your graph but you will need additional observations before you can be sure.

Being able to make sense out of data once it is collected is crucial in experimenting. The preceding activities were designed to give you some experience in searching for data patterns. The developers of many of the elementary-school science curricula have given considerable thought to the significance of data analysis.

In Unit 19, *Comparing Changes,* of the MINNEMAST materials, when describing the data to be collected from planting corn kernels, the authors say:

Lessons 3 through 7 are concerned only with the corn seedlings. In these lessons each child not only has the pleasure of working with a living, changing thing and of speculating about its development, but he also is given the experience of measuring it, and recording and graphing the measurements. Each child should become aware that the height of the plant increases as the days pass, and he should see the connection between the numbers recorded in a table of plant growth and a graph made from such a table.

The child should discover that by using a graph he can "look back" to see how the plant has grown, and even venture to predict how it will continue to grow. He ought to learn that a graph is, in a sense, a picture of the relation between the height of a growing plant and the duration of its growth since planting. He should also discover that the curve that shows his plant's growth is different from that of other similar plants. This illustrates the fact that living things vary.[1]

Karplus and Thier, in describing scope and sequence of the SCIS *Interaction Unit,* point out the importance of patterns.

The interaction concept is being used more and more to explain social and scientific phenomena. At conferences one may find strong interaction among some participants, but weak interaction among others; erosion is caused by the interaction of wind and water with rock; in the laboratory, magnets interact even when they are not touching. In ancient times some philosophers took the view that changes were brought about by an ultimate fate or destiny that was inherent in every object. Now we say that a change is brought about by interaction, and we try to determine the conditions under which the interaction occurs.

Finding regular patterns of behavior is the goal of the scientist who examines natural phenomena. When he finds regularity, he gains some confidence about his ability to predict the outcome of certain experiments because he expects them to fit the same pattern. In this way the scientist is not very different from the rest of us. All of us are uncomfortable in a completely new situation. All of us, from childhood on, accumulate through experience knowledge about what is likely to happen in many circumstances.

---

[1] MINNEMAST, *Comparing Changes,* Unit 19, p. 9.

This gives us confidence in facing the future because we have a pretty good idea of what will happen next.

One of the most important kinds of patterns is the one that leads to cause-and-effect interpretations. If a scientist observes a certain change which always follows when some objects are near each other and which never occurs otherwise, he will hypothesize that the objects are interacting and have a cause-and-effect relationship. The scientist and the layman infer the existence of interaction from observable evidence, from changes that occur in the persons or the objects involved in a phenomenon. Interpreting changes in terms of interaction appears to satisfy a psychological need for explaining observations.

An aim of this unit is to help children recognize regular patterns of behavior. The first step is to identify the system of material objects that is present and seems to be connected with a happening. The second step is to recognize that changes are taking place during the period of observation— changes in shape, position, color, temperature, appearance, or other details. The third step is to determine which object or objects were instrumental in causing the change. This step is the one that leads to the interaction concept. Therefore observation of change is evidence of interaction. The statement that objects interact is merely a statement that they affect or change each other.[2]

Another aspect of the SCIS *Interaction Unit* is organization of data collection and reporting.

An important dimension of science is the recording and reporting of experiments and investigations. It is essential to keep a record of experimental arrangements, factors that are controlled and varied, observations that are made, and unexpected events that occur so that the data that are necessary for interpretations are actually collected. Usually a systematic plan for data collection is a part of the plan for an experiment. The critical test of the plan for collecting data is whether it will lead to the collection of all relevant data.

The investigator in science also has a responsibility to report his experiments and investigations, his findings and interpretations to his colleagues. Ideally, these reports should be brief, but give all the essential information, and be clear and succinct. The critical test of a scientific report is whether it is sufficiently clear and complete so that another investigator in the field can replicate the experiment and check the findings and interpretations. There are some scientists who believe that the scientific report should also be written in such a way that it can be understood by well-educated adults.

In the unit *Interaction* children record data, interpret results, and write reports. Naturally, these reports are not highly sophisticated. Sketches and pictures are used to convey most of the ideas and information, but the reports are useful as records of what has been done and to convey to others the findings and interpretations. In record keeping and reporting, children begin to have experiences with an important dimension of science.[3]

---

[2] Robert Karplus and Herbert D. Thier, *A New Look at Elementary School Science,* © 1969 by Rand McNally & Company, Chicago, pp. 47–49.

[3] Science Curriculum Improvement Study, *Elementary Science Sourcebook* (Chicago: Rand McNally & Company, 1944), p. 296.

One of the process skills of the *Science—A Process Approach* curriculum is interpreting data.

Interpreting data accumulated in an experiment is an important process of science. The accuracy of observations is governed by the design of the experiment and by the skill and integrity of the investigator. The correctness of the interpretation of the data depends on the ability of the investigator to reason logically and also upon his opinions. Data interpretation may include mathematical correlations, predictions, inferences and hypotheses. One purpose of the sequence of exercises which emphasize interpretation of data is to have the child learn to distinguish between the results obtained in an experiment by direct observation and the ideas that are obtained by interpreting data.[4]

1. SCIENCE—A PROCESS APPROACH LESSON: GUINEA PIGS IN A MAZE

Live guinea pigs or gerbils are used for this exercise. The beginning discussion centers on the care of animals, and then leads into a discussion on whether or not animals can learn. The question which is then raised is: how we find out if the guinea pigs can learn. The objectives are for the children to learn to:

1. Describe the changes in an animal's performance of a task which result from repeated trials or practice.

2. Construct a graph showing how an animal's performance depends on the number of trials or the amount of practice.

3. Identify the data that support the statement that the time required to perform an act will in general be shortened after a number of trials.

4. Construct answers to questions about information presented in a graph.

The exercise is based upon having two guinea pigs run through a maze. The children are asked to write down specific questions which they wish to study about the guinea pigs running through the maze. They are asked which variables will be held constant including such things as the time of day when the trials will be made. They then need to identify the manipulated variable and the responding variable, which probably will be the one required for the guinea pig to reach the food at the end of the maze.

A minimum of six or seven trials are made over a period of a week. At the completion of the trials, the tabulated data are converted to graphical form. Once the graphs are constructed attention is focused on the questions which were asked at the beginning of the exercise, and the process of interpreting the data begins. Following a class discussion centered

---

[4] A. H. Livermore, "The Process Approach of the AAAS Commission on Science Education," *Journal of Research in Science Teaching,* Vol. 2, Number 4 (1964), 271–82.

From *Science—A Process Approach* (1968), Part E, Exercise d, p. 1. Reprinted by permission of the American Association for the Advancement of Science, Washington, D.C.

around answering the initial questions, several questions that might lead to further investigation are suggested; such as, how does a guinea pig know where to go, and is one guinea pig smarter than the other?

2. ELEMENTARY SCIENCE STUDY LESSON: ACTIVITIES USING ICE

It is not possible to anticipate all the factors which children may claim affect the melting rate of ice cubes, but this activity describes ways in which to look closely at some. Your class may want to explore others and should be encouraged to do so.

Your students have probably found that ice melts faster in hot water than in room air, but...

Will it melt faster in water at room temperature than it does in air? Does the amount of water in which it melts make any difference?

Does stirring influence the rate of melting? If so, does it matter how fast you stir the water?

How does the temperature of the water affect the melting rate?

If ice melts faster in water than in air, will it melt faster in cold water than in room air?

Does the ice melt faster in or out of its container?

Does the size of the water container make any difference? Does the material of which the container is made have any effect?

Does a crushed ice cube melt more quickly than a whole cube? Does the degree of fineness to which it is crushed make any difference?

Will twice as much ice take twice as long to melt?

To answer questions like that, children will probably propose experiments similar to those suggested below. Information about the experiments has been provided so that you can plan to do at least some of them within class periods of fixed length.

It is not important that all the experiments be done, nor do all the children have to do the same experiments. Perhaps one group of children will want to investigate the effect of crushing, while another group pursues the problem of how the amount of water influences the melting rate, and still another studies a problem not listed here. You may prefer to offer all the questions as research topics and let the children work independently on those which interest them. It is best, however, to let the children raise their own questions and try to design experiments to answer them.

Despite discussions you may have conducted about changing only one variable factor at a time, you will find that students discuss such practice more effectively than they perform it. You can ask questions to help them separate, sort, and examine their ideas. For example, if you see a student stirring ice and water with his finger, you can ask, "Is it the stirring or the heat from your finger that makes the most difference?" Then let the children devise ways to find out. The following are questions that children have asked and experiments they have designed to find answers.

1. Will Ice Melt Faster in Water or in Air If Both Are at the Same Temperature?

Water in pails left in the classroom overnight will acquire a temperature very close to that of the room. In less time, you can easily adjust the water temperature to that of the classroom by mixing hot and cold water. Children can place one ice cube in a pint or quart container full of water and leave a second identical cube in the room air. It will take about ten minutes for a 20cc ice cube to melt in a pint of water at 70°F. If, however, you use water at about 50°F, it will require about a half hour to melt a 20cc ice cube. Consequently, you must deal with water and air temperature at about 70°F or higher, if you wish to carry out this and other melting activities within the span of a normal class period.

2. Does Stirring Ice in Water Affect the Melting Speed? Does It Matter How Fast the Water Is Stirred?

By placing identical ice cubes in three containers with equal amounts of water, children can readily find answers to these questions. Container 1 is left alone. The water and ice in Container 2 are stirred slowly with a stick or spoon, and the contents of Container 3 are stirred vigorously. Should the two stirrers be the same? Should there be a stirring stick or spoon in the container that is not stirred?

Typically, a 30cc ice cube left alone in a pint of water at room temperature takes about 10 minutes to melt.

3. Does the Amount of Water Affect the Melting Time?

Children can place ice cubes of equal volume in different amounts of water at room temperature. The table gives the results for several such experiments, using water initially at 70°F. In which container does the water become coldest?

Volume of water in which cube is placed	Melting time		
	15-cc ice cube	*20-cc ice cube*	*30-cc ice cube*
3 oz.	18 min.	23 min.	50 min.
6 oz.	10 min.	12 min.	18 min.
12 oz.	8 min.	10 min.	10 min.
24 oz.	7 min.	9 min.	9 min.

Notice the differences in melting time with the larger volumes. On the basis of their experiments, can children predict how long it might take one ice cube to melt in a pail of water? Can you think of reasons why doubling the volume of water does not halve the melting time?

Can the students make graphs of their results? If they are not familiar with graphs, this is an opportune time to introduce them. Children can use strips of construction paper or clock number lines. . .to represent melting time. The strips can be pasted or taped to a large sheet of paper. . . .

A greater variety of graphs will be obtained if the children are allowed to develop their own with a minimum amount of instruction. As long as the children's work communicates results, it is not important that their graphs conform to standard style or that they be precise. Enthusiasm can be dampened by a quest for perfection.

If you move about the room while the children are making their graphs, you can help them correct serious errors before the graphs are displayed. From their graphs, children may be able to predict the results of new experiments. Asking questions, such as, "How much water is needed to melt the ice in 11 minutes?" encourages them to use their graphs.

4. Does the Temperature of the Water Affect the Melting Time?

Children will generally realize that they must place ice cubes of equal size in equal volumes of water at different temperatures in order to answer this question.

To insure completion of this experiment within a class period, you should use either small ice cubes or water no colder than 50°F.

The results of one such experiment are recorded below. Which water is coldest after the melting?

Temperature of water (1 pt.)	Time for ice (30-cc) to melt
52°	25 min.
72°	11 min.
103°	4 min.

5. Will Ice Melt Faster in Cold Water Than It Does in Room Air?

Some children will notice that ice in cold water seems to melt faster than it does in air. They will even suggest that ice melts more quickly in its container than it does in air because "It's surrounded by its own melt water." However, children often think that melting is related only to temperature.

They can set up a simple experiment to test this by using two ice cubes of equal volume. Leave one cube in the room air, and place the other in a quart or so of cold water (about 50°F). The experiment can be completed within a class period. Small ice cubes will speed things up.

Following are the results of one such experiment with 20-cc ice cubes and 50°F water.

Ice cube placed in:	*Melting time*
1 qt. of 50°F water	18 min.
72°F air	95 min.

Such results are not easily explained. How can ice melt faster in something cold than in something warm?

Perhaps the substance in which the ice melts plays a role. Children can try melting ice in different liquids, such as alcohol, cooking oil, salt water, vinegar, etc.

6. Does the Size of the Container Affect the Melting Time? Does the Height of the Water in the Container Affect the Melting Time?

Some children may suggest that the size of the container influences the melting time. Their perceptions of the relative sizes of containers, however, are often confused by their shapes. In designing experiments to answer these questions, they may not know whether they should use the same amount of water in different-size containers or different-size containers each filled to the top. (This is common if the problem is suggested by the teacher and does not come from the students themselves.)

The results of two experiments testing the effect of container size are given in the table below. In both experiments, one pint of water at 70°F and one 30-cc ice cube were placed in each container.

Size of container	*Melting time*	
	Experiment 1	*Experiment 2*
1 pt.	12 1/2 min.	12 min.
1 qt., average	11 min.	11 1/2 min.
1 qt., wide	12 min.	13 min.

In another experiment, in which a shallow pan was used, it took twenty-two minutes for the ice cube to melt. . . .

Why do you think it looked as it did?

Why do you think it took longer to melt?

Would it make a difference if a metal container were used instead of a plastic one?

7. Will Ice Melt Faster in Water If It Is Crushed? Does It Matter How Finely the Ice Is Crushed?

Children will probably suggest placing each of three ice cubes—one that is whole, another that is whole, another that is broken into large pieces, and a third that is finely crushed—into separate but identical volumes of water. (Ice can be broken with a hammer and finely crushed if it is first put in a plastic bag.) If the children cannot get all the crushed ice out of a bag, they can put the entire bag of ice into a container, leave the bag in place as a lining, and pour the water onto the ice. . . .

Do they realize that they should also line the other containers with plastic bags?

The results of one such experiment are given below:

State of ice cube	Melting time
Whole	11 min.
Broken into large pieces	7 min.
Finely crushed	5 min.

Typical comments about those results are:

Small ice cubes melt faster than large ones.

When you break the ice, the water can get at the inside of the ice cube, so it melts faster.

You might ask the children how they could make an ice cube that would have more of its inside on the outside. . . .

8. Will Twice As Much Ice Take Twice As Long to Melt in the Same Volume of Water?

Children should have little trouble designing experiments to answer that question. To speed up the process, you can suggest that the children melt the ice in water. . . .

9. Can you Make an Ice Cube Melt Faster in Cold Water Than in Hot Water?

Most children work out this problem by melting ice in both large quantities of cold water and a small quantity of hot water. The results from two such experiments—in one case, a tie—are given below.

	Melting time	
Volume of ice cube	In 1 qt. of cold water	In 1 oz. of hot water
15 cc	18 min.	18 min.
30 cc	21 min.	50 min.

Some children may notice that the ice cube in hot water melts very quickly at first and then slows down as the water surrounding it cools off. In fact, they may dip their fingers in the water and find that the hot water has become much colder than the original cold water.

Background and Teaching Information

Because they do not tend to talk about heat and because heat is difficult to understand, you should not expect children to be able to explain the results of all their experiments. They will be able to answer questions of the "How?" "Will...?" or "Does...?" types more effectively than "Why?" questions. The questions included in this activity were chosen because children have found answers to them by doing something. If your students want to discuss why something occurs, by all means let them, but don't expect textbook conclusions.* Encourage those who do offer explanations to suggest experiments through which they can be tested.

If children recognize that something more than temperature is involved in getting ice to melt, this, in itself, is significant.

Of course, these types of experiments (with no obvious right answer) may initially be uncomfortably strange to both you and your students. Stick to it—the reward of seeing a child pursue a problem in his own way is well worth your effort.

---

* The way in which a question is phrased is important. Asking, "Why does . . . happen?" is less likely to elicit responses than asking, "Why do you think . . . happens?" The first implies that there is one right answer and thus inhibits speculation.

3. MINNEMAST LESSON: SYMMETRY

In popular usage the word symmetry often carries the implication that a thing is pleasantly proportioned or well-balanced. To many, symmetry implies a type of beauty and perfection. In precise usage, a symmetric pattern is one which remains unchanged under a certain rigid motion. One can intuitively notice symmetry in many things such as:

Butterflies

Leaves

Tile floors

Stanzas of poetry

Snowflakes

Arrangement of seeds in a sunflower

Melodies

Rhythms

Weaving in straw baskets

Slices of citrus fruits

Mathematical principles

Certain types of symmetry can be given precise geometric descriptions. Three of these types are emphasized in this unit: (1) rotational or turning, (2) translational and repetitive, (3) bilateral or symmetric about a line. A detailed discussion of them will conclude this commentary. It will be found that symmetric patterns are unchanged by certain motions.

You need not feel that a complete mastery of the introductory material is necessary before you start to teach the unit. Each idea is demonstrated and developed as the lessons progress. This introduction should be regarded as a source of information to which to refer for information during the various studies.

Why Have Symmetry Units in the Primary Grades?

Both the intuitive ideas of symmetry and the precisely defined mathematical ideas of symmetry were considered in the following reasons for having small children study symmetry.

1. The activities provide practice in abstracting concepts, e.g., seeing that several different patterns have the same type of symmetry.

2. The concepts discussed will be used in later topics such as geometry, measurement, wave motion, and classification of biological organisms. Symmetry is a tool in understanding the universe.

3. The principles of symmetry are often applied in art, poetry, and music. Awareness of these principles heightens appreciation of the arts.

4. The activities provide perceptual training for reading readiness. For example, the tracing of patterns aids perception through muscular activities. Practice is given in moving from left to right.

5. The children enjoy the activities and the awareness of symmetry that they develop. Many natural and man-made shapes in the children's environment have some type of symmetry that they can recognize.

OBJECTIVES

On completion of the unit the child should:

1. Recognize symmetry in nature, music, poetry, and art.

2. Recognize turning symmetry (rotational symmetry), repeating patterns (translational symmetry), and symmetry about a line (bilateral symmetry).

3. Be able to make the necessary tests and comparisons for the three types of symmetry studied.

Rotational Symmetry or Turning Symmetry

Consider the letter *S*. Think of it as a shape that can be moved and which leaves its image behind. Can the *S* be moved in a definite way, so that after it has been moved it will coincide with its original image?

1. Simply picking the *S*-shape up and laying it back down is one such operation. This is trivial because it can be done for any movable object.

2. Turning the *S*-shape a full turn, i.e., through 360°, is another move that will leave the shape in coincidence with its original image. This is also trivial because it can be done for any shape.

3. Turning the *S*-shape through one half of a full turn, i.e., through 180°, will also cause the *S* to coincide with its original shape.

This third operation shows that the *S*-shape is symmetric with respect to rotation about an axis perpendicular to the shape at the center. The shape is said to have rotational symmetry or turning symmetry. Note that if the *S* is flipped over to the position *S* it cannot be put into coincidence with its original shape.

Another example of a shape that possesses rotational symmetry is a triangular block with equal sides. The block outlines. . .may help in visualizing the rotations that leave the block in coincidence with its original image. The rotations are one-third of a full turn, two-thirds of a full turn, and the trivial ones of no turn and of a full turn; rotations of 0°, 120°, 240° and 360° leave the pattern of the block unchanged.

Note that in considering rotational symmetry of a pattern, only rotations about an axis through the center of the pattern are considered.

The pattern is not flipped or turned about an axis across the pattern.

A rotation through any amount less than a full turn that yields coincidence with the original position is a test for the presence in a pattern of rotational symmetry or turning symmetry. Further examples of simple patterns exhibiting rational symmetry are stars, squares, ovals, and circles.

A three-dimensional object can't be tested for rotational symmetry exactly as done above, because a solid object won't coincide with a surface pattern. However a variation of the test can easily be made. The solid object can be turned and compared to an exact copy of itself. If after the object has been turned an amount less than 360°, the object and its copy cannot be distinguished, the object has rotational symmetry. . . .

A slightly different point of view is to consider a rotationally symmetric pattern as one that can be generated by rotating an element of the pattern. For example, the shape   can be generated by rotating the shape   into three positions.

Repeating Patterns and Translational Symmetry

Suppose a stencil is used to make the repeating pattern in the strip design shown in [the following figure].

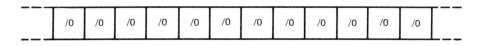

The dotted lines in the figure show that the pattern could be continued indefinitely. If the pattern is imagined as being infinitely long, it can be picked up, moved through a certain distance, and laid down again to cover the entire original pattern. The pattern would then look exactly as it did before it was moved. This is possible because an infinite pattern has no beginning and no end, but extends infinitely in either direction. A mathematician might say that a translation carries the pattern into itself. Because of this, the pattern is said to possess *translational symmetry*.

Repeating patterns are easy to find. For example, they are seen in wallpaper, brick walls, and strings of beads. These patterns repeat only a finite number of times, but they may be thought of as "potentially infinite." This means that the pattern can be imagined to extend indefinitely in both directions. Thus the term "translational symmetry" is sometimes used in talking about repeating patterns which are finite but can be imagined to extend infinitely.

A pattern is a repeating pattern if some part of the pattern (1) can be moved a definite distance along a line to cover an identical part of the same pattern and (2) with a succession of such moves will cover the entire pattern. As in rotational symmetry, comparisons are made after some part of the pattern is moved. This time a part of the pattern is moved in equal-sized jumps and compared to other parts of the same pattern to determine coincidence. The part of the pattern that is repeated can be called a "block," a "cell," or an "element."

In testing the string of beads shown below for a repeating pattern, the block to be compared could be

The block to be compared could also be chosen as
This would again cover the pattern when repeatedly moved in steps along the string. If the beads are formed into a circle, they will show a rotationally symmetric pattern. If actual beads were used, instead of a drawing of beads, the comparison block of beads would of course not be laid on top of another block. It would be placed beside a corresponding block for the comparison.

There are many (imperfect) repeating patterns to be observed in nature. Two examples are bamboo stems and caterpillars. Often only a portion of the object shows the repeating pattern, as in the caterpillar where the middle segments are approximately of equal size and shape but the two ends are not (see Figure 1).

The activities in this unit will extend the concept of repeating patterns to poetry and music. Repeating sound patterns are common in both poetry and music.

Bilateral Symmetry or Symmetry about a Line or Plane

Consider the letter A in Figure 2. Any line drawn perpendicular to the dotted line in the figure cuts the pattern in pairs of points that are equidistant from the dotted line. For example, the points *a* and *b* in Figure 3 are at equal distances from the dotted line.

The letter A is said to exhibit symmetry about a line, or bilateral symmetry. The dotted line is called the line of symmetry or the axis of symmetry.

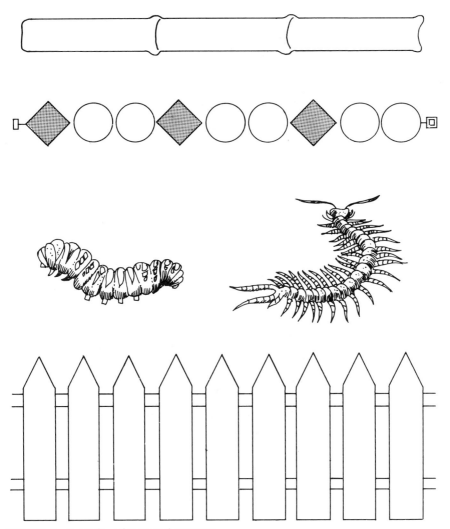

FIGURE 1. Examples of repeated patterns.

Any pattern through which a line can be drawn so that every line perpendicular to this line cuts the pattern into pairs of points equidistant from the line is said to *exhibit symmetry about a line* or *bilateral symmetry*.

A simpler but less exact statement of this idea is that for every point on one side of the line of symmetry there is a corresponding point on the other side. The paired points must be at equal distances from the line of symmetry. Figure 4 shows some almost exactly bilaterally symmetric patterns that occur in nature. There are tests one can use to determine whether or not a pattern possesses bilateral symmetry. Two of these tests are described below.

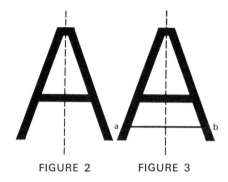

FIGURE 2   FIGURE 3

If a mirror is placed in a vertical position along the dotted line in Figure 2, the pattern viewed (half of A and its image in the mirror) coincides precisely with the original letter A. The *mirror test* consists of holding a mirror

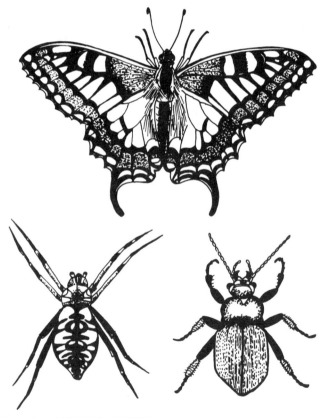

FIGURE 4. Examples of bilateral symmetry.

on the axis of symmetry to show that the pattern can be divided into two parts identical in size, one part being the mirror image of the other. In any bilaterally symmetric pattern, one half of the pattern is the mirror image of the other half. This is the reason that bilateral symmetry is also referred to as *mirror* symmetry. It is interesting to test some non-symmetric patterns with a mirror.

Bilaterally symmetric patterns may also be folded along the axis of symmetry to test for the coincidence of the two halves of the pattern. This gives another test, the *folding test*, for bilateral symmetry.

There are some differences in examining the symmetry of patterns on plane surfaces and of three-dimensional objects. Corresponding to the line of symmetry of plane patterns, bilaterally symmetric three-dimensional objects have a plane of symmetry. Every line perpendicular to this plane cuts the figure in pairs of corresponding points that are at equal distances from the plane. Obviously, a solid object cannot be folded to test for bilateral symmetry. However, a mirror can be placed along the plane of symmetry to show the existence of bilateral symmetry. The human face is an interesting object that has approximate symmetry with respect to a plane. Other objects that might be tested are a cone, a beetle, and toy figures of people or animals.

A picture of a three-dimensional object is, of course, a two-dimensional pattern. Thus the symmetry of a picture of a three-dimensional object may be tested by either the mirror or folding test. Generally the kindergarten and first grade activities will involve only two-dimensional patterns or pictures.

4. SCIENCE CURRICULUM IMPROVEMENT STUDY LESSON: TRACKS

PATHS OF MOVING OBJECTS

There are several demonstrations with which you can initiate a discussion about the motion of objects. For one, you might blow up a balloon in front of the class and release it without tying the opening. The motion of the balloon will be erratic and very difficult to describe, but can spark an informative discussion by children. In another demonstration, you might stretch a rubber band and shoot it across the room. The course of the rubber band will not be so erratic as the balloon's and will be easier for the children to describe. Invite children to trace the ·path of either object with their fingers while the other children watch and comment on the accuracy of the description. The children will discover that the paths would be easier to observe and remember if the balloon or rubber band had left a visible track. Invite the children to compare the paths of the balloon and the rubber band and to name objects which leave tracks as they move. Some examples are a car moving on a dirt road, birds walking on a sandy beach, a jet airplane

From Science Curriculum Improvement Study, *Position and Motion*, pp. 76–79.

flying at high altitude, snakes and turtles crawling across soft ground and so on.

After the children have named some objects that do and some that do not leave tracks as they move, you might pose the following problem. Take a steel sphere (write the word "sphere" on the board while you pronounce it), roll it across the floor, and ask the children how the sphere's path could be made visible. Typical responses are "Put some chalk on the sphere or on the floor; cover the sphere with water or paint; roll the sphere across some sand." If time and materials are available, group the children around a cleared floor area where they can test some of their suggested methods. It is easy for a child or you to coat the sphere with chalk dust and roll it across the floor, where it might leave a track. Wetting the sphere is also easy to do, but this method usually does not produce a "good" track. If you have paint, you should probably roll the sphere across a large piece of newspaper or chart paper, and wash the sphere promptly afterward. Experiments on sand or earth can perhaps be done on the playground.

STEEL SPHERE TRACKS

To introduce the technique the children will use for recording tracks, place a piece of plain paper on the floor or demonstration table, cover it with a sheet of the soft carbon paper (carbon side down), and roll a sphere across it—but do not lift the carbon paper. The procedure making a track, rather than the track itself, is the important thing for the children to observe in this demonstration. Interest in using this technique will be heightened if the first tracks the children see are the ones they themselves produce.

CHILDREN'S EXPERIMENTS

Give each pair of children two sheets of plain paper, one sheet of carbon paper, and one steel sphere. Set the box of remaining spheres in an accessible place, so that the children may occasionally exchange their sphere for another one. We recommend that you do not give them free access to paper supplies at this point. You will have to judge how long one piece of carbon paper can be used and when to supply a new piece.

Most children become very enthusiastic about rolling the spheres across the carbon paper and observing the tracks. Give the children ample time to experiment, and encourage them to compare tracks. The variety of their ideas and observations will be valuable preparation for the following chapters. As you walk among the children to observe their work, look for unusual tracks which stand out from the jumbles of tracks on the papers. Ask the pair of children how they made such a track, and/or whether they could make another track that would be very similar. As you talk with the individual teams, try to discover whether they are aware of some of the possible inferences which are described below, and make a mental note of additional inferences the children make. If some children tire of these experiments, suggest that they play Coordinate Tic-Tac-Toe or Squangle while the others continue their track investigations. Keep the record papers for reference during discussion (below).

INFERENCES FROM TRACKS

The question easiest for children to answer is "Which tracks were made by the large spheres? By medium spheres? By small spheres?" They will be quick to point out the dark wide tracks made by the large spheres and the narrow light tracks made by the small spheres. If there is disagreement about this or one of the other inferences, small groups of children may wish to investigate the various questions and report their results to the class. A related activity is the optional "Track museum."

Another question concerns a sphere's speed. "Was the track made by a fast- or slow-moving sphere?" Or "Was the sphere moving fast or slowly when it made this part of the track?" The children will find that the fast-moving sphere makes a track which is broken with wide spaces between the carbon marks. The slower the sphere rolls, the closer together the carbon marks become until they form an almost unbroken line.

Still another question which frequently comes up in a discussion of tracks is "In which direction did the sphere roll across the paper?" Children will be able to answer this question if they released their spheres slightly off the paper and the spheres bounced lightly as they rolled. The carbon marks left by a sphere when it bounces are usually darker and farther apart than those made while merely rolling. Encourage the children to look for other clues along the track which give clues about the sphere's direction of motion.

After a class or group discussion of these matters, ask the children to name variables which affect the track appearance.... You may want to begin a chart listing the variables which children mention. Children who studied the SCIS *Systems and Subsystems* unit will be familiar with the concept of variables. However, you may want to review it for them—and introduce it to the other children—as suggested in the optional "Bulletin-board display" activity.

OPTIONAL ACTIVITIES

Bulletin-Board Display

At the end of the exploratory session, each child has a paper with many tracks crisscrossing in all directions, perhaps on both sides of the paper. Have them write their names on the papers and then post the papers on the bulletin board to let the class admire them. To review and/or introduce the variables concept, ask the children for reasons why there is so much variety among tracks. Make a list of their answers (speed, weight, distance sphere has rolled, etc.) or point to the chart which was begun earlier. Explain that the items on the list are called "variables." Write the word "variables" as title over the list. Post the chart and refer to it during the later discussions.

Evaluating Tracks

At the beginning of a science class, distribute a sphere, a piece of carbon paper, and two pieces of white paper to each team. Ask each child to make only one track on his piece of paper. After a minute or two, collect the spheres and the carbon paper. Then ask several children in turn to show their tracks to the class. Invite other children to make inferences about the sphere which left each track. They may also compare these tracks to portions of any tracks that are displayed on the bulletin board. We recommend that the child who displays his track not give any hints but let the discussion be carried on exclusively by his classmates. Furthermore, at the end he should not describe how the track actually was made. This could focus the activity more on "getting the right answer" than on observing and evaluating the tracks as evidence about the properties of spheres and their motion.

Track Museum

Tracks which the children make under partly controlled conditions (see "Inference from tracks" and "Evaluating tracks') may be labeled with the conditions and displayed as part of a "track museum." These tracks can serve as standards for comparison with tracks made under unknown conditions, such as the tracks on the bulletin-board display.

5. SCIENCE CURRICULUM IMPROVEMENT STUDY LESSON: CHANGING TEMPERATURES

Interacting Water Systems

Your pupils observe and record the temperature changes taking place when two samples of water in separate containers interact through a container wall, without being mixed. After drawing a graph to describe the temperatures during a ten-minute period, they recognize that the two samples eventually come to the same temperature. They also identify the energy sources, receivers, and variables affecting the energy transfer. This chapter will require one or two class periods.

For Each Team of Two Children

2 thermometers

1 flask

1 styrofoam cup

1 cardboard tray

1 paper towel

For the Class:

2 styrofoam buckets to be filled with cold water—40°F to 50°F

2 styrofoam buckets to be filled with warm water—120°F to 130°F
food coloring

8 aluminum cans

1 temperature graph chart

From Science Curriculum Improvement Study, *Energy Sources,* Teacher's Guide (Chicago: Rand McNally & Company, 1971), pp. 70–73.

2 plastic bags

2 colored felt pens

1 watch or clock with a second hand

ADVANCE PREPARATION

Assemble the children's equipment for rapid distribution. Just before class, place a bucket of cold water or a bucket of warm water and two aluminum cans at each of four stations. Tint the warm water with a little food coloring to identify it. Be sure the plastic bags don't leak.

TEACHING SUGGESTIONS

Introducting the Experiment

Begin the class period by showing your pupils the two plastic bags and putting similar quantities of warm water in one and cold in the other. Ask them to predict what would happen if you poured all the water into one bag. After this question has been discussed briefly, hold the two bags in close contact and ask the class to predict the temperature changes in this system, where the warm and cold water interact but are not mixed. Also, invite children to identify the energy source and receiver. Furthermore, ask them to estimate for how long a time energy transfer would go on and what the temperatures of the two water subsystems might be at the end. Keep this discussion brief, as you are merely trying to arouse the children's curiosity and few of them have any basis for answering your questions accurately.

Children's Experiment

Ask your pupils to...carefully preview the procedure for the energy-transfer experiment in which warm and cold water interact without being mixed. Point out and perhaps demonstrate the following four steps:

1. Each team measures and pours one full can of cold water into a Styrofoam cup, one full can of warm water into a flask. These two samples of water will be the interacting subsystems of the water system in the experiment.

2. Each child records the warm and cold water temperatures before the subsystems interact and leaves his thermometer in the water for later use.

3. When you give a signal, each team immediately places its flask of warm water in the cup containing cold water and records the starting temperatures of both samples in Fahrenheit degrees.

4. On your signal every minute thereafter, each team member reads and records the Fahrenheit temperature of one water subsystem. He might stir his subsystem so all parts will be at the same temperature.

Distribute the children's equipment and give them about two or three minutes to get ready for the first signal, before the water temperatures change significantly. Keep an eye on the second hand of your watch and provide the first and later signals at approximately one-minute intervals. Observe the children's work between signals and help them, when necessary, to read and record the data. After all the data have been collected, the children clean up the equipment and copy data from their partners' manuals if necessary.

Graphing the Data

Ask a few students to describe briefly what they observed in their experiments. After they have mentioned the temperature changes, invite others to describe the energy transfer and to compare the experiment with the mixing of warm and cold water previously.

Then post the temperature graph chart and tell your pupils that they will draw a graph to describe their data. Explain that the numbers along the bottom refer to the time (the minutes that have gone by since the start of the interaction); the numbers along the left side refer to the temperatures of the two water subsystems.

Ask one team to provide its data, beginning with the temperatures at the start (part C). Mark the hot and cold water data in different colors or symbols on the chart. As you graph the data, proceed either fast or slowly, depending on the children's familiarlity and skill with graphs. Finally, draw smooth curves with a broad crayon or marker near the points to display the progressive changes in the two temperatures during the experiment.

Depending on your pupils' interest and the time available, ask them to draw graphs for their own experiments. . . . (See "Discussion" below.) Suggest that they use differing symbols or colors for the warm and cold water data. Help individuals locate their data points . . . , and correct errors they may make inadvertently.

Discussion

Invite students to describe their graphs in terms of heat-energy sources and receivers during each one-minute interval and during the entire ten minutes. Other points that may come up in the discussion, or that you might introduce at opportune moments if none of the students do, include: (1) variables that speed up or slow down the energy transfer; (2) variables that affect the amount of energy transfer; (3) further changes in the systems after the ten-minute observation period; and (4) interaction of the water samples with objects outside the system.

If your class would welcome the challenge, raise a few questions that could lead to additional investigations. Some of these are: (1) How can you compare the amount of energy given off by the energy source with the amount of energy taken up by the energy receiver? (2) How would the energy transfer and the temperature graph be affected if the flask had been made of extremely thin plastic, or of very thick foam plastic? (3) How would the energy transfer and the temperature graph be affected if more warm than cold water had been used, or vice versa?

Now that you have learned how to search for patterns in data and studied some of the suggested approaches for working with children, you are ready for a posttest. Take the posttest and then check your responses.

POSTTEST

You will not need any additional equipment for this posttest.

The following graph was constructed following collection of data by some students.

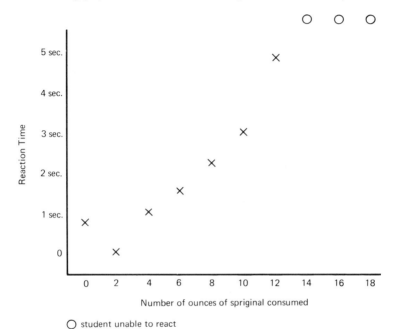

Number of ounces of spriginal consumed

○ student unable to react

1. What was the manipulated variable?

   _____

2. What was the responding variable?

   _____

3. Describe the pattern which is reflected by the graph.

On page 246 you will find acceptable answers to this posttest.

Acceptable Responses for the Posttest

1. The manipulated variable was the amount of spriginal consumed.

2. The responding variable was reaction time.

3. One summary statement is: With consumption of two ounces of spriginal there is a decrease in reaction time; however, further consumption results in rapid increase in reaction time to the point of there being no reaction time when twelve ounces is consumed.

If you find that you are having difficulty, you may either discuss this with your instructor or recycle yourself through this chapter.

11. Generalizing

By the end of this chapter, you should be able to: (1) *distinguish between statements of inference and hypotheses,* (2) *construct an hypothesis,* (3) *accept, reject, or modify a hypothesis as a result of data patterns.*

Check yourself now. If you can successfully perform these tasks, you may omit this part of the chapter and go to page 255.

For this task, you will not need any additional materials.

1. The following sentences were made following observation of a burning birthday candle. The sentences are either statements of inference or hypotheses. Mark each sentence that is an inference with an I. Mark each sentence that is a hypothesis with an H.

_____ 1. The candle is made of wax.

_____ 2. Flames of burning candles are always yellow.

_____ 3. Candles are made of saturated corn oil.

_____ 4. The wick in this candle is made of nylon.

_____ 5. The candle was lit by a father.

_____ 6. Candles are used for birthdays more than for anything else.

_____ 7. The candle is pink because of the hot flame.

_____ 8. The temperature at which candles burn will vary depending on the color.

_____ 9. Birthday-cake candles will not burn unless they are placed on a birthday cake.

_____ 10. The melted wax on the frosting will taste sweet.

2. While attending a band concert you observe that there are two tuba players in the band, each of whom is tapping his right foot and puffing his cheeks. Write a hypothesis that could be tested from your observations.

Now compare your answers with the discussion of acceptable responses on the next page.

Acceptable Responses for Pretest

1. The following is the suggested classification of the ten sentences.

1.	I	4.	I	7.	I	10.	I
2.	H	5.	I	8.	H		
3.	H	6.	H	9.	H		

2. One hypothesis that could be constructed is: All tuba players who play in bands puff their cheeks and tap their right feet. Or, by puffing their cheeks, tuba players are able to make louder sounds.

If you were successful with the pretest, you may go on to the next part of the chapter, page 255. If you were not successful, do the activities suggested below as a way to help you develop skills in identifying and constructing generalized statements.

Whether a scientist discusses an event or he is just thinking about it, it is important for him to distinguish among actual observations, inferences (explanations of what has been observed), and general statements (hypotheses), which include all occurrences of the event, even the ones he did not personally observe.

Based on his observations and inferences, a scientist may generalize to unobserved situations by saying that when variable *A* is added to variable *B*, event *C* will occur. He predicts that whenever the same variables are combined, the same event will result. A general statement of this type is called a hypothesis. A hypothesis can be thought of as an inference that has been made general to cover *all* cases, not only those actually observed.

Once a hypothesis has been stated, it must be tested. An experiment is set up, variables are controlled, and data collected. If the data pattern is consistent with the pattern predicted by the hypothesis, the hypothesis is supported.

A special word of caution is needed at this point. If the data pattern is consistent with the hypothesis, many people will say that the hypothesis is *proved*. However, hypotheses can *only* be proved if *all* possible cases have been tested. Each individual set of observations will *support* the hypothesis but not prove it. On the other hand, the first set of data that is contrary to the hypothesis results in the hypothesis being *disproved*. A disproved hypothesis must be either dropped or restated to account for the new findings.

In summary then, a statement that describes what will happen when variables interact and that is general in the sense that it covers *all* cases, both observed and unobserved, is called a hypothesis. A hypothesis may be disproved when one set of observations is contrary to what the hypothesis describes; however, a hypothesis cannot be proved until *all* possible cases have been tested. Remember that the next set of observations may be the one that disproves the hypothesis! Following are some activities dealing with generalizing. (Remember that activities are more apt to clarify points of confusion than further descriptive reading.)

Activity 1: Driving

You will not need additional equipment for this activity.

While standing next to a busy intersection, you observe a cigar-smoking man in a chauffeur-driven limousine run a red light. The limousine is struck by a young woman driving a foreign economy car. The following list of statements includes observations, inferences, and hypotheses. Mark each statement as being an observation (O), an inference (I), or a hypothesis (H).

_____ 1. The cigar-smoking man will fire the chauffeur.

_____ 2. Women should not be allowed to drive economy cars because they cause accidents.

_____ 3. The woman is hollering at the chauffeur.

_____ 4. When a driver runs a red light, he will have an accident with a woman driving an economy car.

_____ 5. The cigar-smoking man is making a call on the telephone in his limousine.

Now construct a hypothesis for each statement that you marked as either an observation or an inference.

The following is the classification of the statements; where needed, hypothesis is added.

Inference 1. The cigar-smoking man will fire the chauffeur.
Hypothesis: Whenever a chauffeur has an accident, he will be fired.

Hypothesis 2. Women should not be allowed to drive economy cars because they cause accidents.

Observation 3. The woman is hollering at the chauffeur.
Hypothesis: Women always holler when they are involved in accidents with chauffeurs.

Hypothesis 4. When a driver runs a red light, he will have an accident with a woman driving an economy car.

Observation 5. The cigar-smoking man is making a call on the telephone in his limousine.
Hypothesis: All limousines have telephones.

Activity 2 : Bubbling and Headaches

For this task, you will need two drinking glasses and two seltzer tablets.

Fill one drinking glass with hot water and the other drinking glass with cold water. Simultaneously drop one seltzer tablet into each drinking glass and observe the results. What were some of your observations ?

One of your observations might have been that there were a lot of bubbles produced in the liquid when the tablets were dropped in. What would be an inference that would follow from this observation?

Now make this inference into a hypothesis by generalizing to all cases.

One inference that could have followed from the observation was: The seltzer tablet causes the water to boil.

The generalized statement or hypothesis that would follow is: When a seltzer tablet is dropped into water, the water will boil.

One other observation that you are sure to have made was that there was more vigorous bubbing in the glass with the hot water. What would you hypothesize from this observation?

One hypothesis could be: When a seltzer tablet is dropped into hot water, the chemical activity of that tablet is increased more than when it is dropped into cold water.

If you now observe your containers, what do you observe?

If it has happened not too long ago, the cool water will still be bubbling, whereas the warm water will have no bubbles. What hypothesis would follow from this observation?

Would this be an acceptable hypothesis?

For faster relief for an upset stomach drop tablets in hot water, for prolonged relief drop tablet in cold water.

Regardless of whether you answered yes or no, further experimentation would be needed.

Activity 3 : Heights

No additional materials will be needed for this activity.

In the preceding chapter, Activity 1 : *Height of boys and girls,* you studied data collected from one elementary school. In looking for patterns in the data, two patterns were identified.

1. As the grade level increases, the average height of both the boys and the girls increases.

2. At each grade level, the average height of the girls is greater than the average height of the boys.

These patterns were found in data collected from one elementary school. Suppose you now wished to make a more generalized statement covering all elementary schools. What would this generalized statement or hypothesis be?

1.

2.

The following are two possible hypotheses:

H1   In elementary schools, the average height of both the boys and girls increases as the grade level increases.

H2   At each grade level in elementary schools, the average height of the girls is greater than the average height of the boys.

Note that the hypotheses cover *all* cases, not just the elementary school where the observations were made. What would you have to do to test the first hypothesis?

Right, make additional observations, collect additional data, find the average height of the boys and girls by grade level in other elementary schools. What would you have to do to prove the hypothesis?

In order to prove the hypothesis, you would have to find the average height of all boys and girls by grade level in all elementary schools.

What would you do if in collecting additional data you found a third-grade class in which the average height of the boys was greater than the average height of the girls?

First, you would have to reject H2, it has been disproved. You can either drop it all together or modify the hypothesis by saying that "In most schools" or that "In approximately 95% of the schools" the average height of the girls is greater than the average height of the boys at each grade level. Or you could just say that one hypothesis is not valid for third-grade children.

There are different philosophies about whether or not and, if so, how the skill of generalizing should be taught to children. Some curriculum developers do not think the skill should be dealt with at all. Their reason is that the skill is difficult to acquire for adults and therefore even more difficult for children. This argument also suggests that the skill can only be acquired by children who are able to think abstractly.

Other curriculum developers think that the skill of generalizing from the experimental data and the testing of hypotheses are very important skills for children to become familiar with. Of course, there are many individuals in between the extremes, and the following paragraphs are to help you in clarifying your thoughts.

The developers of the *Science Curriculum Improvement Study* state that hypothesis formation and testing are characteristic of a mode of inquiry.

A central objective of the SCIS elementary science program is the development of *scientific literacy*. Essentially, scientific literacy involves an awareness of the modes of inquiry in science and some understanding of conceptual structures of science. The modes of scientific inquiry are among the most powerful intellectual tools available to man. The products of scientific inquiry are developed into the conceptual structures, which are our most reliable views of the nature of the world in which we live. A modicum of scientific literacy is essential for everyone living in a modern scientific and technologically oriented society. It is important that the task of developing this literacy be initiated in the elementary school.

Modes of Inquiry in Science

Science is characterized by the use of certain modes of inquiry. Basic assumptions are made, terms are defined, phenomena are observed, hypotheses are suggested, evidence is collected, data are interpreted, and information is related to existing conceptual structures of science. In most cases scientific work serves to refine or readjust segments of the conceptual structure. Occasionally, major scientific revolutions, such as the Copernican revolution which placed the sun rather than the earth near the center of the solar system, reorient entire fields of science.

To illustrate a mode of inquiry in the sciences, let us consider a fairly simple example and how it might be investigated.

A ball is released and it drops to the ground. Other objects such as pieces of wood, metal, and a feather are also released; they all fall to the ground. We may formulate a hypothesis: "When released, all objects fall to the ground." But, suppose a balloon filled with helium is released; instead of falling to the ground, it rises. That's the end of the hypothesis. It could, however, be modified to state: "All objects fall to the ground when released in a vacuum." (A helium-filled balloon will fall to the ground in a vacuum.) But, even this hypothesis is sensible only near the earth or another large celestial object. In space, far from the earth, the statement "falling to the ground" is meaningless. The objects might very well go into orbit around some celestial body such as the earth or the sun. In order to cover more classes of events, the original hypothesis has to be extended and refined. This process of formulating, testing, revising, and extending hypotheses is an important mode of operation in science. Eventually, a hypothesis that has stood up under repeated testing and covers a wide range of phenomena may be considered a law.

Certain basic assumptions are usually made in science. One assumption is that there is a real physical universe, that there is matter, and that matter is involved in natural phenomena. In the example, it is assumed that the ball, wood, metal, feather, balloon, and the earth actually exist. A second assumption is that natural phenomena are reproducible, that is, if the same set of conditions are set up, the same phenomena will occur. These assumptions are implicitly made by the members of the scientific community, and are a part of what might be called the "scientific point of view."

Hypotheses are suggested explanations for observed phenomena. They are formulated out of other similar observations and experiences. A hypothesis is used to help direct further investigations. If further observations are consistent with the hypothesis, the hypothesis is considered confirmed and tentatively accepted. If the hypothesis turns out to be inconsistent with further observations, it must be revised and subjected to additional testing. For example, the hypothesis that "when released, all objects fall to the ground" was found not to hold for a balloon filled with helium. It had to be revised in order to include what happens when a balloon filled with a light gas is released.

In science, *the ultimate test of an idea is an empirical one.* Is the idea consistent with direct observations? Does it work when it is tried? Based on previous experiences theory, it is tried? Based on previous experiences theory, it is possible to predict with some certainty what will happen when certain operations are carried out. For example, we can predict that, when a ball is released, it will fall to the ground. The ultimate test of this prediction is the empirical one of what actually happens when a ball is released. Sometimes, of course, the empirical evidence does not uphold the prediction. Then, the theoretical framework on which the prediction was based has to be reconstructed in light of the empirical evidence.

The empirical test of ideas is of central importance in science. Even in very theoretical discussions an attempt is usually made to suggest empirical tests for ideas. For example, as a check on one of his ideas associated with relativity, Albert Einstein suggested observations of starlight that could only be made during a total solar eclipse. The observations supported his ideas and were used to substantiate his theory

Theoretical predictions can be checked in empirical tests. Again, ideas associated with the theory of relativity were used to predict that objects accelerated to velocities approaching the velocity of light would gain in mass. These predictions were made even though there were no ways of achieving such velocities at that time. Later, with the invention of the cyclotron, it became possible to accelerate particles to velocities approaching the velocity of light. The prediction was substantiated—the particles did gain in mass.

The significance of empirical evidence in science has important implications for elementary science programs. Certainly, it underscores the importance of children having direct firsthand experiences with science materials and equipment.[1]

The *Science Curriculum Improvement Study* developers also point out the following.

One of the goals of scientists is to find consistent patterns among interactions. These patterns can then be described in terms of generalizations or conceptual schemes. For example, other kinds of acids, such as acetic acid (vinegar) and boric acid, might be put into the solution of bromothymol blue in water to see if color changes take place. If there always is a color change, then it would be possible to generalize and say, "There is usually an interaction between bromothymol blue and an acid as evidenced by the change in color." This statement could be broadened if similar evidence of interaction were obtained with such indicators such as litmus and phenolphthalein. One of the goals in science is to develop broad conceptual schemes that can be used to explain consistent patterns among interactions.[2]

The developers of *Science—A Process Approach* point out:

Thinking about observations leads scientists to seek causes for events. To broaden their understanding of their environment they then generalize their statements of explanation. This process of generalization is what we have called *Formulating Hypotheses.*

In *Science—A Process Approach,* a hypothesis is defined as a generalization that includes all objects or events of the same class. Hypotheses may be formulated on the basis of observations or of inferences. For example, you may observe that a sugar cube dissolves faster in hot water than in cold water. From such an observation, you might formulate the hypothesis that all substances soluble in water will dissolve faster in hot water than in cold water.[3]

In the first *Science—A Process Approach* exercise on formulating hypotheses the teacher is advised of the following.

Rationale

We measure the progress of science partly by the extent to which we can describe our environment in general rather than specific statements. For example, the statement that blue stars are hotter than red stars is more general than the observation that Polaris is a blue star and Arcturus is a red star. It conveys information that might apply to all red and blue stars.

In *Science—A Process Approach,* a hypothesis is defined either as an inference that is generalized to include all objects or events of the same class

1 Science Curriculum Improvement Study, *Elementary Science Sourcebook* (Chicago: Rand McNally & Company, 1944), pp. 18–20.
2 Science Curriculum Improvement Study, *Elementary Science Sourcebook* (Chicago: Rand McNally & Company, 1944), pp. 66–67.
3 *Science—A Process Approach,* Commentary For Teachers, p. 57. Reprinted by permission of the American Association for the Advancement of Science, Washington, D.C.

or as a generalization about observations. For example, we can infer that chalk is a poor conductor of electricity because it cannot be used to complete an electric circuit. We can also infer that chalk is a poor conductor of heat because we can hold it in our hand by one end when we put the other end in a flame. A related hypothesis might be that all poor conductors of electricity are poor conductors of heat. It is a hypothesis because it is a general statement that includes all substances in the class of poor electrical conductors.

In this exercise, the children will make simple observations to suggest a generalized statement. They will then examine further observations to determine whether or not these observations support the hypothesis. In the next exercise, they will select a hypothesis using their own observations, and then test it by extending these observations. The need for careful definitions of terms is stressed repeatedly and is thus a good preliminary of the next exercise which introduces the subject of operational definitions.[4]

The following exercises from various curriculum projects indicate some of the methods of teaching children to think about the way their experiments can be generalized and hypotheses can be tested further. As you will notice, some of the lessons provide opportunities for thinking about generalizing but do not suggest that this should come from the teacher.

1. SCIENCE—A PROCESS APPROACH LESSON: CONDUCTORS AND NONCONDUCTORS

In an earlier exercise, children experimented using electrical circuits to identify electrical conductors and nonconductors. In this exercise, they will be observing thermal conductors and how effective these conductors are. The exercise begins with the teacher using two alcohol burners and holding an aluminum rod and a glass rod with one over each of the two burners. After a short period the teacher drops the metal rod, but continues to hang on to the glass one. A discussion then follows based on examining why the teacher dropped the metal rod.

The objectives are for the children to learn to:

1. Construct an inference based on a hypothesis about conductors and nonconductors.

2. Identify whether or not an observation supports a stated hypothesis, or an inference based on a hypothesis, about conductors and nonconductors.

The term "conductor" is introduced and the idea that objects conduct or carry heat is discussed. The discussion then shifts to asking the children to suggest tests which

[4] *Science—A Process Approach,* Formulating Hypotheses *1,* Observations and Hypotheses, p. 2. Reprinted by permission of the American Association for the Advancement of Science, Washington, D.C.

From *Science—A Process Approach,* Part E, Exercise J, p. 1. Reprinted by permission of the American Association for the Advancement of Science, Washington, D.C.

they could make to determine how good or poor a heat conductor a particular material is. The remainder of the exercise is based upon the procedure of placing some melted candle wax at a particular point on a rod and pressing a marble into the wax. Then the rod can be heated and the length of time taken before the marble drops off can be measured. The difference in time then is related to how rapidly the heat is conducted through the material.

The next step, once the procedure is outlined, is for the class to identify various variables or factors which might affect the time taken for the marble to fall from the rod; such things as the kind of material, the distance from the flame, and the total length of the rod are listed. The class is then divided into groups and the groups are then to test out the kind of heat conductors various rods are. As a result of their investigations, the class should be able to classify the objects tested as being either good or poor conductors of heat.

Next the children deal with a hypothesis relating conductors and nonconductors of electricity with the good and poor thermal conductors. Based upon their observations the children are asked to construct a hypothesis or general statement. Next, the class compared the performance of aluminum, steel, and brass rods as electrical conductors with their ability as heat conductors. Following the investigations the teacher is asked to discuss with each group the interpretations, and then to hold a class discussion to summarize the activities and to further interpret what the children have learned about conductors and nonconductors and constructing, using, and testing hypotheses.

2. ELEMENTARY SCIENCE STUDY LESSON: MEALWORMS

Can Mealworms See?

Students usually become aware of the mealworms' tendency to follow walls. A question which follows naturally from this observation relates to the way in which mealworms do this. If they follow walls, they may have some way of sensing the wall's presence.

See if your children can explain how the mealworm might be able to perceive a wall. Should they lack ideas, you could ask them to think of ways they themselves would have of walking along beside the wall of the schoolroom. One way would be to use one's eyes, as might a mealworm. But suppose the person were blind or it were dark? A child can be blindfolded and watched as he follows the walls of the classroom. Perhaps an arm or leg is dragged along the wall. What could a mealworm use to do this?

Looking at Mealworms

A careful anatomical examination at this time might reveal some organs of sight or touch. Mealworms kept in a jar on top of some ice will become sluggish and therefore easier to examine—until they warm up. Magnifying glasses and microscopes could be used if they are available. Students often

Reprinted from *Behavior of Mealworms*, pp. 11–15, by the Elementary Science Study. Copyright 1944 by Education Development Center, Inc., 55 Chapel Street, Newton, Massachusetts 02160.

say that a mealworm looks like a monster when seen through a microscope. They might make drawings to show details of structures they find on the mealworm's head and body . . . . The drawings could be labeled to indicate the possible functions of the different parts.

When the children have found what they can on their own, they could study photographs of mealworms. . . . You may want to mount them on cardboard before making them available for your class to study.

After they have combined direct observation with study of the photographs, the pupils probably will have seen the pointed antennae, the hooks on the end of each leg, the black, eye-like spots on the head, and the fine hairs on the legs and sides of the body. One or more of these structures could serve as a well-sending device. The function of the so-called "eyes" of a mealworm could be compared with those of other animals. "How are a mealworm's eyes different from yours?" "Do you think a mealworm can see as you can?" The evidence on sight may be contradictory, since mealworms bump into things but do seem to respond to bright lights. "Is it possible to 'see' just light and dark?" A large box could be lowered over the head of a child with his eyes closed. He can't really see, but he is still able to tell when it becomes darker as the box is lowered.

How Can Mealworms Follow Walls?

"What can we do to find out which parts of the body might be used by a mealworm for following walls?" The children might suggest that, to test sight, a mealworm's head could be coated with nail polish or black paint. This may be a good idea, but it should be discouraged since it is harmful to the mealworms and does not show much anyway. A magnifying glass could be used to look at the legs or antennae of a mealworm which is following a wall.

"Would a mealworm still be able to follow a wall in the dark?" Let your children try to work out some techniques for answering this question. The problem, of course, is how to see where the mealworm travels in the dark. If chalk dust or talcum powder is sprinkled on the bottom of the box, mealworm tracks made in the dark can be observed.

In the words of one student: "To find out whether mealworms use their eyes or not we put them in a dark box with flour on the bottom, hoping that the worm would leave tracks showing where he went. It did not work because if there was enough flour for tracks, he would just bury himself and do nothing. If we used too little for him to bury in, it wouldn't leave tracks. What I think should be done is to put the mealworm in a box in a pitch dark place with a fluorescent dot of paint on him. Then we can follow his movements."

In spite of what this student says, a mealworm's path can plainly be seen if the powder is not too deep.

Building Walls for Mealworms to Follow

Building a variety of "mealworm walls" is another worthwhile activity. The idea can be introduced by the teacher if it does not evolve naturally.

"What kind of wall could you build to see if mealworms follow a wall by seeing it?" "Maybe you could make one which the mealworm could not see. How could this be done?" "What would it mean if a mealworm could not follow a glass or clear plastic wall as well as a smooth and opaque one?"

"What kind of wall could be made to show if a mealworm follows a wall by dragging its legs or body along it?" See if the children can figure out some ways to make such a wall. To keep the mealworm's protruding feet from touching, a wall could be made with an overhang. A very low wall would allow only the feet to come in contact with the vertical surface.

"What does a mealworm do when it reaches the end of the wall it is following?" "Does it continue straight ahead while its tail is still in contact with the wall?" If it does, this could mean that the wall is sensed by the tail. Perhaps the mealworm will cease following the wall after its head passes the end. What might this indicate?

"Can a mealworm detect a 'negative' wall (an overhanging edge)?" "Will it slow down when coming to a cliff?" "Does a mealworm walk along a precipice just as it walks along a wall, or does it fall over?" "Can a mealworm follow a wet wall better than a dry one?"

With the foregoing in mind, the construction of test walls can be carried out by the students at home or in school. If done in school, the necessary materials should be provided. Match sticks, toothpicks, popsicle sticks, paper clips, and tongue depressors can be used. Pieces of cardboard and plastic can also be cut up. . . . The walls can be built inside boxes or on separate pieces of cardboard. They can be held together with glue and left to dry before the mealworms are put in.

Students should keep in mind why they are making their walls. This exercise allows children to design and make equipment to test "hunches" they might have in explanation of wall-following. Often the array of materials leads some children to make elaborate structures with little apparent purpose. Walk around and ask, "Why are you making your wall that way?" Perhaps materials should be limited so there is no opportunity to construct more than is necessary.

In one trial class almost everyone made a complex obstacle course . . . . One girl, however, built an effective set of walls very simply . . . . one side was made with a piece of plastic, blackened with a crayon in all but one place. "If he can see, he'll try going through the clear part," she said. Another side was a piece of cardboard with a number of holes punched in it. "If he feels with his antennae, he'll get confused." Pins stuck through the bottom of the third side held the cardboard just off the ground so there was a crack under it. "If he feels with his feet, he'll try to go underneath."

Reporting the Behavior of Mealworms

Students enjoy watching mealworms walk along their new walls. Magnifying glasses can be used if they are available. You might wish to have the children describe their operations in a written report to answer the question of how mealworms follow walls. Many of their conclusions may be quite contradictory, but the important thing is that the conclusions be drawn from real observations.

"I found out that the mealworm follows the wall with his legs, because I put the mealworm in the maze and it followed the wall by touching with the legs."

"I think they use feelers to follow walls, because they didn't seem to be using anything else and they kept touching the walls with them."

"From watching the mealworms travel in and out of the maze, I found that they mostly follow walls with their bodies and not their eyes or antennae. I saw that when they followed the wall, they rubbed their sides against the wall to tell if it was there."

"At first I thought they followed walls with their bodies. But now I think they have eyes, because they tried to walk through the glass walls, but they didn't try to walk through wooden walls."

"I don't think they can see, because they just bump into the walls of the maze. When the mealworm goes into a pointed corner, it doesn't know which way to turn."

"By watching a mealworm in a maze, I found that mealworms have eyes in back of their body. I know this because I had a door that opened and closed. When he got to where he could see the door, the front part of him started to go the other way. But when his back saw the opening at the other end, he started to go towards it. Then I shut the door and he started to go forwards again."

3. MINNEMAST LESSON: TEETH

ACTIVITY A

Give the children mirrors and have them once again observe their teeth. Review the differences in shape between the biting teeth and the chewing teeth.

Suppose your front teeth were broad and flat instead of having thin edges. Would they be better for biting off pieces of food? How can we find out?

At this point we introduce the idea of experimenting with a model. We use a stone and a knife to represent two types of teeth, to see how the teeth are adapted to do their special job.

Is there something that has a thin edge and something else that is broad and flat that we can use for experimenting to see which cuts better?

You should be prepared with materials that children might suggest as models, such as a table knife and a flat stone, or a ruler and a block of wood.

Which of these is more like our front teeth? (The knife.)

In what way is it like the teeth? (It has a thin, sharp edge.)

Touch your front teeth to feel the edge.

From MINNEMAST, *Investigating Systems,* Unit 15, pp. 86–88. Copyright 1944 by the Regents of the University of Minnesota.

Show the children two pieces of Plasticine of the same size, with which they can experiment to see which shape is better for cutting. Have one child cut the Plasticine with the knife and the other with the stone. The one who finishes first should hold up his two pieces. This will dramatize the difference in efficiency of the two shapes.

Which shape is better for a biting tooth? (The thin edge.)

Have the children use their mirrors to look at their biting teeth and see how much the edges resemble the edge of the knife.

Your front teeth bite. What have you seen your back teeth do? (They squash and grind the food.)

Are your back teeth more like the knife in shape or more like the stone? (Like the stone.)

How can we find out which shape is better for squashing and grinding—a knife or a stone? (Try them and see.)

Have one child use the edge of the knife and another the stone on pieces of apple, banana, or nuts and show the results to the class.

The following question is especially important because it draws attention to the relation between the structure and function of an organ.

Now who can tell us how the shape of teeth helps them do their job better? (Biting teeth are thin, which makes them better for cutting. Grinding teeth are flat, which makes them better for grinding and squashing food.)

ACTIVITY B

Now tell us what other parts of your body besides your teeth you use when you eat. (Lips, tongue. Children may also recall using their arms, fingers, fingernails, etc.)

Distribute another piece of apple to each of the children so that they can investigate the part the tongue plays in eating. Ask them to wait until you give them the signal to put their pieces of apple into their mouths. Then they are to take a bite and start chewing, but they are *not* to move their tongues while they chew. After an interval call "freeze." Tell them that when you say "melt," they may use their tongues while chewing, to see what difference the use of the tongue makes in eating. When they have finished eating, continue the discussion.

What job does the tongue do when we eat? (It pushes food onto the chewing teeth and then it pushes food to the back of the mouth so that we can swallow it.)

Have the children use their mirrors again to observe how the tongue moves.

What property does the tongue have that enables it to do its work? (It bends easily in many directions.)

What do your lips do to help you eat? (They keep the food from falling out of your mouth while you chew.)

What parts of your body did you discover to be in your system for eating? (Arms, hands, fingers, fingernails, biting teeth, chewing teeth, tongue, lips.)

Provide an opportunity for children to include other parts of the body in the eating system. Each child who does so should be asked to explain what function the part has. For example, someone might mention the eyes because they see the food, or the throat which is involved in swallowing.

4. SCIENCE CURRICULUM IMPROVEMENT STUDY LESSON: GUPPIES EAT DAPHNIA

Six 1-gallon aquaria, each containing one hungry guppy, are set up at several points around the room. You add the contents of a vial containing ten to twenty Daphnia to each aquarium. The guppies catch and swallow the Daphnia.

The Daphnia had previously eaten algae. The feeding relationship involving these three organisms is diagramed algae   Daphnia   guppies.

For the Class

6 one-gallon containers

6 guppies

6 plastic vials

1 Daphnia culture

ADVANCE PREPARATION

Transfer six guppies to a container of aged tap water. Do not feed them for a week. Prepare six vials, each containing ten to twenty Daphnia in aged tap water.

TEACHING SUGGESTIONS

Guppies eat Daphnia

Add one hungry guppy to each of six containers, and place these around the room so all the children can see them. Ask the children to quietly watch the guppies while you pour one vial of Daphnia into each aquarium. The guppies should eat the Daphnia soon.

Discussion

Gather the children so that they may report their observations. Since all of them should have watched the feeding closely, ask them, "Why did guppies eat the Daphnia?" If no one mentions food, you should say that the Daphnia are food for guppies.

Write on the board "Daphnia are food for guppies." Then say that you will write this idea a shorter way, Write Daphnia   guppies, on the chalkboard. Then ask the children what Daphnia eat. If they do not volunteer

---

From Science Curriculum Improvement Study, *Organisms* (Chicago: Rand McNally & Company, 1974), pp. 53–55.

"algae," you should do so and then write algae   Daphnia
guppies. Leave this on the board where the children can see it for a day or
two. . . .

OPTIONAL ACTIVITIES

Put one hungry guppy in a 1-gallon aquarium and another in a small
plastic tumbler. Add ten Daphnia to each container, and see which guppy eats
all Daphnia first.

What could you do so guppies and Daphnia could live in the same
aquarium without Daphnia being eaten?

Put ten Daphnia in each of two plastic tumblers. Add one hungry guppy
to each tumbler. Put a cover over one tumbler to exclude all light. Wait ten
minutes and then remove the cover. Which cup has more Daphnia in it? Why?

Train the guppies. Mark a corner of one aquarium with an X. Every day
thereafter for a least three weeks, tap the aquarium at spot X and feed the
guppies immediately. Add the fish food or the Daphnia at the same spot in the
X corner every day. In about three weeks the fish will come to the corner when
you tap, even if you do not feed them.

Cleanup

Return the guppies to the original aquaria. Strain the Daphnia through
a dip net, and return them to the stock culture. Rinse and store the containers.

You may put a tumbler of Daphnia and a medicine dropper beside an
aquarium. Your pupils can add Daphnia to the aquarium and watch the fish eat.

The Food Web Concept

The diagram first drawn (on the previous page), algae   Daphnia
       guppies, is further developed. Children find that guppies eat Daphnia
but that their diet includes something besides Daphnia. After making this discovery, children are able to build a more elaborate diagram. Other plants and
animals that are involved in a food relationship may be included. The result
is a weblike diagram—a "food web."

For the Class

1 Daphnia culture
1 package fish food
  drawing paper
1 roll butcher paper
  crayons
  paste
  scissors

TEACHING SUGGESTIONS

Review the previous discussion by asking the children what happened
when Daphnia were put in the aquarium with guppies. Call their attention to
the algae   Daphnia   guppies diagram.

Ask your pupils if guppies eat anything besides Daphnia, if any organism eats guppies, and if another eats that animal. Then ask if any animals (other than guppies) eat Daphnia, and so on. Add to the diagram the names of all organisms the children suggest. A very complex diagram might result, depending on the children's ideas. One class suggested—

$$\text{algae} \longrightarrow \underset{\underset{\text{fish food}}{\uparrow}}{\overset{\overset{\text{goldfish}}{\downarrow}}{\text{Daphnia}}} \longrightarrow \text{guppies} \longrightarrow \text{trout} \longrightarrow \underset{}{\overset{\overset{\text{alligator}}{\downarrow}}{\text{whale}}}$$

Invention

Tell the children that this (the whole diagram) is a picture of a food web—"food" because it shows what object is food for what and "web" because the arrows and the names of organisms spread out and interconnect in a web-like pattern.

If children disagree about whether a certain animal does in fact eat another, encourage them to secure evidence to resolve the disagreement. If the organisms in question cannot conveniently be observed firsthand, your pupils may obtain information about them in encyclopedias and dictionaries. Before the children resort to books, however, you might ask them, "Do the organisms live in the same habitat?"

Expanding the Web.

Children's comments as they construct the Daphnia food web often contain hints for experiments and expansion of the web. For example:

1. "Do other fish eat Daphnia?" If other fish or even tadpoles are available, add Daphnia to their aquaria while the children watch closely.

2. Your pupils will probably mention that guppies eat fish food. Read aloud the list of ingredients on the fish-food package, and let the children decide whether to add some of these names to the web.

The following activities are designed to give children opportunities to discover additional examples of food webs so they may expand their understanding of the concept.

Land Food Web

Ask the children to name an animal that lives on land, and write the name on the board. Then build a food web by asking the children what this animal eats, and what eats it, and so on, until many parts of the web have been drawn. This web is likely to contain the names of many plants as well as animals and may also include "people."

Habitat

Since the concept of habitat has already been introduced, suggest that the children confine the food webs to organisms that live in the same habitat, such as a desert or a forest. In the food web diagram the children constructed at the beginning of this chapter, some of the organisms they suggested may live in freshwater and some in salt water. You can point out that the food web has not been confined to one kind of habitat by asking such questions as, "Where do guppies live? Where do whales live? Is this the same habitat?" or "How does the water in which guppies live differ from the water in which whales live?"

Mural

The class can construct a food web mural, using as large a sheet of paper as you consider feasible. On another sheet of paper each child may draw and cut out a picture of a plant and one of an animal. Select one picture at random, paste it to the mural paper, and write the name of the organism beneath. Ask if anyone has a picture of something that organism eats or of something that eats it. Paste these pictures to the paper and label them; then let children draw arrows to indicate feeding relationships (what is food for what). Organisms can be grouped according to habitat.

After a number of pictures have been placed on the mural, children will discover that more than just a single arrow can be drawn for each new organism. They will begin to see how very complex this web can become. Not all pictures need to be fitted into the web on the day the mural is begun; the class can start building it with just a few pictures, adding more later. By looking at and working on the mural from time to time for several weeks, children will begin to see more and more relationships.

Meanwhile, individual pupils may draw food webs of their own choosing, using either names or pictures of organisms.

In science, there are many opportunities for children to develop skill in generalizing (making hypotheses) and in testing hypotheses. As with the other skills, the amount of emphasis given to development of this skill will vary depending on the philosophy of the curriculum developer and of the teacher.

The main objective of this chapter was *your* ability to identify, construct, and test hypotheses. Take the posttest now.

Posttest

You will not need additional materials for this test.

1. The following statements were made by an elementary-school principal following observation of a science class. Mark each statement with an H if it is a hypothesis and with an N if it is not a hypothesis.

_____ 1. There were an awful lot of children moving around.

_____ 2. Science classes are always noisy.

_____ 3. Children cannot learn when there is noise.

_____ 4. The bulletin boards were very nice.

_____ 5. Teachers who teach science always seem so disorganized.

_____ 6. Large amounts of material are needed to teach science.

_____ 7. Science is not worth the time and effort it takes to teach it.

_____ 8. Science classes are always disorganized; children never sit quietly in their seats.

2. The following graph was constructed by a group of students following a survey conducted at one of the major pedestrian intersections on campus. All people entering the intersection were asked whether they were faculty or students and whether their major field of interest was in the natural sciences or the behavioral sciences. They were then asked to define the word grok.

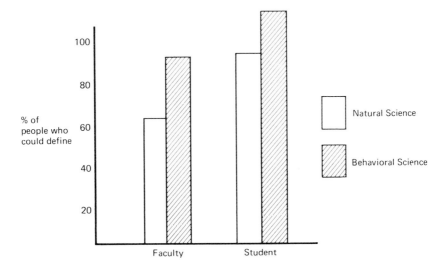

Write two hypotheses that could be made relative to these data.

H1 :

H2 :

On the next page, you will find acceptable answers.

Acceptable Responses for the Posttest

1.   N   1.   There *were* an awful lot of children moving around!

      H   2.   Science classes are always noisy.

      H   3.   Children cannot learn when there is noise.

      N   4.   The bulletin boards were very nice.

      H   5.   Teachers who teach science always seem so disorganized.

      H   6.   Large amounts of material are needed to teach science.

      H   7.   Science is not worth the time and effort it takes to teach it.

      H   8.   Science classes are always disorganized; children never sit quietly in their seats.

2.   Two possible hypotheses are:

H1:   People in the behavioral sciences are more intelligent than people in the natural sciences.

H2:   Faculty are less well read than students.

     If you find that you are having difficulty, you may either recycle yourself through this chapter or consult with your instructor.

12. The Scientist at Work

Introduction

The organization of this chapter differs from that of the other chapters. It has no pretest and no posttest, but it offers an opportunity "to put it all together." You have been involved in a series of activities and readings dealing with the skills that scientists and people in the street should use in solving problems. For each chapter specific objectives have been stated and activities have been described to facilitate your acquisition of these skills. In this chapter the activity is much more open-ended, requiring you to identify and structure the problem and its solution. To do this you will have to integrate and apply what you have learned in the preceding chapters.

Rationale

Science can be thought of as having two components. One is the body of knowledge —that information which has been learned from observation and experimentation. The other consists of the intellectual skills that the scientist uses to identify and solve problems. Until recently, in science teaching the emphasis has been on the *body of knowledge* exclusively. In science classes, in the texts, and on exams the questions generally relate to science information. "Name the parts of the flower." "Describe a third-class lever." "Name the components of a complete circuit." "Draw a picture of the solar system and name the planets." Rarely is the child asked to do anything more with his accumulated knowledge than to print it out.

The point that is being missed is this: in order to compile that body of knowledge, someone had to use his mind to process existing knowledge and build new knowledge through experimentation. This processing, building, and experimenting form the intellectual skills of the scientist—his ability to think and his thinking pattern.

The activities in the preceding chapters dealt with your acquisition of specific intellectual skills thought to be important in doing experiments, that is, in using the available knowledge to develop new knowledge. The time has come for you to combine all the specific skills, from making observations to stating a hypothesis, and to do an experiment.

This assignment must be turned in to your instructor on _____, 19__.

Assignment: Experiment

In doing an experiment, a scientist uses his mind. More specifically, he employs various intellectual skills or processes. You worked with the processes of science in carrying out the activities in the previous chapters. You have learned to identify and describe such processes as observing, inferring, identifying variables, and finding patterns in data. Now you are to demonstrate your understanding of these processes by performing an experiment.

Your experiment does not have to be published in a bulky volume. However, this does not mean that a one-paragraph report will receive enthusiastic reviews.

The problem should be explicitly stated. This might include your initial observations and inferences that lead to the problem. Your instructor will want to find out whether you have operationally defined your terms and if necessary the variables, whether you have considered and controlled the variables, stated one or more hypotheses, looked for data patterns (graphs and tables may be helpful), and whether your hypothesis still stands, was disproved, or was modified.

Do not forget to organize your report in a logical way, which is understandable to others. If you master the skills with which you worked in the preceding chapters, then this experiment should be enjoyable. Of course, you should refer to any resources, including the book, that may be helpful. Remember, the problem area does not have to be science. This goal is that you demonstrate comprehension of the skills employed in doing an experiment, not that you possess scientific knowledge.

POSSIBLE EXPERIMENT TOPICS

One of the first points to consider in deciding upon an experiment is that you need some content to experiment with. Process skills cannot be employed unless there is something to process. Without knowledge and a specific problem experimentation cannot occur.

The following are just a few ideas for problem areas. Of course, these areas would have to be more specific in order to do an experiment. Hopefully the list will act as your stimulus to think of more interesting hypotheses for testing.

1. Moistened bread placed in plastic bags.
2. Evaporation of water from containers that differ in size and shape.
3. Cleaning power of detergents.
4. Rate of melting of ice cubes.
5. Growth of seeds in different environments.
6. Observation of people waiting at a stoplight.
7. Behavior patterns of goldfish.
8. Amount of water containers of different shapes and sizes will hold before sinking.
9. Behavior patterns of people in an elevator.
10. Characteristics of buyers of Volkswagen buses.
11. _____
12. _____
13. _____
14. _____
15. _____

SAMPLE EXPERIMENT

The following is a sample-experiment report. This report has some good and some bad points. You are not expected to have a perfect experiment and report. The following report, which could be considered representative, should give you some helpful ideas in designing, doing, and describing your experiments.

ICE MELTING IN DIFFERENT ENVIRONMENTS

Initial Observations.   While eating dinner in a restaurant I observed that the ice in the iced tea glasses and that in the water glasses appeared to melt at different rates. Somewhere I had learned that dark-colored objects absorb more heat than light colored and also that thermos bottles and coolers seem to be of different colors and that a thermos left in a car on a hot day does not keep things cool as long as when left outside the car.

Inference.   The ice in the iced tea melted faster than the ice in the water because the tea was darker in color. I also inferred that everything in my car was getting warm quickly.

Hypothesis.   After thinking further I decided to test the following hypothesis.

Ice cubes will melt faster in a dark-colored car than in a light-colored car.

Materials

Ice cubes.

Cars of different color.

Stopwatch.

Procedure.   To test hypothesis, four cars of different colors were selected. The cars, all four-door sedans, were of approximately the same size. They were parked heading in the same direction next to each other.

In order to prevent direct sunlight from hitting the ice cubes an ice cube was placed on the *back seat* of each car. The doors were closed and the windows rolled up. Another ice cube was placed on the roof of each car. Another ice cube was placed on the ground next to each car. The melting time of each ice cube was measured using a stopwatch.

The procedure was done twice since several observations are needed to obtain accurate measurements.

Definition of Terms

Melt time—the time elapsing between the positioning and the melting of the ice cube.

Melted—an ice cube is melted when not the slightest piece is visible any longer, or when the last air bubbles that were trapped in the ice leave the water.

Dark-colored cars—black, dark brown, red, or navy cars.

Light-colored cars—white, yellow, or light blue cars.

Variables

Constant variables:

a.   Source of ice cubes.

b.   Sun.

c.   Time of day.

d.   Outside temperature.

e. Geographic location.

f. Size of ice cubes.

g. Beginning temperature.

h. Ice cubes on the ground next to each car.

Manipulated variable:
  Color of the car.
Responding variable:
  Melt time.

Data Collected

  Time for ice cube to melt.

Car	Navy	White	Black	Yellow
Trial 1				
Cube inside	2'55.3"	3'05.1"	2'46.4"	3'03.2"
Cube on top	2'20.5"	2'59.7"	2'15.5"	2'56.5"
Cube on ground	4'48.9"	4'48.1"	4'52.3"	4'50.0"
Trial 2				
Cube inside	2'58.9"	3'05.3"	2'44.3"	3'07.2"
Cube on top	2'22.3"	2'53.1"	2'08.6"	2'57.0"
Cube on ground	4'47.6"	4'54.4"	4'50.1"	4'53.6"

Looking for Patterns

The data were put into a graph to facilitate identification of data trends that would help in testing the hypothesis.

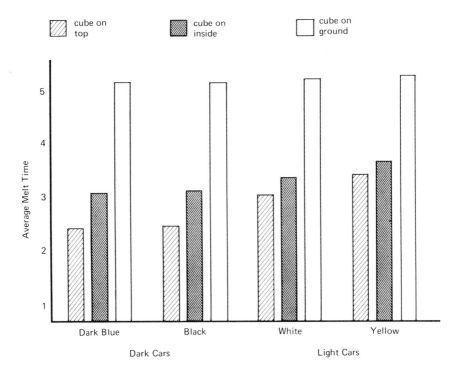

Conclusion. From the data it appears that ice cubes melt faster inside dark cars than they do inside light cars. Therefore the data support the hypothesis.

However, there is also a basis for constructing a new hypothesis, which holds that ice cubes melt faster on top of dark-colored cars than they do on top of light-colored cars. Another hypothesis which could be tested is that ice cubes melt faster when placed on car tops than when placed on car seats.

Summary. It seems that for people living in warm climates it would be advisable to buy light-colored cars. People living in cold climates should buy dark-colored cars.

Another implication of this experiment is that coolers should also be of a light color, in order to keep their contents cold longer.

Investigations are basic to many of the activities in the recently developed science curricula. Elementary-school children have opportunities to experiment with many different kinds of objects and organisms. The amount and types of suggestions to the teacher will vary, but the emphasis is on the fact that the children do investigations which are practically identical to the work of the scientists.

The summary for Elementary Science Study unit *Microgardening in the Classroom* is a good description of how the developers planned the sequence of activities to provide opportunities for open-ended experiments parallel to the historic sequence of events.

...*Y OF THE FIVE AREAS OF INVESTIGATION*

1. What Are Molds Like?

(Four activities, about 1–2 weeks)

With hand lenses the children observe mold growing on bread and discuss what they see. The class starts a mold garden to determine what things will mold. Challenged to grow mold on a piece of bread and given the freedom to try whatever they think will work, children immediately become involved with basic questions. As their bread begins to mold, they try to sort out the reasons for this development. If microscopes are available, the students can examine the details of mold structure and make comparisons among different kinds of molds.

2. What Influences the Growth of Molds?

(Four activities, about 4–5 weeks)

The children are encouraged to set up experiments to show the factors that influence the growth of molds. At first their experiments may be indeterminate and confusing, but through mistakes and successes they encounter the need to sort out and test variables such as water, light, and temperature, one at a time. The children are given a chance to apply the knowledge thus gained by investigating how to prevent mold from growing on bread.

3. Where Do Molds Come From?

(Five activities, about 4–5 weeks)

The children are introduced to a fundamental technique—sterile procedures. The children expose culture dishes of sterile media to the air and discover a flourishing growth of mold a few days later. They then try to grow just one kind of mold by placing spores on sterile media. Further experiments confirm the fact that spores, although invisible, are nearly everywhere; but they are not to be found in healthy living tissue. These experiences help the children to grasp the significance of historic events, such as Pasteur's experiments on the presence of spores in the air, and to understand some of the principles of aseptic surgery and the germ theory of disease.

4. What Influences the Rate of Mold Growth?

(Three activities, 2–3 weeks)

This area offers an opportunity for experimentation with more precision. Using growth tubes containing sterile potato agar inoculated with pure cultures of molds, the children compare rates of growth of various molds. They also investigate the effect of alternating daylight and darkness on the rate of spore production of certain molds. With the growth tube as a tool, children with special interest and motivation can go on unendingly devising experiments as time and equipment allow.

Looking further into what molds can do, the children refer again to the mold garden, and discuss the role of molds in breaking down materials.

5. What Can Molds Do?

(Three activities, about 3–4 weeks)

The children grow pure cultures of a species of Penicillium which produces penicillin and then seed the cultures with harmless bacteria. The results of this experiment lead to a discussion of antibiotics in general and of Fleming's discovery of penicillin.

After observing some seedlings that have begun to mold, the children develop the idea of isolating the mold, growing it, and then inoculating healthy seedlings. Having thus followed the historic steps of establishing that a microorganism such as a mold can be the cause of disease, they discuss the story of Robert Koch, who first worked out this procedure.

The developers of the Science Curriculum Improvement Study also have planned for the children to investigate and develop an understanding of the conceptual structure of science.

SCIENCE AND THE SCIS PROGRAM

The implications of the modern view of science are manifested throughout the elementary science program developed by the Science Curriculum Improvement Study, and only a few of them can be highlighted here. Throughout the teacher's guides, experiences are suggested that will help children achieve some degree of scientific literacy. These experiences have been developed with the following principles in mind.

Children Need Direct Experiences with Phenomena

It is much better for children to handle and examine directly a snail or a magnet than to study a sketch or listen to a description. In many of the activities in the SCIS program, children have an exploratory confrontation with materials and phenomena. After concepts are introduced that help children understand the phenomena, further direct experiences are developed in which children apply these concepts in other situations. These firsthand experiences are essential if the science concepts that are introduced are to have meaning for children.

From Science Curriculum Improvement Study, *Elementary Science Sourcebook,* (Chicago: Rand McNally & Company, 1944), pp. 23–32.

Children Should Engage in Investigations

If children are to have some understanding of the modes of operations that are used in the sciences, they must carry out investigations themselves. To carry out such investigations, it is important that children approach problems with a sufficiently developed "scientific point of view" so that they can sense the existence of a problem and can construct a tentative approach to its solution. Early experiences in the SCIS program are designed to begin the development of this scientific point of view.

As children undertake investigations, they gain experience in the use of some of the modes of operation that are characteristic of the scientific endeavor. For example, they delineate appropriate systems and suggest hypotheses that can be used to guide their investigations. They also gain a better understanding of scientific work and continue to extend their comprehension.

The Child Develops His Own Conceptual Structure of Science

The child is introduced to some of the major generalizations of science that have been developed over the centuries. He has a variety of experiences in which he "discovers" how these generalizations apply in different situations. As the child is introduced to various ideas and discovers operational meanings of these statements, he develops and extends his own conceptual structure. The conceptual structure that he develops provides him with an approach to the investigation of problems in science.

Guidance and Discussion Are an Integral Part of the Program

While it is an extremely important fact that children have the opportunity to explore and experiment, there should also be substantial guidance and discussion. Some of the guidance takes the form of the introduction of ideas that can help youngsters interpret observations. Through discussion, the child's experiences and the concepts are related to other experiences and to the conceptual structure of science.

Science Activities Lead Children into Additional Science Experiences

Science is not a closed undertaking; it has an "endless frontier." Similarly, SCIS science activities have been planned to lead children further and deeper into the study of science. There is an emphasis on "divergent" as contrasted to "convergent" questions. It is hoped that the divergent questions will lead children to seek new relationships. There is little room in a science program for the neatly packaged lesson in which all loose strings are carefully tied together. Instead, it is to be hoped that there will be many "loose ends," and that children will be attracted into investigating some of them.

It has been said that in science instruction our aim should be to "uncover" rather than to "cover" science. A neatly packaged lesson could have been developed around falling objects—all of them heavier than air. But, much would have been missed if the behavior of lighter-than-air objects when they are released had not been considered.

Scientific Statements Are Considered to Be Tentative in Nature

Scientific "truth" is not absolute and permanent. The early exploration of falling objects had to be revised as a result of Galileo's experiments. Our common sense consideration of the nature of "falling" has to be revised in order to explain the experiences of an astronaut in an earth satellite who releases a camera that does not fall to the floor of the satellite. It is conceivable that when we gain further experience with falling objects on the moon, and possibly other planets, we may have to change our concepts of the nature of "falling" again. In science, such changes are to be expected and not necessarily to be feared.

Through their science experiences, children become aware of the tentative nature of truth and the importance of adopting a questioning attitude toward statements. Just because a statement is written in a book or voiced by a noted authority does not mean that the statement is "true." It may be consistent with the facts as currently known, but it is quite likely that it will be subject to change.

In using the MINNEMAST materials the teacher is advised to remember that he is dealing with children and to make sure that the children can understand the procedures and equipment utilized.

How the Children Participate

Even though the children are not able to contribute many ideas at first, always invite them to participate in planning the experiments. You may have to step in with a system the children have not themselves devised, but even so they still have much to learn from setting up and working with the systems provided in the unit. It will be necessary for you to point out to the children what they are trying to do in each experiment and why they are doing it. It will also be necessary, as the children do one experiment after the other, to show them that in each experiment they are applying the techniques of a general scientific method.

Standards of Experimentation

As far as equipment and recording data are concerned, the experiments in this unit are controlled to the degree that is suitable for third-grade children. Even if more sophisticated, expensive equipment does give more exact conditions for experiments, its complexity makes it less useful for young children. By using methods and equipment that are understandable to the young child, the experiment itself can be more meaningful, and it can be duplicated or extended by the child at home working with simple equipment. It is important for the children to realize that the results of their experiments point in particular directions, but that because their measurements and the conditions of the experiments are not perfectly exact, they can not say, "This would always happen," about any of the factors that they have tested. But the children can say that they have enough evidence to make some predictions that can be tested further. For instance, after the experiment with mealworm beetles and different conditions of light, the children can say, "The mealworm beetles we experimented with went to the dark side of the container more often than they did to the light side." This is a comment about what they directly observed and may not generalize to all mealworm beetles. Similar statements that say, "Thus, this appears to be so," can be made about the other moisture, light and temperature experiments.

The following are samples of how several of the developers of elementary-school science curricula have suggested that teachers involve children in doing the work of the scientist.

1. MINNEMAST LESSON: GROWTH OF SEEDS

PREPARATION

You may wish to have the soil for the lesson brought in by a few children. If so, make sure they all bring in the same kind.

Assemble the materials for the groups on trays, and have ready a tray with materials for only two plantings for your demonstration. Mark all the medicine droppers with a grease pencil about three-fourths of an inch above the open end. Water to this mark will be called "one squirt."

Preselect a floor space where all the groups can put their trays after they have set up their experiments. This should be a place where the light and temperature will be as nearly the same as possible for all the trays.

PROCEDURE

Conduct a brief review of the bulletin-board information. Then ask the children:

> Why couldn't we tell whether or not the amount of moisture in our pieces of nature affected the growth of the grass? (There were differences in the amount of light each setup had, as well as in the amount of heat. Some children used one kind of soil and some another kind. Some planted their seeds in the soil, and others sprinkled them on the surface. There were too many variables.)
>
> How could we set up an experiment to find out if different amounts of moisture affect the growth of plants?

Let the children discuss this. Gradually guide them to establishing the criteria for a controlled experiment with the following:

> What would we have to do about the moisture? (We would have to use different amounts of water in each container. Then we could watch to see how the different plantings grew.)

MINNEMAST, *Conditions Affecting Life,* Unit 23, pp. viii and ix. Copyright 1944 by the Regents of the University of Minnesota.

How could we make sure that something else—the light, the temperature, or the soil—did not cause the differences in growth? (We would have to keep all these the same for each planting.)

Ask the children to name all the conditions that would have to be the same in every planting. List these on the chalkboard, as the children suggest them. Then ask them to name the one thing that must be varied and put this on the chalkboard, too. Your list should include the following:

Keep the same	*Vary*
Temperature.	Moisture used in each planting
Light.	(amount of water).
Number of seeds planted.	
Kind of soil used.	
Amount of soil.	
Depth at which seeds are planted.	
Type of container.	

It is important to emphasize to the children that the amount of moisture to be used is the only condition that should vary in such an experiment.

Bring out the demonstration tray and tell the children that, using the conditions they have specified above, you are going to do two plantings. Have them watch closely, because they will be doing the same experiment, but with more plantings. Before demonstrating, ask:

How can I make sure that my two setups will have the same amount of soil, seeds, light, and temperature? (By measuring.)

When it has been established that everything in this experiment will be carefully measured, whereas in the pieces of nature there was no quantification, show the children what they are going to do.

Step 1

Place two level quarter teaspoons of soil into each of your two containers. Show the children how to use a craft stick or ruler for leveling.

What condition is to be different for each planting? (The amount of moisture.)
How much water should we use in each setup? (Let the children make suggestions, but lead them to the realization that if they put measured amounts of water from "no water" to "lots of water" and keep all other conditions the same, they may be able to find out what amount of moisture is best for the radish seeds they are going to plant.)

Step 2

Show how to fill the medicine dropper to the one-quart mark, and how air sometimes enters the dropper after it is taken from the water, pushing the water up. Say that this is no problem, since the amount of water in the dropper remains the same. Say that the different setups will have different numbers of squirts.

Step 3

After adding no squirt (zero squirts) to one of your containers and one squirt to the other, stir the soil in each to distribute the water. Then smooth the surface of the soil. Label each container with the number of squirts (0 and 1). Tell the children that each group will have nine containers, which should be labeled 0 through 8 according to the number of squirts in each.

Step 4

Count out ten radish seeds and spread them out on the soil in one container. Then count out ten more seeds and spread them on the soil in the second container. Tell the children that they will plant ten radish seeds in each of their containers. The seeds are to be pressed down even with the soil.

Step 5

When you have pressed the seeds even with the soil, cover each setup with a small piece of plastic wrap and secure it with a rubber band. Ask the children if they can tell you why each container should be so carefully covered. (To keep the moisture in.)

Step 6

Ask the children to tell you how to measure the temperature. When they suggest using a thermometer, show them how to measure the temperature beside each container with the thermometer. Tell them they must read the thermometer at *eye level*.

Step 7

Ask the children how you might measure the light that each container is receiving. If they don't suggest a light meter, show them yours and how it works. Tell them that all groups will measure the light with this meter when their plantings are set up.

Divide the class into groups of six and have a tray of materials distributed to each group. Assign a letter (A, B, C, etc.) to each child in every group, then list the duties on the chalkboard.

Child A: Puts 2 level quarter teaspoons of soil in each container.

Child B: Puts measured squirts of water in the containers, as follows:

Container	Number of squirts
1	0—no water at all
2	1
3	2
4	3
5	4
6	5
7	6
8	7
9	8

Child C: Writes the number of squirts on each container.

Child D: Stirs up the soil to distribute the water evenly and smooths the surface.

Child E: Spreads 10 radish seeds in each container and presses them down until they are level with the soil.

Child F: Covers the top of each container completely with plastic wrap and a rubber band. He places the containers in order on the tray.

Have the children carry out their tasks. When they are finished, show them the place on the floor where they are to put their trays. When all the trays are in place, have one child measure the temperature and another the light to make sure that these are as nearly the same for all trays as possible.

Explain to the children that it will take four or five days for the seeds to grow enough for conclusions to be drawn about the effects of different amounts of moisture, but that they should make daily observations to see which. seeds germinate first, which seem to be growing best, etc.

Conclude the lesson by spending a few minutes on predicting. Ask:

How many of you think the seeds will grow best in the 0 to 2-squirt containers?

In the 3 to 5-squirt containers?

In the 6 to 8?

Write on the board the number of children who responded to each prediction. Tell the class that, when observable growth has taken place in the containers, these predictions will be checked. Say that, in the meantime, the children will be doing some experiments with the effects of moisture on small animals.

2. SCIENCE CURRICULUM IMPROVEMENT STUDY LESSON: PENDULUMS

Controlling the Variables (Optional)

Your pupils plan and carry out sets of experiments with the whirly bird to learn more about the variables affecting the number of turns the arm makes or the time interval the arm coasts after it is released. They compare their findings on histograms and record their conclusions in their manuals. In a separate activity, they investigate the whirly bird pendulum, in which the arm swings vertically rather than rotating horizontally. This chapter has been designated as optional because it is too demanding for many children in the middle elementary grades. However, your pupils' work in one or more of these activities will help you evaluate their understanding of the concept of variables.

For each team of Two Children

1 whirly bird set

From Science Curriculum Improvement Study, *Subsystems and Variables,* Teacher's Guide (Chicago: Rand McNally & Company, 1944), pp. 102–4.

For the Class

chart with variables

time-measuring device (provided by the teacher)

ADVANCE PREPARATION

Post the chart with the list of variables for the children's reference. Provide a time-measuring device for children who wish to measure the coasting time of the whirly bird arm.

TEACHING SUGGESTIONS

Your pupils may measure either the number of turns or the time interval that the whirly bird arm coasts. The effect of changes in any one of the variables listed on the chart can be studied. To do so, permit one variable to change while the others are fixed. You might plan a set of experiments with the whole class, or let each team plan its own, or form groups of two or three cooperating teams. If several teams duplicate a set of experiments, their mutual checking will result in more reliable results, but there will be less variety of information. The children's ability to plan and carry out investigations will help you estimate their progress toward reaching the objectives of this unit.

In each experiment, one variable changes while the others do not. The rivet positions, rubber band twists, and other conditions of the experiments are recorded in the boxes. It is not necessary to use all the space, however, if fewer experiments will answer the children's questions. If only two or three teams carry out similar experiments, each team should check its results by repeating its observations at least once. Then two sets of data will be recorded in each box.

Arrange a discussion by the entire class or by groups carrying out similar investigations so the children may compare their results. They may also construct histograms to show the number of times the arm turned under each condition they explored and write their conclusions at the bottom of the student-manual page.

Graphs

If your pupils have learned how to draw line graphs, they may be interested in showing the results of their investigations by this means. . . . The children might predict the coasting time for an intermediate placement of the rivets, basing their predictions on the graph. Some predictions can and should be tested experimentally as well.

The Whirly Bird Pendulum

A pendulum is a body suspended from a fixed point that swings freely back and forth under the action of gravity. The pendulums used to regulate the movement of clocks are the most familiar examples. Perhaps you used a pendulum as a timing device in the "Optional Activities" section of Chapter 18.

Since the whirly bird includes a freely moving subsystem, you can construct a pendulum by turning the whirly bird base on its side so the arm moves in a vertical plane. Remove the base crosspiece and anchor the other piece on a desk or table with a weight. The children can measure either the number of swings or the units of time before the arm stops moving. The pendulum operation is influenced by many variables, such as the placement of rivets, the hole where the arm is attached to the post (this need no longer be the center hole), and the height to which the arm is raised before it is released to swing. Interested children may use their ingenuity to think of other experiments to test the influence of these variables. They may make drawings and otherwise describe their observations on page 32 in the student manual.

3. ELEMENTARY SCIENCE STUDY LESSON: MEALWORMS

How Does a Mealworm Know It Is under Bran?

This question of how a mealworm knows it is under bran provides a chance for new experiments. One difficulty is that there is almost certainly more than one stimulus involved in the mealworm's ability to stay under the bran. ... At all events, the question cannot be solved conclusively, because the number of variables is so great that it is impossible to control them sufficiently. This is the most important lesson to be learned from the exercises.

The children can be asked how mealworms know they are under a bran pile once they find it. Some possible explanations for this behavior, as offered by the pupils, might be that mealworms remain in the bran because it affords food, darkness, weight on the back, quietness, or pleasant odor. Of these ideas, the first three are the most suitable for further study and can be treated separately in some detail.

Any other possibilities might be disposed by a discussion to show why they are probably not the cause. Loud noises have no apparent effect on a mealworm. Even so, how much quieter would it be under the bran? A quick check will show that bran has little or no smell. But does this mean that mealworms cannot smell it?

The questions of weight on the back, darkness, and food can be explored by all the children, by smaller groups within the class, or by interested individuals. Oral reports could be given to describe the experimentation that was carried out. Students can demonstrate in their reports any special equipment which they made to help solve their problem. Appropriate charts should be designed and used for recording data from these experiments.

Do mealworms stay under bran because they eat it? Piles of other materials such as pencil shavings or chalk dust could be put into a box along with bran. Will the mealworms show a preference for bran? Do they behave differently when they are hungry? How can you make mealworms hungry?

Testing for the Effect of Light

Does a mealworm know it is under bran partly because of darkness? How could this be found out? Many ways will probably be suggested and can be carried out. Among the most convincing is to see that mealworms do not collect under the bran nearly as much when the box is dark. Does this show that mealworms go under bran to avoid light? Or is this because they can't see the bran in the dark and are unable to find it?

The question could also be raised of just how dark it is under the bran pile. How could you find out? It might be possible to make a huge mount of bran so children could crawl under. But this is not too practical. How dark is it under a pile of leaves? One way to find out about the darkness under a little pile of bran would be to get a box and cut a small (one-inch) hole in the bottom. A window can be made by covering the hole with a piece of glass or clear plastic, or plastic wrapping taped at the edges. Then a pile of bran can be made over the window. Children can see how dark it is under the bran by looking into the box from underneath or through a peep hole in the side.... Is it dark inside the box? Suppose a light is placed under this glass-bottomed bran pile; will mealworms still stay under the bran?

Testing for the Effect of Weight

Does the mealworm know it is under bran partly because of the bran's weight on its back? What kind of material must be used to test this idea? See if your children can realize that something is needed under which a mealworm can crawl, but which will not provide darkness or food. Why wouldn't a pile of sawdust or chalk powder be good? How would you know if mealworms stayed under sawdust or chalk because of the weight on their backs or because of the darkness? What could be used for these experiments that would be better? You can have the students offer ideas, and the suggestion of shredded cellophane or similar transparent flakes might be given. A piece of such material could be cut up for experimentation.

Behavior of Mealworms in the Wild

You might want to discuss with the children the significance of what they have learned about the behavior of mealworms in relation to the mealworm's natural life. The children could try to explain how a mealworm's "liking" for dark places might be useful. Suggestions such as hiding from enemies might come up. Could this idea be tested? If a toad, field mouse, circus chameleon, or some other animal which eats mealworms is placed together with buried mealworms and mealworms in the open, which mealworms are eaten most frequently? Perhaps the mealworms' tendency to back away from light and to follow walls enables them to find dark places.

Suppose a predator ate more mealworms in the middle of an empty box than along the edge. This might show that the mealworms were protected by their wall-following behavior. It could be, however, that the predator would "know" where to look and would eat no mealworms out in the open. What might this show?

The survival of a mealworm population depends, perhaps, more on the location of a good supply of food than on the protection from predators. Experiments may have already indicated that wandering and chance "bumping" into food enables the mealworm to locate it. Is the mealworm hatched in a supply of food or does it wander until a supply is located? The adults could be given a variety of egg-laying sites to see where most eggs are laid. If wandering is found to be the means of locating food, does the newly hatched larva wander more?

You have now had an opportunity to learn various intellectual skills important in experimenting or problem solving for both scientists and laymen. In addition, you have read sample activities from several of the recently developed science curricula for the elementary school. The activities illustrated that there are many approaches to teaching science; all of these have in common that they focus on children doing rather than on talking by the teacher.

You have now arrived at the time when it is your turn. Ducks only learn to swim by getting into water. From this point on, only experience will teach you how to become a good science instructor. Knowing all the answers is less important than evoking interest in the course you teach by actively involving your children. It should prove rewarding in terms of your personal satisfaction. We hope that you find science teaching to be as enjoyable, noisy, and messy as we have!

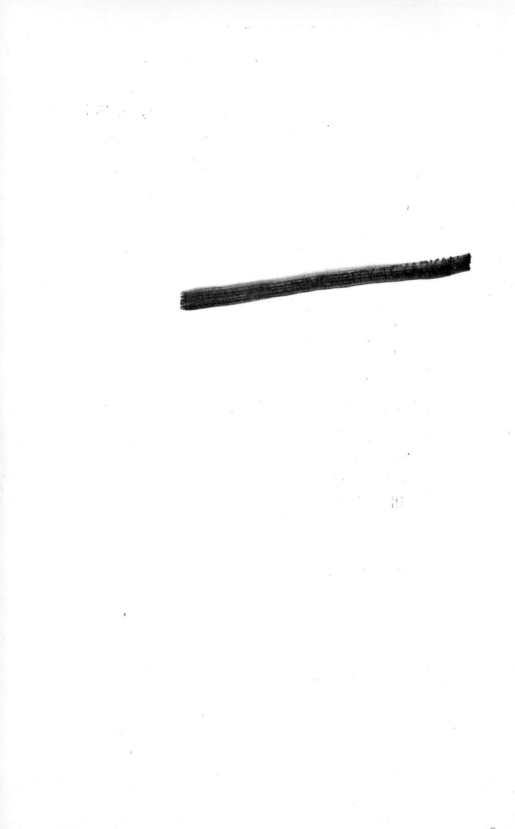